POETS TEACHING POETS

Poets Teaching Poets

Self and the World

Edited by
Gregory Orr and Ellen Bryant Voigt

Ann Arbor

THE UNIVERSITY OF MICHIGAN PRESS

The editors would like to thank Ruth Anderson Barnett and Laura Newbern, without whom this project would not have materialized, for their generous organizational and editorial help; Friends of Writers, Inc., *for proposing and encouraging the project; Donald Hall, model and conduit; and the writers at Warren Wilson College, whose book this is.*

Copyright © by the University of Michigan 1996
All rights reserved
Published in the United States of America by
The University of Michigan Press
Manufactured in the United States of America
⊗ Printed on acid-free paper
2004   2003   2002   2001   9   8   7   6

A CIP catalog record for this book is available from the British Library.

LIBRARY OF CONGRESS CATALOGING-IN-PUBLICATION DATA

Poets teaching poets : self and the word / edited by Gregory Orr and
    Ellen Bryant Voigt.
        p.   cm.
     ISBN 0-472-09621-4 (hardcover : alk. paper).—ISBN 0-472-06621-8
(pbk. : alk. paper)
     1. Poetry—Study and teaching.   I. Orr, Gregory.   II. Voigt,
Ellen Bryant, 1943–
PN1101.P585 1996
809.1—dc20   96-4234
                                                                   CIP

Contents

GREGORY ORR and ELLEN BRYANT VOIGT

Introduction

The essays in this collection emanate from the first low-residency
graduate program in writing, established at Goddard College in Ver-
mont in the mid-seventies. In American higher education, "poets
teaching poets" most often occurs in workshops, a mentor guiding a
group of less experienced writers in critiques of their own work. The
low-residency model sought a supplement and an alternative to this
method, within a pragmatic semester structure designed for adults:
two weeks on campus to initiate six months of independent tutorial
through correspondence.

The term "low-residency," however, fails to suggest the instruc-
tional advantages of those two intense weeks of conferences, work-
shops, seminars, and lectures. Tutorial requires a low student-faculty
ratio, which in turn brought together a greater number of practi-
tioners in each genre than is possible in wholly residential programs.
Tutorial also needs its correction: a variety of aesthetics, team teach-
ing, and a mixture of new and returning faculty every term. And it
was faculty, not design, that provided the crucial element: innovation
does not *always* attract, as it did in this case, the serious and the gifted.

Residency craft lectures, presented to the full community, became an
increasingly significant feature of the program following its move from
Goddard to Warren Wilson College in North Carolina in 1981. These
were occasions primarily for teaching—vital demonstrations of how
writers think about their craft, how one can analyze, absorb, and chal-
lenge traditional or contemporary work—but also for exploration, for
articulation, and for argument, with elders on the page and with peers
in the listening audience. What the occasions fostered was a remarkable
cross-fertilization among some of the country's most impressive writ-
ers, and a sustained conversation about writing, poetics, and literature.

This collection gathers a sample of the lectures on poetry, all but
one delivered in Swannanoa, N.C., about ten miles from the site of
Black Mountain College, so influential in the arts mid-century. Insight-
ful, eclectic, sometimes contentious, the pieces are notable first for
their variety and passion, even when grouped here, loosely, by
method of approach. In this way, they provide an interesting reflection
of the state of the art in the past two decades—a period both attacked
for its "democratization" of the art and praised as a renaissance. At the
same time, a recurrent ground note looks forward, to the end of the

millennium: broadly, what are the poet's responsibilities in contemporary American society? Specifically, what are the hazards and the achievement of the lyric preoccupation?

To note this shared attention is not, however, to confess to exclusion or narrowness. The lyric is no longer a circumscribable genre, distinct within verse from the other Aristotelian categories of drama and narrative, but may be said to have subsumed the best of all the old modes and become the hardier and more diverse for such involvements. Current American poetry, certainly, exhibits a remarkable range of hybrids—variations of the lyric moving either *outward*, following Whitman's lead, toward the dramatic, narrative, meditative, metaphysical, or political; or *inward*, following Dickinson's, toward the personal, confessional, psychological, existential, or ecstatic. Precisely in its post-Romantic escape from generic confines, the lyric refutes the charges of solipsism so long brought against it.

Rhymed or unrhymed, metrical or open, discursive or imagistic, autobiographical or masked, the contemporary American lyric derives from forces thrown into conflict as the worldview held in eighteenth-century England was undermined by the Industrial Revolution, the accompanying rise of the middle class, and the seeds of political transformation. When the old social and economic orders eroded, the cultural, intellectual, and aesthetic structures supporting them collapsed as well. The Enlightenment's view of order and reason had claimed a universal (even divinely ordained) hierarchy—a strict and reassuring vision to which Alexander Pope's didactic verse epistles gave memorable expression:

> Vast Chain of Being! which from God began,
> Natures ethereal, human, angel, man,
> Beast, bird, fish, insect, what no eye can see,
> No glass can reach; from Infinite to thee. . . .
>
> ("Essay on Man," i.237–41)

Biologic order was paralleled by social and political orders of equal clarity, a series of concentric, harmonious rings:

> God loves from Whole to Parts: But human soul
> Must rise from Individual to the Whole.
> Self-love but serves the virtuous mind to wake,
> As the small pebble stirs the peaceful lake;
> The centre moved, a circle straight succeeds,
> Another still, and still another spreads;
> Friend, parent, neighbor, first it will embrace;
> His country next; and next all human race. . . .
>
> (iv.361–68)

Where all this begins and ends is the wisdom of the status quo:

> And spite of Pride, in erring Reason's spite,
> One truth is clear, WHATEVER IS, IS RIGHT.
>
> (i.292–93)

In poetry these metaphysical and social assumptions encouraged the poetic satire, the verse essay and epistle, the translation of classical epic, but not the lyric outcry. The heroic couplet, orderly and summative, was the exact formal equivalent to a vision of art as a force for teaching the single "human soul [to] rise from Individual to the Whole." The self was simply the pebble that initiated those concentric circles of attention: friend, parent, neighbor, country, "and next all human race."

A crucial half-century of history and a difference in class perspective separate Pope from William Blake. While ruling-class vantage celebrated "order" as stability, Blake's lower-middle-class view, from beneath, saw such order as crushingly oppressive:

> I wander through each charter'd street,
> Near where the charter'd Thames does flow,
> And mark in every face I meet
> Marks of weakness, marks of woe.
>
> In every cry of every Man,
> In every Infant's cry of fear,
> In every voice, in every ban,
> The mind-forg'd manacles I hear.
>
> ("London," ll. 1–8)

From Pope to Blake poetry switches sides—the energy, imagination, and moral commitment of poetry change their allegiance from the rulers to the ruled, from the controllers to the controlled, from Pope's "order" to Blake's "Liberty." Whether in Byron's and Shelley's radical politics of rebellion, or in Wordsworth's "incidents and situations from common life . . . in a selection of language really used by men . . ." (preface to the *Lyrical Ballads*), the revolution that is literary Romanticism was interwoven with a parallel turning point in history.

Having lost faith in the sort of external ordering principles that sustained Pope and the long poem, the Romantics replaced reason with feeling. How then to order feeling into the coherence of poetry? With the personal lyric. It would be brief: the arc of feeling and personal urgency will not sustain an epic, intent as the lyric is on what Robert Frost would later call "momentary stay[s] against confusion." It would introduce radical new subject matter: the urban poor with

Blake, the rural poor with Wordsworth (and with Whitman, the equally disturbing matter of sex). It would admit greater disorder than the poetry that preceded it, and there would be new orderings also: Wordsworth's vision of enduring and sustaining natural forms; or the more subjective thematic faiths of Keats, "the holiness of the Heart's affections, and the truth of Imagination" (Letter to Benjamin Bailey, 22 November 1817).

Should we be surprised that this revitalized, even politicized lyric took deep and permanent root in American soil? A fairly straight line runs there from Wordsworth's youthful infatuation with the French Revolution. Alexis de Tocqueville, having disparaged the possibilities for poetry in a democracy, changed his mind and proposed instead, in his 1847 study *Democracy in America,* a new kind of poetry and a new kind of subject matter for the new world:

> I need not traverse earth and sky to discover a wondrous object woven of contrast, of infinite greatness and littleness, of intense gloom and amazing brightness, capable at once of exciting pity, admiration, terrors, contempt. I have only to look at myself.

American poets who did so, he predicted, would "enlarge and throw light on some of the obscurer recesses of the human heart." And there was this from Emerson:

> The modern mind believed that the nation existed for the individual, for the guardianship and education of every man; this idea, roughly written in revolutions and national movements, in the mind of the philosopher had far more precision: the individual is the world. ("Historic Notes of Life and Letters in New England")

That reciprocal fluidity of identity is exactly what we find in Whitman's confident opening invitation to his "Song of Myself"—

> What I assume you shall assume
> for every atom belonging to me as good belongs to you . . .

a reciprocity that takes us *through* the lyric "I" and beyond it, toward the narrative possibilities his great poem reveals.

In the opening pages of that founding document of American consciousness known as *Walden,* Thoreau tells us that the "I" is where all testimony begins:

> In most books, the "I," or first person is omitted; in this it will be retained; that, in respect to egotism, is the main difference. We

commonly do not remember that it is, after all, always the first person that is speaking.

The lyric likewise prefers "I" to "we" as the ground of authenticity and authority without which it cannot come into being—it is the voice of personhood, of individual identity singing out in pain or exultation, agony or rage or tenderness. Whenever the lyric is suppressed, one can be confident that political and economic oppression have been institutionalized—for this, not only Stalin's silencing of Mandelstam, Akhmatova, Pasternak, and Tsvetayeva, but the historic absence, only recently finding correction, of women's and minority voices, are ample and costly evidence. Critics charge that the lyric risks mediocrity in its egalitarian assumptions, and risks retreat into the self to the world's exclusion, but without the lyric the inner life of democracy vanishes: the world is also the individual.

It is hard, however, for the isolated poet in East Machias, Maine, or West Lafayette, Indiana, to feel the breath of Whitman's thousands at her shoulder. Hard, too, for the beginning poet to find, and use, among the current lyric hybrids or in the canon preceding him, those models that can instruct and enable his particular voice. And hard for all those driven to make poems to do so in the face of our culture's indifference to that effort.

The essays in this collection have been arranged in three groups. As with the opening—and oldest—selection, Robert Hass's lecture on Tranströmer and his imagery, delivered at Goddard College in the late seventies, the writers in the first part have begun with texts by a poet or poets and sought to induce and clarify the foundations of those "airy Citadels." Louise Glück's shrewd collective of Hass, Jeffers, and Milosz, juxtaposed with Joan Aleshire's classical defense of lyrics by Glück, Lowell, Akhmatova, Yeats, and others, continues the characteristic note of open inquiry, and, with Marianne Boruch's inclusive and lyrical treatment of Sylvia Plath, the issues of self and world are enjoined. The broad arc of concern inscribed by those issues is traced at the end of the section from Carl Dennis's close readings of voice in Homer and Dickinson, O'Hara and Zagajewski, to Alan Williamson's examination of Rilke and the implications of "innerness" in contemporary work.

Part two offers a richly informed retrospective approach and establishes a context for what Eliot called, in "Tradition and the Individual Talent," "the present moment of the past." Returning us to early Greek poetry, Renate Wood locates the emergence of the sense of self necessary to the lyric, while Allen Grossman examines and contrasts the mythic prototypes of the poet, Orpheus and Philomela. Both pieces query history with the urgency of current dilemma, and through the lens of current knowledge, as do Eleanor Wilner's "Medusa Connection," her correction of history and myth, and Michael Ryan's thorough treatment of "Poetry and the Audience" from the tribal bards through Whitman and Pound.

In part three, Reginald Gibbons's essay on revision as modeled by Dickinson, Vallejo, Yeats, Celan, C. K. Williams, and others ("Poetry and Self-Making") yokes the issues of poetic source and poetic craft to initiate a superb set of classrooms for both beginning and advanced students of poetry: Heather McHugh explicating movement in poems by William Carlos Williams and Elizabeth Bishop ("Moving Means, Meaning Moves"); Ellen Bryant Voigt isolating the function and power of the image in Eliot, Roethke, Bogan, and others; Stephen Dobyns analyzing, with Aristotle, Chekhov, Baudelaire, Merwin, and Larkin, clarity of structure ("Writing the Reader's Life"); and Tony Hoagland, in the collection's most recent essay, defining—and challenging—the Horatian ideal of balance and proportion. The volume ends, appropriately, with Gregory Orr's "Four Temperaments and the Forms of Poetry," an overview of the principles by which the poet orders the disorders we experience.

A map, then, of the thickets around us, and a path through them. From open fruitful exchange among these fine poets, and others unrepresented here, has come not a set of prohibitions but a cluster of permissions, not a "school" of poetry but a community of poets. It is our hope that making available this unique volume will extend that community, and we offer it in particular to those young poets lost in the culture but thankfully, as Hart Crane would have it, "loosed in the pattern's mastery."

PART ONE *A Beautiful Circuiting*

Now it appears to me that almost any man may spin from his own inwards his own airy Citadel—the points of leaves and twigs on which the spider begins her work are few and she fills the air with a beautiful circuiting.

—John Keats, 19 February 1818

ROBERT HASS

Tranströmer's *Baltics*
Making a Form of Time

Thinking about Tomas Tranströmer's *Baltics* in midwinter and mid-Vermont; lots of snow: white, gray, smoke blue; dark green pines, windrows of snow-burned cedar. I had hardly seen snow until I was eighteen and so the intensity and neutrality of the New England landscape is permanently strange and vivid to me. And present. Because it does not belong to childhood, it calls up no longing, is the afterimage of nothing lost; and it makes me completely happy, except for a small sensation of wonder that is like an itch. The happiness is like an experience of pure being; the itch is wondering what it means or what to do with it. This seems like a huge question and it reminds me of what I had first valued in Tranströmer's poems, or in the translations of them I've seen:

> 2 A.M.: moonlight. The train has stopped
> out in a field. Far off sparks of light from a town,
> flickering coldly on the horizon.
>
> As when a man goes so deep into his dream
> he will never remember that he was there
> when he returns again to his room.
>
> Or when a person goes so deep into a sickness
> that his days all become flickering sparks, a swarm,
> feeble and cold on the horizon.
>
> The train is entirely motionless.
> 2 o'clock: strong moonlight, few stars.

This poem feels like it is about the social man waking up to the fact of his being. It feels very austere. In the translation there is—or I imagine there is—a secondary drama in watching the poem discipline Robert Bly's hunger for excited states of mind. The middle stanzas are

"Tranströmer's *Baltics:* Making a Form of Time," from *Twentieth Century Pleasures* by Robert Hass. © 1984 by Robert Hass. First published by The Ecco Press in 1984. Reprinted by permission.

9

a kind of war between the Whitmanic possibilities of the long, en-
jambed line and Tranströmer's quiet precision. The result is a very
strong poem in English. The stanzas breathe long and then freeze in
place. What holds them, and what haunts me, is the metaphor or fact
of the stopped train. The poem is called "Track," and the track be-
comes a figure for time, for the preordination with which our social
life glistens pointlessly into the future, while the train in a moment of
clarity—like an eye opening suddenly—is stopped. The moonlight is
a figure for that; for pure consciousness, without object. Because it is
pure, because it just is, it means nothing special; and its not meaning
anything is what fascinates me about Tranströmer.

When I look across the page, with edified ignorance, at the Swed-
ish, I see that the main musical device of the poem seems to be the
repeated vowel rhyme on *flimrande* and *synranden,* flickering and hori-
zon. At the end of the first stanza,

> flimrande kallt vid synranden

and at the end of the third

> att allt som var hans dagar blir några flimrande
> punkter, en svärm,
> kall och ringa vid synranden

make an insistence. *Synranden,* I have been told, means "horizon," but it
is not exactly the same word. Something more powerful than the En-
glish word is buried in the Germanic root of the Swedish: *syn*=vision,
randen=border. I find that etymology, in the context of the poem,
wrenching and mysterious. The held, vivid moment and life flickering
out there at the vision-border. It is not lonely exactly, but it's so pure I
don't know what to do with it. I don't know what its relation to the
track is. And Tranströmer's early poems call up this feeling in me again
and again.

I have said to myself that it has something to do with the epistemol-
ogy of the lyric poem. Novels and narrative and discursive forms of the
poem imitate life in time. They move and accumulate, ripen; some
things fall away and other things come up. But the lyric imitates in-
sight, or being, or consciousness without object, or waking up to one-
self on the stopped train, or my two-week stint at Goddard College in
the New England snow that has for me no past or future. This morning,
walking to breakfast—trying to think about Tranströmer, about a lec-
ture the poet Stephen Dobyns had given yesterday on metaphor, about
a note I had written in my journal for no apparent reason, which went
"The *Cantos* are a long struggle between image and discourse"—I
passed a bird feeder under pine trees and saw suddenly against the snow

twin flashes of pure yellow and bright blue, a jay and an evening gros-
beak swooping up fast to perch at a safe distance, and the color and
surprise made my heart leap in my chest, and there it was again.

This is the way I come at *Baltics,* which I like to read. I can't know
how good a poem it is because I know it only in Samuel Charters's
translation, but it is very interesting to me. Tranströmer is one of the
most remarkable European poets of his generation, and I had thought
of him as a deeply private writer. That he had written a poem called
Baltics surprised me. Though my paternal great-grandfather had emi-
grated from a small village outside the Baltic port of Stettin, now
Polish and Szczecin, no stories survived in my family and all I knew of
that part of the world was Günter Grass's novels about Danzig, now
Polish and Gdansk. I was also struck by the fact that the Irish poet
Seamus Heaney had just addressed the North Sea region in *North.*
Maybe something was up. And this curiosity reawakened wonderings
I have had about Tranströmer's politics and about the relation between
image and discourse or, to make a long jump, between history and
pure moment, story and song. The political question enters in this
way: in a poem like "Track," Tranströmer seems to feel that the social
man is not quite real and, if that is true, the social relations between
men cannot be quite real either. He doesn't say that in the poem; he
doesn't say anything quite like that in any of the poems that I know
but in all the poems, including *Baltics,* which explores the relation of
people to a place, it does seem to be something that he feels at least
some of the time. Look, for example, at the metaphor he develops
from the baptismal font at the beginning of the third section. It looks
like a gloss on "Track":

In the half dark corner of the Gotland church, in the mildewed
    daylight
stands a sandstone baptismal font—12th century—the stone cutter's
    name
still there, shining
like a row of teeth in a mass grave:
                    HEGWALDR
                        the name still there. And his scenes
here and on the sides of the vessels crowded with people, figures on
    their way out of the stone.
The eyes' kernels of good and evil bursting there.
Herod at the table: the roasted cock flying up and crowing "Christus
    natus est"—the servant executed—
close by the child born, under clumps of faces as worthy and helpless
    as young monkeys.
And the fleeing steps of the pious
drumming over the dragon scales of sewer mouths.

(The scenes stronger in memory than when you stand in front of
    them,
strongest when the font spins like a slow, rumbling carousel in the
    memory.)
Nowhere the lee-side. Everywhere risk.
As it was. As it is.
Only inside there is peace, in the water of the vessel that no one sees,
but on the outer walls the struggle rages.
And peace can come drop by drop, perhaps at night
when we don't know anything,
or as when we're taped to a drip in a hospital ward.

"And peace can come drop by drop": I don't know what the reso-
nances of this line are in Swedish; in English it echoes a famous poem
so directly that it seems to refer to it:

> And I shall have some peace there, for peace comes dropping slow,
> Dropping from the veils of the morning . . .

Tranströmer's lines may not be a "better" poem than "The Lake Isle of
Innisfree," but the translation is certainly a more interesting poem,
because there is nothing in Yeats that has the power of "nowhere the
lee-side." And "Track" is also a more interesting poem to me because
it renders an awakening that has no form but itself; it is not the fantasy
of a paradisal form that exists elsewhere.

It is easy to see how this raises political questions. The figure is so
completely and exactly realized that the self seems to be separated
from the world by eight inches of old sandstone. It has made a wall of
the body, with social life outside in a stylized medieval frieze and
inside the held, blessed water, and this is achieved through the unargu-
ableness of metaphor. It is typical of the power of Tranströmer's po-
etry and almost a perfect embodiment of the hermetic attitude toward
art and experience. There can be no picking and choosing. If you want
to object to it, you have to dismiss it outright, saying, as the social
poet will say about the hermetic poet, that it's very well done but all
wrong, that the figures for inwardness in "Track" are dream and
sickness, that there must be some other solution than a gnostic one to
this long European disease of alienation and solipsism. And I would
say all of this about Tranströmer, and say more, that the poems reek
existentialism, reek the ambience of Tranströmer's youth in the late
forties and early fifties, which I was already sick of at second hand in
my youth in the late fifties and early sixties, when my teachers tried to
persuade me that the dead, affectless voices of *Nausea* and *The Stranger*
were the very form of freedom.

Only my experience tells me that, tone and period feeling aside, there is something about what Tranströmer is saying that is permanently true, and especially true to the form of the lyric poem. That clean sense of wonder in "Track" is something I have heard in Sappho and Tu Fu. Besides, another disconcerting fact about Tranströmer's poetry is that it always seems to be the work of a deeply rooted man. Friends have told me about his Swedishness, in "Evening—Morning" for example, where the image of the dock and the half-suffocated summer gods seem inseparable from the paradisiacal long days of the short Swedish summer, and in "Sailor's Tale," how the *barvinterdagar,* the dark winter days without snow in November and December, are so central to the poem that it can almost not be felt without knowledge of that experience. It is this completely local and rooted sense conveyed in a poetry that always wakes stunned from the rooted and local into a place where the self throbs with itself and the world seems elsewhere that makes me inclined not to mount arguments but to shut up and listen.

And it is what fascinates me most about *Baltics.* Partly because of its length, partly because of its subject, this poem focuses Tranströmer's themes more intensely than anything else of his I have read. Samuel Charters describes its shape and occasion in his introduction: "The poem is largely about his family and the island in the archipelago off the east coast of Sweden where they lived for many years, and where he returns each summer with his wife and his own children. The poem is in some ways almost like taking a summer walk with Tomas across the island's stretches of forest and overgrown fields." Another fact of its occasion is the death of his mother after a long illness. If you look back at the final image in the passage I have already quoted, you can see some of the ways in which the fact of death refocuses the whole passage. The mystery of the solitary self, because it is the mystery of any human being's last hours, becomes already a social thing; it aches with a question about the ways in which we can and cannot reach out to others.

The poem is in six sections, framed by an account of his grandfather in the first and an account of his grandmother in the last. There is no apparent progression; it wanders, as Charters says, and it seems to wander partly through the island and partly through a sequence of Tranströmer poems and fragments of Tranströmer poems. The connections among the sections and among the parts of the individual sections are rarely logical or discursive. And yet everything in it tugs against everything else. Fact has the pull of metaphor and one metaphor pulls against another. Here, for example, is the whole first section of the poem:

It was before the time of radio masts.

My grandfather was a newly licensed pilot. In the almanac he wrote
down the vessels he piloted—

name, destination, draft:
Examples from 1884:
Steamer Tiger Capt Rowan 16 feet Hull Gefle Furusund
Brig Ocean Capt Andersen 8 feet Sandofjord Hernosand Furusund
Steamer St. Petersburg Capt Libenberg 11 feet Stettin Libau
    Sandhamn

He took them out to the Baltic, through that wonderful labyrinth of
    islands and water.
And those that met on board, and were carried by the same hull for a
    few hours or a few days,
how well did they get to know each other?
Talking in misspelled English, understanding and misunderstanding,
    but very little conscious lying.
How well did they get to know each other?

When it was thick fog: half speed, almost blind. The headland coming
    out of the invisibility with a single stride, it was right on them.
Foghorn blasting every other minute. His eyes reading straight into
    the invisible.
(Did he have the labyrinth in his head?)
The minutes went by.
Lands and reefs memorized like hymn verses.
And the feeling of we're-right-here that you have to keep, like
    carrying a pail filled to the brim without spilling a drop.

A glance down into the engine room.
The compound engine, as long-lived as a human heart, worked with
    great soft recoiling movements, steel acrobatics, and the smells
    rising from it as from a kitchen.

When I first started reading *Baltics,* I wanted to make a joke to
someone about the influence of Charles Olson, whom I am quite sure
Tranströmer has never read: "Hmm, Steamer Tiger Capt Rowan 16
feet Hull Gefle Furusund. Where have I heard that rhythm before?"
But Tranströmer is right, as Olson was right in his insistence on it,
that we know the man through the specifics of his trade. If this were
Olson, it would send us reeling back from this first laconic fidelity of
the written word to its origin in Phoenicia and, although Tranströmer
is free from the majesty of that imperialist ambition of American
poetry, the transcription does circle back profoundly for me to all the
unvarnished records of half-lettered men that called writing into be-
ing. And rightly: the poem patently becomes a metaphor for the con-
nection between poetry and navigation, grandson and grandfather.
Did he have the labyrinth in his head? All of this is fairly obvious. His

curiosity about the men raises the theme of communication. The "pail filled to the brim" looks forward to the baptismal font. The knowledge secure as "hymn verses" looks longingly to the secure pieties of another age. And the final metaphor of the engine is packed in enough ways that I won't insult it with explication. The passage does not become allegory; the facts stay solidly facts, but the pull of metaphor almost overwhelms it at the outset. So much so that, if this were a poem by itself, however surprising as a Tranströmer poem, it would seem finally nostalgic and familiar, full of easy longing.

Instead, it introduces us to a labyrinth of islands and water that seems to be absolutely the terrain of modern poetry. It explains to me why, in the middle of thinking about it, I made a note to myself about Pound. One of the impulses of the modernist poem is to leap out of time, or to record those moments in which we seem to. In English poetry the process began as soon as Wordsworth tried to make an account for himself of the way, when he was a boy skating, the heavens spun when he pulled up abruptly and silence fell all around him. It was intensified as soon as Baudelaire started reading Swedenborg. Imagism was its surest expression. Pound makes a joke of it in one poem by including a date in the title, "Pagani's, November 8": "Suddenly discovering in the eyes of the very beautiful Normande cocotte / The eyes of the very learned British Museum assistant." Not *déjà vu* exactly, but the way resemblance empties time of time. If there was ever an inappropriate method for embarking on a long poem that must somehow make a shape over time, imagism is that method. And it is no accident that *The Cantos* begins with a mariner and a navigator: "And then went down to the ship." Or: "It was before the time of radio masts."

I don't know how much of this bears on the traditions of Swedish poetry. What does seem clear is that the proposal of this poem, the haunting presence of the grandparents, the death of the poet's mother, his love of the island, compels Tranströmer in a new way, to struggle with the materials of his art. *Baltics,* as I've said, is an anthology of Tranströmer poems, an archipelago. The baptismal font passage in the third section is an instance. So is section one. Here, randomly, are some others:

> The strategic planetarium rotates. The lenses stare into the darkness.
> The night sky is full of numbers, and they're fed into
> a blinking cupboard,
> a piece of furniture,
> inside it the energy of a grasshopper swarm that devours the acres of
>   Somalia in half an hour.

> Bullhead.   The fish that's a toad that wanted to be a butterfly and
>   made it a third of the way, hiding himself in the seaweed,

but pulled up in the net, hooked fast by his pathetic spikes
and warts—when you untangle him from the mesh of the
net your hands shine with slime.

ঌ

Sometimes you wake at night
and quickly throw some words down
on the nearest paper, on the margin of a newspaper
(the words glowing with meaning!)
but in the morning: the same words don't say anything anymore,
     scrawls, mis-speakings.
Or fragments of a great nightly style that dragged past?

ঌ

I don't know if we're in the beginning or in the final stage.
No conclusion can be made, no conclusion is possible.
The conclusion is the mandrake—
(see the encyclopedia of superstitions:
     MANDRAKE

                    miracle working plant
that gave such a dreadful shriek when it was torn from the earth
that the person fell dead. A dog had to do it . . .)

ঌ

The wind that blew so carefully all day—
all the blades of grass are counted on the furthest islets—
has lain down in the middle of the island. The matchstick's flame
     stands up straight.
The sea painting and the forest painting darken together.
Also the foliage of the five-story trees is turning black.
"Every summer is the last." These are empty words
for the creatures at late summer midnight
where the crickets sew on their machines as if possessed
and the Baltic's near
and the lonely water tap stands among the wild rose bushes
like an equestrian statue. The water tastes of iron.

Each of these is wonderful in its way. They have the carefulness and
surprise and sardonic tenderness and despair and sheer intelligence that
make Tranströmer always worth reading. There is not a false note, and
I even had that fatuous feeling of the exhilaration of creation that
sometimes overtakes literary criticism, when I typed them out. If I
have a criticism of them, it is that they have for me the aftertaste of *17
Dikter,* the sensation that they could be engraved in stone under the
superscription "Twentieth Century Sentiments" and survive for centu-
ries as an emblem of our mortal weariness with living in our time.
     The first passage makes an emblem of alienation by physics. The

second figures despair in the face of evolutionary theory, saved some-how by the shiny slime of the sculpin, which is like the mystery of the stuff of the spirit but feels like semen. The third is our haunting by the unconscious and by the fragmentation of our speech. The fourth is our literal rootlessness, our having been hauled, half-dead and half-alive, out of traditional and organic forms of society by industrial and techno-logical revolution. The fifth is that Tranströmer poem of the self that is like water; it is almost too beautiful, too deft, the poet and the poem, each man on the edge of his own Baltic, a "lonely water tap" standing "among the wild rose bushes / like an equestrian statue." By them selves, they become an irritation, and Tranströmer's striking talent doubles back on him, as if the style were the face of a man who appeared to have answers and had instead a stunning repertoire of methods for describing the predicament.

But the passages don't occur by themselves. They are parts of a longer poem that take their central weight—at least I have chosen to believe Charters when he says they take their central weight—from the fact of his mother's death, which draws the whole sequence down-ward toward a place where there can be no satisfaction in the iterated revelation of a self without meaning in a world that is busy, admirable, terrible, and pointless. The reference to his mother's death is the most opaque passage in the poem and I don't know if I could have seen it if Charters had not pointed it out:

> The Death lectures went on for several terms. I was present
> together with classmates I didn't know
> (who are you?)
> —afterwards everyone went off on his own, profiles.
>
> I looked at the sky and the earth and straight ahead
> and since then I've been writing a long letter to the dead
> on a typewriter that doesn't have a ribbon, only a horizon line
> so the words beat in vain and nothing stays.

It is one thing to wake up to the solitariness of one's own being, to recognize that solitariness as a fact about each of us, and to contemplate its extinction in oneself; it is another to experience it happening to someone you love. The figure of "the Death lectures" gets the relentless-ness and desperation of it. And it recurs in the meditation on his grandfa-ther's death, which leads him in turn to wonder about the fate of a stranger in a nineteenth-century photograph, some anonymous human whose life must mean whatever the idea of a *Baltics* means:

> But in the next brown photo
> someone I don't know—

by the clothes from the middle of the last century.
A man about thirty, the powerful eyebrows,
the face that looks me right in the eye
whispering: "Here I am."
but who "I" am
is something no one remembers anymore. No one.

TB? Isolation?

Once he stopped
on the stony, grass streaming slope coming up from the sea
and felt the black blindfold in front of his eyes.

This perilousness of our individual lives is what makes the insight of
the isolated lyric poem untenable. It creates the need in the wandering
fragments or islands of *Baltics* to somehow transform image into dis-
course, into a form of time, as the terse notations of the poet's grandfa-
ther had turned the isolated towns his ship visited into a rudimentary
culture: "Steamer St. Petersburg Capt Libenberg 11 feet Stettin Libau
Sandhamn." It makes the form of the poem its deepest and most
urgent subject.

There are metaphors for this throughout the poem, metaphors of
writing, speech, misspeech, communication. The men on shipboard
in section one prefigure it, "Talking in misspelled English, understand-
ing and misunderstanding, but very little conscious lying. / How well
did they get to know each other?" It appears in the second section in
what seems to be a reference to the Soviet Union: "where a conversa-
tion between friends is a test of what friendship means," but could be a
reference to America in the late sixties, or to any repressive society. In
section four, it appears in an image that is particularly crucial because it
calls up our distrust of abstract thought, which is the traditional
method or form of discourse: "the seaweed holding themselves up
with air bladders, as we hold ourselves up with ideas." In section five,
he speaks of the problem directly:

August 2. Something wants to be said, but the words don't agree.
Something that can't be said,
aphasia,
there aren't any words but maybe a style . . .

The style is, simply, the attentive, loose wandering of *Baltics,* a
sort of slowly turning mobile of mind and island, in which discourse
occurs because the separate parts tug at one another and everything
seems metaphorically related to everything else. I had better pause
over that phrase: metaphorically related. In the lecture I heard yester-
day, Stephen Dobyns began by talking about the wonder he felt at

the swiftness of the mind's perception of metaphorical connection, the speed with which it takes in, connects, and generalizes that perception. The example he used was taken from W. S. Merwin's *Asian Figures*:

> Spits straight up
> learns something

Almost before he had finished saying it, the audience laughed—as if to illustrate his point. He used this to demonstrate that metaphor is a participatory act; it surprises the hearer into self-knowledge. It heightens his relationship to himself. I loved his saying that, because I had always thought more or less naively that a metaphor connected two things; in fact, in metaphor, *we* connect two things, or have connected things, and metaphor calls up the work already done. Dobyns quoted this to the audience: "When he draws a tiger, it's a dog"; and asked us to feel our whole minds drawn to its solution, so that we experienced what the natural and incessant work of the imagination was. Art, he concluded, allowed the reader to establish an intimate relationship with himself and to become aware of how relationship formed his own sense of the world.

What happens quickly in the Merwin aphorisms is what happens slowly as the mind moves through the parts of *Baltics*. It is not a wisdom poem; it does not try to arrive at some healed knowledge, comic or tragic. And it is not a political poem, though its themes include community and isolation. But it enacts the qualities of a consciousness that knows it has been outside of time and is going to die, two thousand miles below words like *socialism* and *intentional anarchism* and *bankbook,* and it knows that the discovery and enactment of those qualities in our art are the spiritual precondition for a viable politics. That last sentence sounds so grand, I have scared myself a little. The proof, finally, is in the poem, for which I don't mean to advance these propositions as claims of complete success, but as an indication of Tranströmer's compelling seriousness as an artist. The reader should really apply the Dobyns test for himself by watching himself read section five of *Baltics* with a whole mind.

July 30.   The channel has become eccentric—today it's teeming with jellyfish for the first time in years, they pump themselves along with calm consideration, they belong to the same shipping company: AURELIA, they drift like flowers after a burial at sea, if you take them out of the water all of their shape disappears, as when an indescribable truth is lifted out of the silence and formulated into a lifeless mass, yes, they're untranslatable, they have to stay in their element.

August 2. Something wants to be said, but the words don't agree.
Something that can't be said,
aphasia.
there aren't any words but maybe a style . . .

Sometimes you wake up at night
and quickly throw some words down
on the nearest paper, on the margin of a newspaper
(the words glowing with meaning!)
but in the morning: the same words don't say anything anymore,
    scrawls, mis-speakings.
Or fragments of a great nightly style that dragged past?

Music comes to a person, he's a composer, he's played, has a career,
    becomes director of the conservatory.
The trend turns downward, he's blamed by the authorities.
They put up his pupil K——— as chief prosecutor.
He's threatened, demoted, sent away.
After some years the disgrace diminishes, he's rehabilitated.
Then comes the stroke: right side paralysis, and aphasia, can only
    grasp short phrases, says wrong words.
Can, as a result of this, not be touched by advancement or blame.
But the music's still there, he still composes in his own style,
he becomes a medical sensation for the time he has left to live.

He wrote music to texts he no longer understood—
in the same way
we express something with our lives
in that humming chorus of misspeech.

The Death lectures went on for several terms. I was present
together with classmates I didn't know
(who are you?)
—afterwards everyone went off on his own, profiles.

I looked at the sky and the earth and straight ahead
and since then I've been writing a long letter to the dead
on a typewriter that doesn't have a ribbon, only a horizon line
so the words beat in vain and nothing stays.

I stand with my hand on the door handle, take the pulse of the house.
The walls so full of life

(the children won't dare sleep alone up in the attic—what makes me
   feel safe makes them uneasy.)

August 3. Out there in the damp grass
slithers a greeting from the Middle Ages: Helix pomatia
the subtly grey-gold shining snail with its jaunty house,
introduced by some monk who liked *escargots*—yes, the Franciscans
   were here,
broke stone and burnt lime, the island was theirs in 1288, a donation
   from King Magnus
("Thes almes and othres he hath yeven / Thei meteth hym nu he
   entreth hevene.")
the forest fell, the ovens burned, the lime taken by sail
to the building of the monastery . . .
                              Sister snail
stands almost still in the grass, feelers sucked in
and rolled out, disturbance and hesitation . . .
How like myself in my searching!

The wind that blew so carefully all day—
all the blades of grass are counted on the furthest islets—
has lain down in the middle of the island. The matchstick's flame
   stands straight up.
The sea painting and the forest painting darken together.
Also the foliage of the five-story trees is turning black.
"Every summer is the last." These are empty words
for the creatures at late summer midnight
where the crickets sew on their machines as if possessed
and the Baltic's near
and the lonely water tap stands among the wild rose bushes
like an equestrian statue. The water tastes of iron.

I think I like especially the crickets sewing on their machines as if
possessed. It is what the stitching of Tranströmer's writing in this
passage feels like to me.

   In speaking about long poems, Charles Olson often quoted White-
head: "The process of creation is the form of unity." This has been,
more or less, the justification for most poems of any length since *The
Cantos,* and it has always seemed to me to be a question-begging
formulation. Because, by not saying how the process of creation
comes to closure, it tells us nothing about either form or unity. It
doesn't tell us the difference between a thing coming to form and
those experiments in pure seriality that seem to end either in exhaus-
tion or the death of their author. *Baltics* ends because the poem arrives,
in the sixth section, at a figure for itself. I have read the poem many,

many times, and I guess I should say that I don't think its conclusion is entirely achieved. That is, I don't feel, haven't yet felt, that its circling movement through many dark places to this last bright leap is accomplished rather than wished into being. I can't think of many places in literature where it is. *The Tempest,* the end of *The Cantos.* But the conclusion for which it reaches is surprisingly similar to Pound's, the place where the light of intelligence, of metaphor, discourse, and relation becomes indistinguishable from love, that word Pound avoided by plugging in a scrap of Italian Neoplatonism: *intelleto d'amore.*

Tranströmer comes at it in his own way when he focuses the poem at the end on the family house, a two-hundred-year-old fisherman's house, and discovers the pattern of his own mind in the tiles that ornament and encircle its roof:

> So much crouching wood. And on the roof the ancient tiles that
>   collapsed across and on top of each other
> (the original pattern erased by the earth's rotation through the years)
> it reminds me of something . . . I was there . . . wait: it's the old
>   Jewish cemetery in Prague
> where the dead live closer together than they did in life, the stones
>   jammed in, jammed in.
> So much encircled love! The tiles with the lichen's letters in an
>   unknown language
> are the stones in the archipelago people's ghetto cemetery, the stones
>   erected and fallen down—
>
> The ramshackle hut shines
> with the light of all the people carried by a certain wave, a certain
>   wind,
> out here to their fates.

I don't know if he has brought it off. I don't think that anyone without a knowledge of Swedish could know for sure, even in the misspeech of Samuel Charters's clear, strong translation, but it is hard not to feel that those last lines—"a certain wave, a certain wind"— have deeply touched the mystery of place and of the shape of the poem.

LOUISE GLÜCK

Obstinate Humanity

Robinson Jeffers appears to be a poet other poets chastize eloquently. That is: the inducement to literary reprimand is in proportion to the stakes: the grander, the more fundamental the objection, the more inviting the project. The remarkable poems of this little genre, Milosz's and Hass's, are devoid of flamboyant condescension, at least insofar as the living can avoid flaunting their ongoing development at the immobile dead. "So brave in a void / you offered sacrifices to demons": so Milosz addresses Jeffers. If not exactly tribute, this is nevertheless a particular species of reproach: giant to giant.

The reprimand is moral: at issue is humanity, the definition thereof. And Jeffers's crime, in Milosz's poem, "to proclaim . . . an inhuman thing." Hass concurs, pretty much, though his formulation changes the emphasis, focusing on causes: "human anguish made him cold."

What's odd to me is that Jeffers in all his hardness and obstinate fixity and dogmatic revulsions is, of the three, the most poignantly, albeit cheerlessly, human.

I read Milosz in translation, which makes discussion of tone problematic. And yet, at issue in his poem "To Robinson Jeffers" is the placement of the speaker relative to his subjects and, in fact, Milosz speaks as a diplomat, an envoy, his mission being to explain, or represent, one form of paganism to another.

The paganism he defends is maternal. Earth centered. Moon centered. Fruitful. Predictable. Cyclical. This is the same fecund earth Hass reveres. Both approve it as the wise man approves woman, radiant in otherness. Homage to the source, the root, but homage paid, in Milosz, by someone well beyond primitive gesturing.

The mathematical equivalent of feminine earth is multiplication: increase, whatever its metaphoric manifestation, seems inherently life-affirming. Whereas the corresponding, the declared metaphor for Jeffers's earth, the "massive mysticism of stone," is elimination: a dead end, presumably.

In "The Return of Robinson Jeffers" Hass puts all this more eloquently: "though rock stands it does not breed." He sees the lure of rock but names its spiritual danger: sterility. To stand, to not breed, is to be finally inhuman, and, pragmatically, *not* lasting: the future of the species is more profitably assured through reproduction than through endurance. In Hass's mind, mutability, not fixity, sponsors ongoing existence. And yet the manner in which Jeffers espouses rock is immensely human: exposed, rash, extreme, vulnerable. Rigid, where Hass and Milosz are lithe-minded, evolved.

Jeffers writes out of enraged, disappointed romanticism: civilized in his expectations, he cannot forgive civilization in that it wasn't worth his faith. This can seem, to a reader, cumulatively trying: repetition deprives a last stand of its dramatic force.

Whereas Hass characteristically resists resolution: a mark of intellect, but also a temperamental inclination that can create its own form of stasis, in that it lacks not motion but momentum.

Hass hates disappointment, hates being imprisoned in its continuing and limited range of attitudes, of tones: rue, regret, plangent lament. When Hass *sighs* in *Praise* he does so with a kind of savage fury, constrained by perspective, by habitual poise; in these moments, he comes closest to being what Milosz has always been, since to write as an ancient soul is to write as an ironist (the alternative, I suppose, being to sing the purest and briefest of lyrics).

Hass's method of poetic development has always been exposure: he uses his empathetic capacity to extend his range. Though he is not, I think, at home in irony (unless there is irony in the Buddha's composure), he has most certainly, as Milosz's translator, been exposed to its most subtle and resourceful practitioner.

Hass and Milosz have in common astounding intellectual gifts and the virtuoso's mastery of tone, which contrives to endow natural speech with a sometimes unbelievable subtext of resonances. But the sources of flexibility differ: Milosz's detachment differs from Hass's empathy, as irony is distinct from ambivalence.

It will be interesting to see whether Hass ripens into the sort of poet Milosz is: ironic, but with an irony by turns delicate, malicious, passionate, judgmental, tender. He already has Milosz's 360-degree gaze, as opposed to Jeffers's fixity.

Jeffers's ferocity is alien to Hass; his landscapes less so. Like Jeffers, Hass is attracted to the absence of the human. There have been, from the first, counterparts in Hass to Jeffers's harsh, unpopulated world. And this is an aspect of the work even in *Field Guide,* even before human presence or human agency come to be characterized as that contaminating "steady thoughtlessness." But where Jeffers's imagination settles on rock and hawk, Hass gives us frog and pond, a bowl of oranges. Into these worlds, human beings, men and women, come as intrusions.

Most poets are, in Frost's phrase, acquainted with the night. Hass is unique in having inhabited, as an adult, a sunlit world. Exiled from Eden, he's like the man who's always been healthy and gets sick: when the amazement passes, he simply can't stand feeling this way. And the tonal problem of *Praise,* the collection that registers this change, is to avoid petulant irritability.

The earlier work, "The Return of Robinson Jeffers," is built around a move typical of Hass's work, early and late, an extended enactment of empathy. Hass imagines Jeffers's return from death: "I imagine him thinking . . .": so the meditation starts. Hass's projected epiphany duplicates Milosz's bias; this is not curious, since they address the same figure, the same perceived limitation. Jeffers, in Hass's imagination, ". . . feels pain as rounding at the hips, as breasts." And the form reeducation takes is the birth of feminine empathy and suffering to replace male arrogance.

It is either very touching, very feminine (on this grid) or extremely arrogant that Hass prefers to imagine these revelations as occurring to Jeffers himself, while at the same time refusing to abandon his own position as narrating, as sponsoring intelligence: the epiphany occurs in Hass's imagination. The fact is, Hass has learned much from Jeffers. There are tastes in common: the long, rhythmic, complicated sentences, with subsequent sentences beginning on a repeated phrase, like a thread picked up in a complex tapestry, so that one is always aware of, always hearing the human voice (the danger of complex syntax being that voice will be lost and, with it, intimacy, directness). The similarities are, in any case, easy to hear, for all the difference in ambiance: ". . . what a festival for the seafowl. / What a witches' sabbath of wings / Hides the water." That's Jeffers, but Hass has moments very like.

What Hass does, what no one else now writing does with such skill, is a kind of spiritual ventriloquism: he is able to project not merely voice but a whole sensibility. On the surface, this resembles Keats's ideas of negative capability; in fact, it differs profoundly from Keats, in motive and effect. Always Keats's excursions conclude, and the act of conclusion marks a restoration of self. This is the romantic journey: it might be, it can be imagined, it is not. Hass may assert the fact of limitation, but limitation does not seem to be an attribute of the voice. And the romantic sound is not one Hass seems especially eager to make. His poems are, regularly, a flight from self; what they lack, when they lack anything, is a sense of the restrictions of self, of singleness, which perception necessitates acts of judgment, decision, assertion of priorities. His poems repudiate self in its romantic role: bedrock, shaping principle.

It is appropriate that Jeffers attracts moral criticism: he is himself, in the manner of the darker prophets, obsessed with morality. At stake is the salvation of the race. Always he hungers after large simplicities: "Why does insanity always twist the great answers? / Because only / tormented persons want the truth."

As for mankind in general: "Truly men hate the truth; they'd liefer / Meet a tiger in the road." He built into his poems the romance of not being listened to. He wanted not to be coddled; often, he seems to try to see humankind without human bias, aspiring not to the communal "cordiality and affection" but to the isolated falcon's "Realistic eyes and act."

The "act," for the artist, was not simply to see, but also to judge. The aesthetic that refuses judgment forfeits, for Jeffers, moral density. Thus the Chinese anthology: "These men were better / Artists than any of ours, and far better observers. They loved landscape / And put man in his place. But why / Do their rocks have no weight? They loved rice-wine and peace and friendship, / Above all they loved landscape and solitude, / —like Wordsworth. But Wordsworth's mountains have weight and mass, dull though the song be."

The Chinese poets share certain of Jeffers's biases, but they refuse to substitute speculations on the eternal for fastidious notation of the temporal. If, for Jeffers, they do not satisfy, at least they do not commit the more dangerous errors of self-delusion that occur primarily in the moral or spiritual spheres. As both reader and writer, Jeffers wants what "only tormented persons want"; he is correspondingly suspicious of comfort, of the distractions of pleasure. He despises those spiritual or ethical systems that encourage self-forgiveness; it may be this adamant horror of mercy to which Milosz particularly objects.

The anthropomorphic impulse that, in his address to Jeffers, Milosz commends produces life-enhancing miracles that seem the substance, or confirmation, of "grace and hope"; it is this impulse that makes domestic realities potentially the site of the divine: "Then, under the apple trees / Angels in homespun linen will come parting the boughs . . ." So ravishingly tender is the image as to make one forget that human culture is not, in fact, so wholly benign. But Jeffers's struggle has been to see the sun without an intervening image, not as a "farmer's ruddy face"; his vanity is to believe in the possibility. Jeffers's poems do not "implore protection"—to be protected is to not see, and Jeffers makes a cult of exposure—even as they regularly confess helplessness, despair. Jeffers wants to see the world with a gaze approximating the falcon's "realistic" one; what Jeffers calls "realistic" Milosz sees as "inhuman."

"No one with impunity / gives himself the eyes of a god," Milosz says. Clarity is not within human capability. And yet the preference for clarity over solace and the striving toward it is, in Jeffers, both moving and honorable. If Jeffers was brave "in a void" it was in part because he rejected the conditions of the "white kolkhoz tablecloth": his vanity was his vision of himself in relation to a single truth, but there are other and dangerous vanities, intolerances: the tribe's automatic allegiance to itself, for example. "Cordiality and affection" exclude those who do not participate in the social contract.

Jeffers lived in a terrifying time; it was not his nature to seek tolerable arrangements despite the world's state. Nor could he pray to the available projections; he did not find the world better for its religions. For Jeffers, the central fact of the founders of these religions is their inflamed humanity:

> Here was a man who was born a bastard, and among the people
> That more than any in the world valued race-purity, chastity, the
>   prophetic splendors of the race of David.
> Oh intolerable wound, dimly perceived. Too loving to curse his
>   mother, desert driven, devil haunted,
> The beautiful young poet found truth in the desert, but found also
> Fantastic solution of hopeless anguish. The carpenter was not his
>   father? Because God was his father,
> Not a man sinning, but the pure holiness and power of God. His
>   personal anguish and insane solution
> Have stained an age; nearly two thousand years are one vast poem
>   drunk with the wine of his blood.

In his stubborn, desperate way, Jeffers sought a plausible and sustaining vision, sought it explicitly outside the human circle, but sought it with an unremittingly human yearning. He wanted to find something in the world that was not corrupt, not the product of corruption:

> I think, here is your emblem
> To hang in the future sky;
> Not the cross, not the hive,
>
> But this; bright power, dark peace;
> Fierce consciousness joined with final
> Disinterestedness;
>
> Life with calm death; the falcon's
> Realistic eyes and act
> Married to the massive
>
> Mysticism of stone,
> Which failure cannot cast down
> Nor success make proud.

JOAN ALESHIRE

Staying News

A Defense of the Lyric

At a time when the world is threatened with nuclear annihilation—as well as regional wars and acts of repression that demand attention—many writers have criticized the self-absorption that has dominated poetry in the last twenty-five years, and have urged their fellows to include greater historical awareness and social empathy in their work. The term "confessional," first used to describe the self-revealing poetry of Lowell, Snodgrass, Berryman, Plath, and Sexton has become—often with justification—pejorative. At the same time, however, all poems with a high emotional content in which the speaker can be identified as the poet are being labeled "confessional," as if all were, willy-nilly, overly subjective.

Jonathan Holden, in an essay called "Postmodern Poetic Form: A Theory,"[1] describes Louise Glück and Carolyn Forché as confessional poets as a matter of course. Sandra Gilbert in "My Name is Darkness: The Poetry of Self-Definition" calls Yeats a "male confessional poet,"[2] along with Berryman and Lowell, without trying to distinguish whether the intent of their poems is self-display, or an argument with the self or the world with which the reader may identify.

What has happened to "lyric" as a descriptive term? It is used most often in its meanings of "rhapsodic" or "spontaneous" or "songlike," but rarely in its original sense: as a poetry directly expressing the poet's thoughts and emotions. Such a poetry has often been, in itself, a political statement; Mandelstam and Akhmatova wrote insistently and subversively of the self in a period that demanded political and artistic conformity. As their work shows, the poem of personal experience—the true lyric poem—can, through vision, craft, and objectivity toward the material, give a sense of commonality with unparalleled intimacy. A poem from Russia in the 1930s or from fifth-century Greece becomes new in the reading.

When contemporary poets are praised for their objectivity, all too often this means that they have excluded emotion from their work; too often their poems are bits of filigree rather than true bridges from the poet's consciousness to the reader's, carrying essential information.

The Kenyon Review 10,3 (Summer 1988): 47–64.

Direct expressions of emotion are suspect, particularly in English. Poets who write out of their own lives have reason to be uncertain, even defensive—but they may be writing not confessionally but lyrically. The lyric tradition allows for the expression of direct emotion but imposes a degree of objectivity on the material by formal—but not always traditional—devices.

As a reader, I've always been drawn to poems where the first person speaker is indistinguishable from the poet, because those poems give access, on an elemental level, to intimate experience. In the poems I admire, the personal details convey the essence of the poet's communication without drawing attention to themselves. The "I" of the poem is the fulcrum on which the action of the poem turns, the agent by which the reader can enter the experience, can—in that overused but apt word here—"share" experience with the speaker. The lyric "I" of the poem is the medium of communication, and in its partial quality, its singularity, there is a certain—because limited—reliability. The effectiveness of the speaker lies in his or her vulnerability, when the "I" makes no claims to knowledge outside its own experience. This clear limitation, this bias can convince the reader that the speaker is telling the truth—at least at the moment of composition. Eliot in "The Three Voices of Poetry" defines the lyric as the voice of the poet speaking to himself, oppressed by a burden that he must bring to relief.[3] But this conversation with oneself is not necessarily private, for, as Eliot continues, the voice of the poet speaking to himself and the voice of the poet speaking for an audience of any size are often found together. "Even though . . . the author of a poem may have written it without thought of an audience, he will also want to know what the poem which has satisfied him will have to say to other people, . . . the unseen audience."[4]

Shakespeare in the sonnets, Keats and Yeats speak from the self's particular viewpoint, but for these poets, it's not only life's experience that interests, but how what has been thought and felt—the burden seeking release—can be made into the experience of a poem. The act of making the poem as a piece of work outside the self draws the poet's attention away from the self and into the work, which makes its own demands. True concentration on craft is an act of forgetting the self.

In the confessional poem, as I'd like to define it, the poet, overwhelmed or intoxicated by the facts of his or her life, lets the facts take over. To say that a poem is "confessional" is to signal a breakdown in judgment and craft. Confession shares with the lyric a degree of self-revelation but carries implications that the lyric resists. The *Oxford English Dictionary* defines confession as the declaration or disclosure of something that one has allowed to remain secret as being prejudicial, humiliating, or inconvenient to oneself; the disclosure of private feeling; a plea of guilty, an admission of what one has been charged with; a formal confession made in order to receive absolution. I see the confessional poem as a plea for special treatment, a poem where the poet's stance is one of particularity apart from common experience. Confession in art, as in life, can be self-serving—an attempt to shift the burden of knowledge from speaker-transgressor to listener.

Lowell's poetry shows the shifting borders of lyric tradition and confession. Stephen Yenser, in discussing *The Dolphin,* makes a useful distinction between "gossip (fact, data, raw material)" and "gospel (parable, pattern, truth)" emphasizing that where there is more gossip than gospel, "The pattern of experience cannot emerge."⁵ The poems in *Life Studies* and *The Dolphin* are particularly full of the sort of factual detail that reveals the speaker's life and only intermittently conveys larger, impersonal truth. In "Unwanted," from his last book, Lowell writes: "Alas, I can only tell my own story— / talking to myself, or reading, or writing, / or fearlessly holding back nothing from a friend, / who believes me for a moment / to keep up conversation." The concern with himself and with truth—often in the literal sense, not the metaphoric—is the ground note of the poetry. In "Father's Bedroom," a short but not atypical example of the family poems in *Life Studies,* the sharp eye and ear can't compensate for the lack of communicating metaphor or myth or "gospel." The facts lie, separate and particular, on the page; though the father's precision and a bit of his history are suggested, the speaker-son makes no imaginative entry into his inner world:

FATHER'S BEDROOM

In my father's bedroom:
blue threads as thin
as pen-writing on the bedspread,
blue dots on the curtains,
a blue kimono,
Chinese sandals with blue plush straps.
The broad planked floor
had a sandpapered neatness.
The clear glass bed-lamp
with a white doily shade
was still raised a few
inches by resting on volume two
of Lafcadio Hearn's
Glimpses of Unfamiliar Japan.
Its warped olive cover
was punished like a rhinoceros hide.
In the flyleaf:
"Robbie from Mother."

Years later in the same hand:
"This book has had hard usage
on the Yangtze River, China.
It was left under an open
porthole in a storm."

It seems to me that this poem is interesting only if one is already interested in Lowell; it conveys little sense of the unseen connections, the emotion that draws a reader to identify and to participate in the experience of the poem. The poem places a demand on the reader's indulgence rather than helping the reader to see as the poet does. Even in poems at the end of *Life Studies* where the speaker's emotion is conveyed—"Waking in the Blue," "Home After Three Months Away," "Man and Wife"—Lowell's focus is on the self rather than on life as seen through the speaker's eyes. In "Waking in the Blue," the poet's evaluating and controlling intelligence dominates the emotional experience, and prevents the reader from reacting to the poem's experience without always being conscious of the poet himself. Even though Lowell acknowledges, "We are all old-timers here," after distinguishing himself from the other inmates at McLean's Hospital, the tight control and the encapsulated presentation work to keep the reader, like those "locked razors," at bay.

There are moments in the poems—notably in *History,* in "For the Union Dead," in "The Public Garden," in "Skunk Hour"—where Lowell loses himself in meditation on something other than himself. In "Skunk Hour," the sense of the poet watching the "love cars" and finally, the skunks—who are given a full and attentive description— allows the reader to share the poet's experience most fully without the interference of the poet's mediating self-consciousness. Lowell learned from Bishop's objectivity, and through it actually became most truly lyric. The poems in *The Dolphin* war with detail, including verbatim quotes from Elizabeth Hardwick's letters, but clearly try to discern a larger meaning in the facts. "On the End of the Phone" is one couple's separation but it's also all ruptures, because ambivalence is so brilliantly shown:

My sidestepping and obliquities, unable
to take the obvious truth on any subject—
why do I do what I do not want to say?
When everything matters, ask and never know?
Your rapier voice—I have had so much—
hundred words a minute, piercing and thrilling . . .
the invincible lifedrive of everything alive,
ringing down silver dollars with each word. . . .
Love wasn't what went wrong, we kept our daughter;

what a good father is is no man's boast—
to be still friends when we're no longer children. . . .
Why am I talking from the top of my mouth?
I am talking to you transatlantic,
we're almost talking in one another's arms.

In *The Classical Tradition in Poetry* Gilbert Murray describes the first form of expressive ritual that preceded the lyric: the *molpê,* or dance-and-song. The song was "inspired," or breathed into by the gods; the dance mimicked the longing for what can't be expressed in words. The *molpê's* chief subjects were Love and Death, and then Strife—about which Murray writes: ". . . [I]t is largely strife which gives to love or death its value. The world is not greatly interested in a marriage which has involved no difficulty and no opposition, or even in a natural and expected death. It is Love won in spite of obstacles and enemies; it is Death in the midst of strife and glory, especially Death averted or conquered."[6] In the thwarting of Death, some idea of transcendence arises, simply through the observation of the seasonal cycle; or through *mimesis* and *methexis.* Murray defines *mimesis* as the striving to be like something one longs to be, and *methexis* as participation and communion through ritual. Both mimesis and methexis, according to Murray, involve transcendence of the self: "some ecstasy or 'standing outside' of the prison of the bard's ordinary identity and experience."[7] The bard performed the *molpê* with the dancers, singing words the maker or poet had composed.

The epic, as recorded by Homer and other singers, grew out of the *molpê;* the lyric grew out of the epic but is informed by both traditions. In the earliest known epics, singers reported the old stories without reflection, as pure narratives of the exploits of heroes and gods. Precise detail made the narratives more vivid, and the use of simile stimulated the audience's imagination. The singers performed at feasts, where they were questioned by their listeners, who often asked them to repeat or to give more detail. The German scholar Hermann Fränkel describes these exchanges as "free conversations."[8] Someone would ask, "How did Agamemnon die?" and the singer would make that part of the story more vivid without, however, changing the basic plot. The epic singer, Fränkel says, was "poised, phrase by phrase, verse by verse, between enduring tradition and momentary improvisation."[9] Though the speaker didn't comment on the action, and appeared detached, he conveyed emotion through the details he chose. Sometimes, a singer would seem to the audience to *become* the character whose words he was speaking, giving the listeners a shock of surprise and the sense of intimacy.

Gradually, as people tired of the old stories, singers abandoned the epic masks and began to sing in their own words, often to the accompaniment of Apollo's instrument: the small harp or lyre. In reaction to the epic, the lyric can be seen as antiheroic, realistic, idiosyncratic; in short, it was subversive. Hesiod, writing about peasants' lives in *Works and Days* (eighth century B.C.) prepares the way for the individuality and specificity of the lyric:

> Take good note when you first hear the cranes flying over, coming each year without fail and crying high in the heavens. They will give you the sign for ploughing and tell when the winter's rains are at hand: at their call the man without oxen trembles. Then give your oxen plenty of fodder—if you have oxen. It is easy to say: "Please lend me your oxen and wagon," easy also to answer, "I'm sorry, I've work for my own oxen." (Fränkel translation)

The lyric song emerged as a short improvisation based on the singer's life at the moment of writing, but this improvisation, Murray points out, was prepared for by the poet's mode of living and by the constant exercise of technique. The singer could change his or her mind from song to song, and often within single lyrics several emotions coexisted, in the union of opposites that's characteristic of Greek thought. The lyric was specific, of the present and of the singer; it centered, Fränkel says, on "the personality of the singer, the time of delivery and the particular circumstances of its origin. In a certain sense, the lyric stands in the service of the day and is ephemeral."[10] The singer might reflect on how the song occurred to him and on the paradox of his effort to capture in words a moment always in flux. Mostly, however, the material was presented without evaluation or explanation. The material was drawn from the poet's life and shaped by imagination. The narrative element never disappears in the lyric; as in the epic, vivid detail and gesture express emotion in the poems that have come down to us.

Archilochus is the first lyric singer whose words were copied and preserved. He was working around 700 B.C., but his lyrics were copied from memory and stored in Alexandria when Egypt became the repository for Greek culture in the Roman Empire. The verses we have may be faulty transcriptions, but a strong personality speaks through them. If lyric has been diluted to mean "poetic" or "pretty" or "graceful," Archilochus was none of those things. The bastard son of a noble and a slave from a marble-quarrying island, he was a mercenary soldier as well as a singer. Like Hesiod, he made money singing his impressions of the hard life he knew. "So my shield, which I left unwillingly—it was a good one—somewhere behind a bush, is now a Thracian's delight," he sang. "Still, I came off with my skin: the shield is not so important. Well, let it go. Very soon I'll buy another as good" (Fränkel translations).

Fränkel notes that Archilochus "takes the first and nearest data of the individual: the now, the here, the I,"[11] and there is an appealing sturdiness to his work. This singer learns from conflict and defeat: "The fox knows many things, the hedgehog one big one. . . . [O]ne big thing I know how to do—terribly repay with sorrow sorrow what is done to me." (All translations from the Greek, except those as noted by Mary Barnard and Guy Davenport, are by Hermann Fränkel.) Archilochus's language was colloquial, clear, and seemed to fall naturally into rhyme.

Of his accuracy and immediacy, Fränkel writes: "The primary data . . . are for Archilochus also the final data. . . . [His] lyric proceeds wholly out of the personality of the poet or leads to it; but it is not subjective in the sense that it wishes to give a picture of life individually shaped or colored."[12] The lyric singers used a transparent language through which reality—of the physical, intellectual, and emotional worlds—could be seen. In fact, in a universe animated by the gods, there was no distinction between body and soul, tangible and spiritual; precise detail could embody emotion completely and inevitably.

Accuracy in the expression of one individual life allowed the songs to be personal yet not idiosyncratic. As Fränkel expresses it: "Greek lyric poets did not aim to make themselves interesting by their peculiar sensibilities, but sought rather to demonstrate the general and the basic by the example of themselves."[13] Archilochus makes such an example by saying:

> Such a desire for her love rolled up under my heart, poured a great darkness on my eyes, and robbed from my breast its tender wits. . . . Miserable I lie under desire, lifeless, with harsh pains, because of the gods, pierced to the very bones.

But he's nothing if not resilient: "Heart, my heart, by countless sorrows much bewildered and perplexed, pluck up courage. . . ." At his brother-in-law's funeral he sings:

> Let us sink the painful gift of Lord Poseidon in the deep. [Pain for his death would be lighter] had the funeral fire taken his head and the fair frame of his limbs, wrapped in robes of white, as is seemly. [But] nothing is made any better by tears; nor, if I seek pleasure, company, friendship, and joy, do I make anything worse.

Archilochus is capable of confessing to faults, but, in the same breath, reminds his audience that such failings are human: "I have erred; this very blindness fell on many men before."

Sappho, born about a hundred years later, echoes Archilochus's frankness, humor, specificity, and worldliness—and adds her own note of longing, at least in the fragments that have come down to us.

In two translations, Mary Barnard's intuitive and imaginative render-
ings and Guy Davenport's more literal versions, a strong personality
emerges from scraps of language. The range represented in the exist-
ing fragments—whatever strips of papyrus survived the trash heaps of
Alexandria—is extraordinary. Sappho loved gossip, clothes, and both
men and women; she could be funny and celebratory and grieving in
her songs.

The fragments we have are of songs meant to be sung in public, yet
they are intimate, conversational, often addressed to a specific "you."
Maurice Bowra says of Sappho's Greek: ". . . [I]t looks like ordinary
speech raised to the highest level of expressiveness. In her great range
of different meters there is not one which does not move with perfect
ease and receive her words as if they were ordained for it."[14] Mary
Barnard describes Sappho's style in the original as "spare but musi-
cal . . . the sound of the speaking voice making a simple but emotion-
ally loaded statement."[15]

In Barnard's versions, one has the sense of the translator perceiving
meaning in the fragmentary details and conversations:

47: I was so happy   53: With his venom

Believe me, I   Irresistible
prayed that that   and bittersweet
night be doubled for us
                                           that loosener
                                           of limbs, Love

13: People do gossip   reptile-like
                                           strikes me down
And they say about
Leda, that she

once found an egg   72: Of course I love you
hidden under
                                   But, if you love me,
wild hyacinths   marry a young woman!

                                   I couldn't stand it
                                   to live with a young
                                   man, I being older

79: Really, Gorgo,

My disposition
is not at all
spiteful: I have
a childlike heart

In Davenport, the voice is a bit muted, the tone less sure; #32 in his volume *Archilochus. Sappho. Alkman* is clearly Barnard's #72:

> Though you are my lover,
> Take for wife a younger woman;
> Find a newer bed to lie in,
> I could not bear to be the older.

And his #148 is a flatter version of the poem Barnard translates as #13:

> Once upon a time, the story goes,
> Leda found a hyacinthine egg.

Davenport's translations are valuable because he points out missing sections of the fragments by using brackets, and because he translates more of the songs than Barnard does, but he lacks her ability to elicit the poetic argument, the surprising juxtapositions from the elements at hand. Fränkel's prose translations give a sense of Sappho's use of memory and her ability to present a dramatic situation:

> In good faith, I wish I were dead. She left me, crying bitterly, and said to me: "How terrible it is for us, Sappho; truly I go unwilling." I answered: "Go and think of me, happily. You know how I worshipped you. If not I wish to remind you what fair and lovely things we enjoyed. With many garlands of violets and sweet roses on your tresses you sat by me, on your soft neck many necklaces woven of flowers. Your hair you drenched with myrrh . . . laid upon soft coverlets. . . . No sacred grove nor shrine was there which we did not fill with the sound of our songs and music of the lyre."

The remembered scene is so sensuously described that it comes to life, putting the present in shadow. In spite of the dubious authenticity of the originals, the spirit of lyric poetry—immediate, precise, personally expressive—survives the barrier of translation. There is a sense of shape, of argument in the fragments: poetic intelligence powerfully at work.

Archilochus and Sappho are still read and translated; the singers who followed them are largely forgotten—probably because they became more instructive than expressive, more general than tactile. External pressures may have brought more public considerations into lyric song; in any case, poets began to talk about "the good," and as Fränkel says, "of 'riches,' 'wealth,' 'poverty,' 'distress,' not of wheatfields, herds of oxen, flocks and sheep, ships bearing produce from country to country."[16] Accepted meanings changed in ways familiar to us from bureaucracy and advertising; *psyche,* which had meant *breath,* had become *soul* by the fifth century B.C.

The last great lyric singer, Pindar, placed a premium on a quality called *kairos* that serves as a crucial element in the continuation of the lyric. *Kairos* has no single equivalent in English; it translates as: "the rules of accurate choice and prudent restraint, the sense of what suits the circumstances; tact, discretion."[17] "Kairos alone produces maturity in any field," Pindar wrote, and showed his sense of balance by setting opposite points of view against one another before making a summation or resolution. Pindar's strategy of argument continues in the sonnet as invented by Petrarch, who set forth his songs of courtly love as dialectics in two four-line stanzas followed by two three-line stanzas, with a rhyme scheme of *abba / abba / cdc / dcc.* Petrarch's form has been played on in various ways; what seems consistent is the use of argument, the turns and attempt at reconciliation of opposites.

In Shakespeare's sonnets and in Keats's, the sense of lyric poem as argument is particularly clear. Shakespeare's sonnets are objects of such solidity, so well made that they rival the finest watch. Many of the sonnets contain particular information and direct emotion, but they are about the nature of love and of the lover, more than they are directly about the speaker. The speaker separates his own frank emotions from the making of the poem, and attempts to reach a resolution of a conflict he's presented in the poem. In making the formal turn, the poet often moves to adopt the lover's point of view or to work toward a general good as apart from his own needs. *Kairos* is evident in the formal elements of the poem, but also in its vision. The speaker's concern in all the sonnets is how to arrest the flow of time, not how to express personal longing and grief—though longing and grief are often present in large measure. The poems focus on the self only so that the "you" will be better seen, so that the experience will be fully convincing. The "I" is an agent of experience that, if not immediately intelligible to us in its particulars, becomes so as the argument is presented through sound, syntax, and imagery.

Though Milton is a more general, more descriptive writer than the Greek lyric poets, there is lyric emotion and *kairos* in abundance in the autobiographical sonnet "To Mr. Cyriack Skinner upon his Blindness" (Sonnet XXIII). The "you" addressed is a specific person; the details come clearly from Milton's life, but the poem is no confession, no plea for special treatment. The concentration is on the poem; the juggled phrases and shifts in expected syntax demonstrate how difficult it is to draw good from misfortune. Milton works from the particulars of his life, but turns toward the poem and ultimately to his friend:

> Cyriack, this three years day these eyes, though clear
> To outward view of blemish or of spot,

Bereft of light their seeing have forgot,
Nor to their idle orbs doth sight appear
Of Sun or Moon or Star throughout the year,
Or man or woman. Yet I argue not
Against heaven's hand or will, nor bate a jot
Of heart or hope; but still bear up and steer
Right onward. What supports me, dost thou ask?
The conscience, Friend, to have lost them overplied
In liberty's defence, my noble task,
Of which all Europe talks from side to side.
This thought might lead me through the world's vain mask
Content though blind, had I no better guide.

Milton is always aware of what is beyond the self—the larger cause: of liberty, of reassuring a friend; the guidance of heaven's will. The turns of language make the conflict and its resolution convincing; the reader is drawn into the forging of an argument. *Kairos* is a more discernible element than direct emotion.

The romantic poets adapted and revitalized the lyric; direct expression of personality, and the use of colloquial diction and of specific detail were part of Wordsworth's aesthetic. In the sonnet to Catherine Wordsworth, his dead child, the sonnet form, the *kairos,* barely restrains the expression of grief—but does shape it. What Maurice Bowra said about Greek funeral friezes applies to Wordsworth here: "Greek art, at least in its archaic and classical periods, so masters its subjects that it passes beyond realistic or naturalistic representation to show another sphere. What might be unbearably painful is so controlled and transformed that it does not distress, but exalt."[18]

SONNET XXI—CATHERINE WORDSWORTH
(DIED JUNE 4, 1812)

Surprised by joy—impatient as the wind
I turned to share the transport—Oh! with whom
But Thee, deep buried in the silent tomb,
That spot which no vicissitude can find?
Love, faithful love, recalled thee to my mind—
But how could I forget thee? Through what power
Even for the least division of an hour,
Have I been so beguiled as to be blind
To my most grievous loss? That thought's return
Was the worst pang sorrow ever bore,
Save one, one only, when I stood forlorn,
Knowing my heart's best treasure was no more;

That neither present time, nor years unborn
Could to my sight that heavenly face restore.

The poet openly expresses emotion in a tone so intimate it's as if the child could hear him. Though the syntax and diction seem a bit arch at times—"Oh! with whom / But Thee, deep buried in the silent tomb"—we know that Wordsworth used the speech of his time and was criticized for not being sufficiently "poetic." The most direct moments seem absolutely contemporary—"But how could I forget thee?" The poem keeps turning in its propositions, the syntax working against the lines; it breaks apart in questions as the speaker discovers new dimensions to his grief. There is denial and shocked remembrance, but the fact that the poet has actually lost a child is not as important as the demonstration of the ways loss works on the soul. The strength of the form enables the poem to accommodate so many turns, to break apart so often in shifts of tone, and yet be all of a piece in its expression.

Keats too was able to use the stuff of his own life and at the same time to find form and language to express not the facts of that life but his concerns. We know of Keats that he watched two brothers die of tuberculosis and that he may have noticed symptoms of the disease in himself by the time he wrote the sonnet "When I Have Fears." The poem is located in a moment, a specific "when," but this very designation shifts the focus away from the poet, as it wouldn't so quickly if he'd begun, "I have fears," and then gone on to detail them. The *when* broadens the approach to include everyone—assuming almost conversationally that others share those fears—and sets up a sort of argument; if there's a *when* clause, the expectation is that a *then* clause will follow and possibly resolve the proposition. A sense of balance is established, not only by form but by syntax; if *this* is true, then *that* must follow, at that moment. We read, drawn by argument, by music, by syntax, by image—but there is finally, movingly, no resolution of the fears. The turn is down, to the revelation that the mind is unable to comprehend its own death, even as it knows that death is inevitable.

When I have fears that I may cease to be
    Before my pen has gleaned my teeming brain,
Before high-piled books, in charactery,
    Hold like rich garners the full ripened grain;
When I behold, upon the night's starred face,
    Huge cloudy symbols of a high romance,
And think that I may never live to trace
    Their shadows, with the magic hand of chance;
And when I feel, fair creature of an hour,
    That I shall never look upon thee more,
Never have relish in the faery power

Of unreflecting love;—then on the shore
Of the wide world I stand alone, and think
Till love and fame to nothingness do sink.

The poem is the object Keats puts in the way of oblivion; the only resolution to the fear of no longer being able to trace the shadows is to trace them. The sonnet is remarkably specific and personal, yet it also speaks for us; we go beyond sympathy for the speaker to the sense that the speaker is ourselves.

Akhmatova, too, wrote poems that are scenes from a specific life in a particular time and place, but her interest is not in the self. Rather, she focuses on relationships between people, and on the relationships between sounds and images that make a poem. In her best poems, though this is hard to see in even the most sensitive translations to date, there is a sense of unity, an interlocking structure of images that brings to mind the quote from Donald Justice that Michael Ryan uses in his essay "Flaubert in Florida"[19] to describe Justice's own work:

In a good short poem a fine sense of relations among its parts is felt, word connecting with word, line with line: as in a spider web, touch it and the whole structure responds.

This could be an echo of Aristotle's "A thing whose presence or absence makes no difference to a whole is not part of that whole."

It's said that readers memorized Akhmatova's poems and would recite back to her the lines she'd forget when giving a reading; the degree of identification is high, because there is just enough detail to create an experience that may be the speaker-poet's, but is also known in essence to the reader. In Akhmatova's poetry, complex histories—personal and often public—are conveyed by precise details, but these specifics are also general, available, and analogous to the reader's experience, as Lowell's details are not. Akhmatova, like a Greek lyric poet, exemplifies the personal without being idiosyncratic. Her sense of what the poem demands supersedes any concentration on autobiographical data.

In the 1917 poem usually translated as "We Don't Know How to Say Goodbye," the speaker addresses a specific "you." The couple's predicament is particular, their relationship is outside convention, but the inevitability of parting resonates beyond the particulars. The poet takes the reader on the couple's wandering, and ends with an image of illusion that becomes clear in its implication as the "you" draws it in the trampled snow. The reader's imagination is elicited to complete the picture, and does so because the poet has also made the poem an experience to be entered as a participant.

We don't know how to say goodbye—
we wander all over shoulder to shoulder.
It's already starting to get dark;
you're thoughtful, and I keep quiet.

Let's go into the church, watch
a funeral, a christening, a wedding;
let's leave, not looking at each other . . .
Why don't we live like that?

Or, let's sit in the cemetery,
in trampled snow; let's breathe lightly,
and let you trace with a stick palaces
where we will always be together.

(Aleshire translation)

Akhmatova is the reader's representative; she articulates what we have known. Along with Mandelstam and her first husband, Nikolai Gumilev, Akhmatova believed that poetry would find resonance in the immediate and concrete; the Acmeist movement, which they founded, was a reaction against the static abstractions of Russian symbolism in the late nineteenth century. "Long live the living Rose!" Mandelstam proclaimed, tired of flowers that were merely representations of ideas. Both Mandelstam and Akhmatova were classicists and made the lyric tradition their own.

Though I have no evidence that Yeats was familiar with the Acmeists in Russia, he made a conscious break with the French symbolists and, at the same time in the early twentieth century, began to write poems that were clear and expressive of personality. In "Discoveries," an essay published in 1906—just a few years before Mandelstam celebrated the "living Rose"—Yeats wrote:

> . . . [W]hat moves men in the arts is what moves them in life, and that is, intensity of personal life, intonations that show them . . . the strength, the essential moment of a man who would be exciting at the market or at the dispensary door. They must go out of the theater with the strength they live by strengthened from looking upon some passion that could . . . strike down an enemy, fill a long stocking with money or move a girl's heart.[20]

He began to write directly out of his own life, in a conscious shift from his earlier, more fanciful and more distanced poems. With "No Second Troy" of 1910, Yeats forges a poetry that is particular in personal detail, that deals clearly with the poet's self, but which focuses on the poet-speaker's relationships with the world, with others. In "No Second Troy," the poet is speaking to himself, acknowledging anger and sorrow, but he concentrates on the beloved, opposing reason and sympathy to anger and pain. But then Maud Gonne—the undisputed "you"—becomes not so much the subject of the poem as does her experience, which is then, through the dimension of simile, set in the context of myth. The "I" transmits experience but almost disappears in the process, indicating that the self, where the poem began, is not as important as the story. The poem moves through the particular life of the "she," and then shows that life as history, as part of human endeavor, is more than an individual life.

> Why should I blame her that she filled my days
> With misery, or that she would of late
> Have taught to ignorant men most violent ways,
> Or hurled the little streets upon the great,
> Had they but courage equal to desire?
> What could have made her peaceful with a mind
> That nobleness made simple as a fire,
> With beauty like a tightened bow, a kind
> That is not natural in an age like this,
> Being high and solitary and most stern?
> Why, what could she have done, being what she is?
> Was there another Troy for her to burn?

If there is anger at the "she" as destroyer, there is also a sense of inevitability, which subsumes raw emotion. Yeats speaks not only of himself and Maud Gonne in this poem, but also for Maud Gonne and the nature of her idealism; the poem moves into a dimension of empathy that instructs us and enlarges our sense of human possibility. The argument of the poem—and Yeats believed that a poem is always a quarrel with oneself—is against the part of the self that *does* blame, that is heartbroken and enraged. It is an argument waged in hard, clear terms; the struggle is conveyed in the rhetorical questions—"rhetorical" in the sense that the answer is implicit in the question. "No Second Troy" stops two lines short of being a traditional sonnet, and its rhyme scheme indicates a structure of three quatrains—*abab / cdcd / efef*—submerged in the one long stanza. That the rhymes move outward, rather than repeating or interlocking, conveys the outward movement of the thought: from personal to other, to other's experience and finally to myth. The syntax works against the rhyme scheme to give density and complexity to the strands of argument.

So far in this discussion, the use of traditional forms has been suggested as a way of organizing the material of personal experience—the material that as Mandelstam said, "always resists you." Free verse could be suspected of introducing the self-indulgences I am defining as "confessional poetry," but traditional forms have not always guaranteed a poet's self-restraint or *kairos*. Poets working in free verse have rather had to create their own forms, suited to their temperaments and voices. A poem in free verse can—in fact, must—have its own inner coherence, what Eliot calls in "The Music of Poetry," "the inner unity which is unique to every poem, against the outer unity which is typical."[21]

William Carlos Williams, that great improviser, might have resisted the notion that he is a close relation of the Greek lyric singers, but I share Mary Barnard's sense that Williams's immediacy, his attention to detail, and his interest in speech patterns are truly lyric qualities. Also, his sense of the object as conveying emotion, ideas, meaning is particularly in the Greek tradition. "Waiting" is an argument with the self, but it is meant to be overheard. It arises out of a specific moment of sensation and conflict. The poem's focus moves from the poet's sensations to the external objects, events, and human beings that move him. There is a struggle between desire and sense of duty, honesty, and an attempt at balance. The abrupt line breaks, pauses, and swift transitions are expressive of the speaker's state of mind through the poem: his untroubled, sensual solitude; his despair at his children's demands; his doubt and attempt at distance. The poem resolves in a question that takes the focus away from the poet-speaker and into the dimension of self-knowledge and its expression. There is a struggle for balance and for reconciliation, but the demands of love are recognized as demands, and the sorrow is that of inadequate response. The honesty of the exploration is relentless, unsparing of the self.

WAITING

When I am alone I am happy.
The air is cool. The sky is
flecked and splashed and wound
with color. The crimson phalloi
of the sassafras leaves
hang crowded before me
in shoals on the heavy branches.
When I reach my doorstep
I am greeted by
the happy shrieks of my children
and my heart sinks.
I am crushed.

Are not my children as dear to me
as falling leaves or
must one become stupid

to grow older?
It seems much as if Sorrow
had tripped up my heels.
Let us see, let us see!
What did I plan to say to her
when it should happen to me
as it has happened now?

"Let us see, let us see!" The dilemma is insoluble; the natural world is more vivid, more loved than the children, but knowledge—the hard clarity of the truth—arrives, and the poet articulates it. "Waiting" seems at first glance a mysterious title—for whom? for what? isn't directly apparent. But the title indicates that the poem's true subject isn't the poet's moods or his conscience, but the gaining of wisdom. At the time of this poem, the poet sees that he is still waiting to reconcile his opposing impulses; the poem moves from specific situation through turns of awareness to achieve universal resonance.

Louise Glück has been described as a confessional and idiosyncratically subjective poet, but her sense of restraint gives to her poems a mythic dimension. She is interested in "gospel," not in "gossip," the experience itself, not the literal details. Nowhere is this clearer than in the poem "Mock Orange," which contains a statement of such startling intensity—"I hate them [the mock orange blossoms]. I hate them as I hate sex"—that it may at first seem a confession of the poet's secrets. The poem, however, is more than an outburst; it is an argument between two parts of the self: the one that needs to believe—in love, in union with another; and the one that knows such belief is self-deception, but will go on being deceived. The tension of the argument places the focus of the poem on experience, on human relationship, not on the speaker, who at first seems to be carrying on an actual argument with a "you." The poem begins in midargument, with the speaker correcting the "you's" contentions that it is the moonlight that illuminates the yard, and that it's the moon, or the speaker's moods, that trouble her. The hatred of the flowers for appearing to be what they are not (real orange blossoms, the wedding flowers, the ones that bear fruit) and for not truly, though they glow whitely, casting a light is not expressed as an absolute statement. It is rather part of an equation: I hate them as I hate sex. The terms of the equation—*as* is the crucial syntactical signal here—give qualification, a sense of degree to the hatred of sex. Sex then is shown in vivid terms as domination by the man of the woman, but it is entered into; the cry of abandonment always does escape. The longing for union combined with the knowledge that union can't be truly achieved makes the poem's argument acutely complex and dramatic. The "one sound," the fusion of longings—the "you's" question and the speaker's "pursuing answer," which is no answer but another searching question—falls apart on the acknowledgment of essential, irreparable separation. And yet, the deception is played out, works over and over on the speaker, pervasive as the mock orange scent, until the speaker is left with the question of how to reconcile, how to live with, these conflicting pieces of emotional truth. It is a poem not about the poet but the human dilemma. When the speaker says, "We were made fools of," the "you" and "I" and the readers are included, joined in their imperfection.

MOCK ORANGE

It is not the moon, I tell you.
It is these flowers
lighting the yard.

I hate them.
I hate them as I hate sex,
the man's mouth
sealing my mouth, the man's
paralyzing body—

and the cry that always escapes,
the low, humiliating
premise of union—

In my mind tonight
I hear the question and pursuing answer
fused in one sound
that mounts and mounts and then
is split into the old selves,
the tired antagonisms. Do you see?
We were made fools of.
And the scent of mock orange
drifts through the window.

How can I rest?
How can I be content
when there is still
that odor in the world?

This poem is the first in Glück's collection, *The Triumph of Achilles,* a book that shows its roots in classicism and makes the tradition new. It's also possible, though, to see the lyric tradition alive in much less formal, slangy, even gossipy poems like Frank O'Hara's. O'Hara filled his poems with dailiness, with the detail of a particular life of prominence and privilege, but the underlying concerns, the universal passions are almost always apparent. "The Day Lady Died" is a poem of private grief for a public figure (Billie Holiday) in which the power of music and the shock of death in the midst of life are conveyed with lyric immediacy.

THE DAY LADY DIED

It is 12:20 in New York a Friday
three days after Bastille day, yes
it is 1959 and I go get a shoeshine
because I will get off the 4:19 in Easthampton
at 7:15 and then go straight to dinner
and I don't know the people who will feed me

I walk up the muggy street beginning to sun
and have a hamburger and a malted and buy
an ugly NEW WORLD WRITING to see what the poets
in Ghana are doing these days
                    I go on to the bank
and Miss Stillwagon (first name Linda I once heard)
doesn't even look up my balance for once in my life
and in the GOLDEN GRIFFIN I get a little Verlaine
for Patsy with drawings by Bonnard although I do
think of Hesiod, trans. Richmond Lattimore or
Brendan Behan's new play or *Le Balcon* or *Les Nègres*
of Genet, but I don't, I stick with Verlaine
after practically going to sleep with quandariness

and for Mike I just stroll into the PARK LANE
Liquor Store and ask for a bottle of Strega and
then I go back where I came from to 6th Avenue
and the tobacconist in the Ziegfeld Theatre and
casually ask for a carton of Gauloises and a carton
of Picayunes, and a NEW YORK POST with her face on it

and I am sweating a lot by now and thinking of
leaning on the john door in the 5 SPOT
while she whispered a song along the keyboard
to Mal Waldron and everyone and I stopped breathing

It is hard, finally, to talk about poems that take my breath away. I'm reminded of Marina Tsvetayeva's comment on criticism: "There is no approach to art; it is a seizing." In no art form is this seizing more apparent than in the lyric poem, which gives the shock of hearing a human voice speaking intimately, from the heart.

NOTES

1. Jonathan Holden, "Postmodern Poetic Form: A Theory," *Poetics: Essays on the Art of Poetry* (Green Harbor, Mass.: *Tendril Magazine*, 1984), 20.

2. Sandra Gilbert, "My Name is Darkness: The Poetry of Self-Definition," *Poetics: Essays on the Art of Poetry* (Green Harbor, Mass.: *Tendril Magazine,* 1984), 99–100.

3. T. S. Eliot, *On Poetry and Poets* (New York: Farrar, Straus and Cudahy, 1957), 107.

4. Ibid., 109.

5. Quoted in Ian Hamilton, *Robert Lowell: A Life* (New York: Random House, 1982), 432.

6. Gilbert Murray, *The Classical Tradition in Poetry* (Cambridge, Mass.: Harvard University Press, 1927), 43.

7. Ibid., 45.

8. Hermann Fränkel, *Early Greek Poetry and Philosophy,* trans. Moses Hadas and James Willis (New York: Harcourt, Brace, Jovanovich, 1962), 13.

9. Ibid., 8.

10. Ibid., 133.

11. Ibid., 139.

12. Ibid., 151.

13. Ibid., 151.

14. Quoted in Mary Barnard, *Sappho: A New Translation* (Berkeley: University of California Press, 1958), 103.

15. Ibid., 103.

16. Fränkel, 423.

17. Ibid., 447–48.

18. Maurice Bowra, *The Greek Experience* (Cleveland: World Publishing, 1957), 146.

19. Michael Ryan, "Flaubert in Florida," *New England Review and Bread Loaf Quarterly* 7, no. 2 (Winter 1984): 224.

20. W. B. Yeats, *Essays and Introductions* (New York: Collier, 1961), 265.

21. Eliot, 31.

MARIANNE BORUCH

Plath's Bees

Nearly thirty years to the month, the days had turned unexpectedly warm. October—a word so rough and rich to say—stood ancient, and brilliant as usual, if any sort of genius is usual. A friend of a friend had promised to show me bees; now was the time. The odd summerlike temperatures had roused and gentled them, he said as we turned off Route 26 into woods, the quiet its own sudden creature.

I had imagined a winding road—there it was—and of course a meadow. Then a ring of grub maple and tulip trees, and because we weren't far from the river, two great, sad sycamores. These were the university's bees. I had wanted to see a home site, something closer to Sylvia Plath's own venture in Devon where she kept one colony through its first real season, the summer of 1962, before her death the following winter. But my companion said this was exactly *like* such a place, more so than his own backyard where trees had gradually, over twenty years, encroached on the hives to cast them into shade that made them cross, easily angered. We stopped, and I saw the hives: nine gleaming layered boxes set evenly apart in the clearing's wild grass, cool and restful and weird. They seemed to hover there, the trees behind them just turning—red, and a yellow almost blinding.

October still, and almost thirty years before Plath crossed through this stillness and wrote her bee sequence, five poems, in one sleepless week. Say the words: bee box, pupa, pollen, venom. The busy dark interior I had yet to see. I had been warned to wear light colors. It calmed the bees, my companion told me over the phone. If you wear white, he said, to them you're almost invisible.

To be invisible. To be observer. "How shall I describe it?—" Plath wrote that last year about poetry itself, "a door opens, a door shuts. In between you have had a glimpse: a garden, a person, a rainstorm, a dragonfly, a heart, a city. . . . So a poem takes place." But nothing is as brief or as happenstance, nothing so unasked for. It starts stubbornly in the body, and beyond—father and mother, even back of that. Which is to say, it starts in memory; we want to repeat. "What do

From *Poetry's Old Air* by Marianne Boruch, 82–101 (Ann Arbor: University of Michigan Press, 1995). Copyright © 1995 by Marianne Boruch. First published in *Parnassus: Poetry in Review* 17,2/18,1: 76–95.

I remember / that was shaped / as this thing is shaped?" Williams keeps insisting in "Asphodel, That Greeny Flower." A door opens and shuts, a glimpse. And it begins—the long unfolding into image, specific image culled from a life, two lives or more. Faced without sentiment or nostalgia, such images *release*. Coming first those last months, Plath's bee sequence did this; in its fierce incandescence, twenty-two other poems followed, and *Ariel* began to burn and take form.

The bees, of course, seemed to be waiting for Plath, arriving a full generation earlier. A coincidence, maybe a dark luck, but first there was a boy with a taste for honey almost a century ago in Germany, in the Polish corridor. And this boy, Otto Plath, filched a glass straw from the kitchen, wandered through fields and woods to find the underground bumblebee nests, carefully lowered his straw and—two to one—struck the cool secret in spite of the bees' fury. Soon he was keeping bees carried home gingerly in cigar boxes, set up in the garden. At this distance, the boy becomes a tiny romantic figure on the horizon, the *Bienenkönig*—the bee king—his childhood friends called him, half jeering. Still, he is at it, bent forward in the grass, alert for a sign.

All this equals; it is a cycle we will see in the daughter: solitude and danger, a palpable reward. *Ariel* in general and the bee poems in particular carry—are carried by—this electric pulse and focus. It's in the relentless questions that push the poems forward; it's the repeated words, phrases, whole lines, which, like a narrowing to the sexual instant or like some frenzied mantra, slow the narrative press while speeding up every lyric mystery beneath. Her repetitions break through time, give glimpse of a stranger place—"sweetness, sweetness" the poet nearly singsongs, painting the hive to call to the bees by color, or chanting "she is old, old, old," deepening the pitch, making the queen bee primal, a *first thing,* of myth.

But it isn't myth, not completely. The bee poems aren't all lost to trance and sadness, though these tempt us with their poison and splendor. Ordinary cause and effect is here, the bit by bit of things. Plath's brilliance is that balance. Certainly loss and rage, and a calm that might well be madness, but it's the bees we understand, the sound of them in a box or, come fall, the dark of the cellar with its silent honey jars. How far away now is the boy who stands listening in the grass for what might be hidden underground? Not science or art, not yet. This watchfulness is habit; he is merely curious.

Simple tools for such a habit: I dutifully submitted to the veil, the gloves, part of the "moonsuit," Plath called it. But it was the smoker I loved. Half bellows, half oilcan, something out of Dickens in its epic but domestic no-nonsense feel, the smoker is exactly that: it smokes. And as we moved toward the bees and opened the first hive, my companion puffed into it small rapid clouds from the smoldering wood chips in the firepot.

Instantly the bees, furious at our invasion, calmed into slow drunkenness, flew away or back to the combs to anchor themselves against the pollen or honey cells. The smoke, my companion told me, excites then subdues them. They give up the notion *predator;* the issue is larger, more catastrophic—a fire near the hive, it's pointless to fight. Instead they take off, or begin to gorge themselves with honey in preparation for flight.

But don't they know we're doing this, just the same? I asked, helping him lift off the next heavy wooden layer—he called it a super—so we could see the combs up close. We're just the jiggling to them, he said. We're just what happens when the supers are moved. It's not in their code of responses to figure us out. But the smoke, it's older than we are; they know what to do with that.

I thought of our own codes locked in the brain, buried in cells, a prehistoric riddle. In college, I had a friend who knew all the things the mind refused to do; she had a list from class. One of them was picturing one's own body from a distance. Imagine you're sleeping, she liked to say. Now look down at yourself from the ceiling. But I couldn't. I got everything else in the dorm room right: the cinderblock walls, the pale linoleum. But when I approached the bed, the sense of myself sleeping there, the whole scene grayed out, a quick dissolve. I opened my eyes, then closed them, kept trying until it scared me to try.

Now in the open air, it was the wheeze of the bellows, the swirling dazzle of smoke and the sharp smell of it, the ominous buzzing suddenly lowered in volume and pitch. We were not ourselves but an element—a kind of charm to the bees in our perfect fraud.

I looked down into the hive and saw what Plath saw. "The men were lifting out rectangular yellow slides, crusted with bees, crawling, swarming. . . ." This from the journal account of her first "bee-meeting," what Ted Hughes calls the "loose prose draft" toward her poem of the same name, the beginning of her famous sequence. "If a poem is concentrated, a closed fist," Plath wrote, "then a novel is relaxed, and expansive, an open hand. . . . Where the first excludes and stuns, the open hand can touch and encompass a great deal in its travels."

Plath's journal piece is just such an open hand, distinctive in its wit and description, its fine shifts of tone: an *English* beekeeping meeting, with all the quirky village findings of a Barbara Pym. Before us is the rector, his headgear a dark affair with a screened box attached ("I thought the hat a clerical beekeeping hat," Plath tells us), then the midwife and her "moony beam," and one of the local dowagers "cadaverous as a librarian." Throughout, the poet is alert to all the polite conversation in orbit around Charlie Pollard—his are the bees everyone's come to see—though gradually it is loosened by the oddity of the gathering and the donning of its costumes.

"See all the bees round the rector's dark trousers," whispered the woman. "They don't seem to like white." I was grateful for my white smock. The rector was somehow an odd man out, referred to now and then by Charlie jestingly: "Eh, rector?" "Maybe they want to join his church," one man, emboldened by the anonymity of the hats, suggested.

All this is drawn with sense, even affection, and with the complexity that humor often supplies, but because this isn't Barbara Pym but Sylvia Plath, the inevitable darkness and weight enter. "The men were lifting slides," she writes:

Charlie Pollard squirting smoke into another box. They were looking for queen cells—long, pendulous honey colored cells from which the new queens would come. The blue-coated woman pointed them out. She was from British Guiana, had lived alone in the jungle for eighteen years, lost 25 pounds on her first bees there—there was no honey for them to eat. I was aware of bees buzzing and stalling before my face. The veil seemed hallucinatory. I could not see it for moments at a time. Then I became aware I was in a bone-stiff trance, intolerably tense, and shifted round to where I could see better. "Spirit of my dead father, protect me!" I arrogantly prayed. A dark, rather nice, unruly-looking man came up through the cut grass. Everyone turned, murmured "O Mr. Jenner, we didn't think you were coming. . . ."

In her lightning shifts—from description and fact, through the solitary near hallucination, to the distraction and camaraderie of the group welcoming one of its members—we have not only the authentic flash of thought, we have the *lens* through which the poem will move out of the prose. Not the sweet welcoming, that lens, nor even the smoky quest for the queen. The bee sequence is launched in that moment of personal stillness: the bees stalling outside the veil, the slow alarm of that "bone-stiff trance," two lifetimes—father and daughter—in the desperate, affirmative prayer. So the open hand closes to the fist Plath speaks of. "I could not run without having to run forever," she admits halfway through her poem about that meeting.

> The white hive is snug as a virgin,
> Sealing off her brood cells, her honey, and quietly humming.

Smoke rolls and scarves in the grove.
The mind of the hive thinks this is the end of everything.

Here they come, the outriders, on their hysterical elastics.
If I stand very still, they will think I am cow-parsley,
A gullible head untouched by their animosity,

Not even nodding, a personage in a hedgerow.
The villagers open the chambers, they are hunting the queen.
Is she hiding, is she eating honey? She is very clever.
She is old, old, old, she must live another year, and
she knows it. . . .

A poem, Plath insisted, "excludes and stuns." And the precise strangeness of the imagery here—the hive "quietly humming," the bees' confused flight as "hysterical elastics," and later, in the final stanza, the mob of them rising as "a blackout of knives"—does stun. The significance of this passage can be understood if by *excludes* she means that our witness has ruined us, at least briefly, for polite conversation, that we are outside, abruptly hypnotized by beauty that, as Rilke put it, is terror, or rather that part of terror that we can—but barely—endure.

Poetry like Sylvia Plath's is not *good doggy* work; it neither behaves nor comforts. One doesn't like it in any usual affectionate sense of that word, but that's only the beginning of its power. The winnowing pressure that takes the bee meeting's prose version to its poetic form strikes me as careful and fevered as her father's writing in his book, *Bumblebees and Their Ways,* published when his daughter was two years old, in 1934, when he was teaching at Boston University.

As a collection of straight facts on bees, Otto Plath's effort is a failure. It reads differently than most modern treatises, which is to say, it *thinks* differently. The book doesn't conclude as much as it lets us bear witness. Otto Plath's old childhood habit, a restless, very physical research, is here. The winter digging by ice pike, whole hives sometimes, that close attention to flight patterns and defensive postures, those endless returns to the sites to note every season's effect on the colonies: these are the things that matter. The book reads, in short, as field notes, with modesty and containment and absolute purpose. Still we are never far from that boy with nerve enough to lower his straw down to the underground nests; one is startled, again, by his fearlessness.

Example: Otto Plath writes at length about the bumblebee's defense of her nest. Either queen or worker will raise her legs in threatening ways, sometimes showing her stinger's droplet of venom. Not infrequently, she will shoot a stream of liquid at the intruder. He quotes an authority, one "Huber (1802)," insisting it is venom that is expelled, that "it does no harm, unless preceded by a perforation."

"In order to determine whether Huber's assertion is correct," Plath continues, "I pricked my finger with a pin and rubbed the liquid which had been ejected by an irritated worker of B. *terricola* into the wound but found it did not cause any pain. It is evident, therefore," he writes with a mild flourish, "that the liquid is not venom." Not venom but honey, a fact that comes to us after five pages of ingenious observation of robber bees, katydids, and others who lap up the drops after flying off—if they survive the attack. More surprisingly, Plath comes up with the evidence himself. "It has," he assures us, "a sweet taste."

Having little experience in science, I might romanticize its famous method. Still, what moves me about Otto Plath's work is its curious blankness of mind. The man seems to know nothing when he confronts the bees. In their own habitat, he waits for them *to show him something*. Then he carefully goes about finding reason. What is kept intact is wonder for the alien world. There is no knowing except gradually, firsthand.

"Spirit of my dead father, protect me," Sylvia Plath either thought, or, in writing of it, liked to think she thought, going blank herself— howbeit in a more dangerous, perhaps richer way—before the bees.

We were looking for the queen now, scanning the combs for a clue. An hour had passed; I was having trouble with my helmet and veil though the wind was mild. I kept adjusting it.

The bees never stopped. (Do they ever sleep? I asked. Well, not sleep as we think it, he said. They rest maybe two minutes an hour, that is, we think they rest. They just hang motionless on the comb.) I tried to find one resting but gave it up. They seemed to have forgotten us, forgotten, that is, our smoke. Hundreds, perhaps thousands of black-winged things, layers and layers moved over the brood cells, the honey cells. They were frantic, the work surprisingly specific—nurse bees feeding the pupae and the larvae, house bees cleaning and taking out the dead, the foragers returning with pollen and honey and looking for an empty cell in the combs to discharge their treasure. At least that's what my companion told me they were doing, expertly pointing out who was who; all, to my eye, caught up in the same tiny gyrations. They made me dizzy; they looked like the onslaught of a migraine, the moment after the floating sensation has passed. They were austere and ornate and entirely self-possessed. One felt hopeless and inexact before them. I thought of Plath's poem, "The Arrival of the Bee Box":

> I put my eye to the grid.
> It is dark, dark,

With the swarmy feeling of African hands
Minute and shrunk for export,
Black on black, angrily clambering.

How can I let them out?
It is the noise that appalls me most of all,
The unintelligible syllables.
It is like a Roman mob,
Small, taken one by one, but my god, together!

There it is, in that high exclamation—"but my god, together!"—
the poem's heart, its moment of release. And after the silence of the
stanza break, we are returned to the calmed down, the rational.

I lay my ear to furious Latin.
I am not a Caesar.
I have simply ordered a box of maniacs.
They can be sent back.
They can die, I need feed them nothing, I am the owner.

I wonder how hungry they are.

The rest downshifts further, full of *ifs* and misgivings and sensible,
weighted questions. "I am no source of honey," she writes reasonably
in the famous final lines,

So why should they turn on me?
Tomorrow I will be sweet God, I will set them free.

The box is only temporary.

In the first draft of this poem, however, written by hand in Devon
that last October, on pink memorandum paper she collected years
before from Smith College and on whose reverse side she typed *The
Bell Jar,* the movement in those lines is more complex, more open to
meditative pause. She adds two full lines.

I am no source of honey.
Tomorrow is soon enough to think of that.
Is it a brain that rages, is it a heart?
So why should they turn on me?
Tomorrow I will be sweet God, I will set them free.

The box is only temporary.

It's the third line I love, the one she crossed straight out in black ink—"Is it a brain that rages, is it a heart?" It could have been a chant, this thing she threw away.

I stooped, eye level to the hive. My companion had gone to retrieve something from the car, and I was alone with them.

How does imagery take hold, what burning buried thing in us demands that return to certain rooms or gestures, certain plain nightmares and recognitions, to those and not to others, retelling them in whatever new odd focus, whatever disguise?

In a short story, written in her early twenties, Plath describes a father in a garden after supper. It amazes his small daughter, Alice, how he'd catch a bumblebee, hold it in his closed hand to her ear. She liked "the angry, stifled buzzing of the bee," Plath tells us,

> captured in the dark trap of her father's hand, but not stinging, not daring to sting. Then, with a laugh, her father would spread his fingers wide and the bee would fly out, free, up into the air and away.

In this small scene, composed and heightened as something in a locket, a whole childhood—its fear and wonder—might be compressed. The bees, a real fact of her early years given her father's work, are more than stage trappings. They are danger and romance; they claim the father even as both he and the girl who identifies with him are defined by the simple heroic light against them. "Among the Bumblebees" she called the story, though only a small bit of the piece concerns them. So images, triggered most of all, perhaps, by longing—Otto Plath died when she was eight—begin their long-term settlement in the imagination.

Meanwhile, it's impossible to figure fully what Sylvia Plath really learned about bees from her father, or whether, later, she had read his book at all. Certainly his bees were a very different sort than those that finally intrigued her. Bumblebees don't survive as a colony over winter as honeybees do, for instance (though the bumblebee queens hibernate alone). Neither do bumblebees make enough honey for people to take interest. They burrow in the earth to nest, unlike the honeybees who make their combs—things of great formal beauty in themselves— either in man-made hives or high in trees or eaves.

Yet images speak, and in two earlier bee poems—both elegies for her father, written at least three years before the bee sequence—Plath uses what she does know of her father's world. But it is grief that transforms it. In "The Beekeeper's Daughter," she borrows a detail for the last stanza that was both recorded in Otto Plath's book on bees, and, according to Ted Hughes, demonstrated to her by him.

"In burrows as narrow as a finger," she writes in that poem, "solitary bees / keep house among the grasses. Kneeling down / I set my eye to the hole-mouth and meet an eye / Round, green, disconsolate as a tear." The second poem, "Electra on Azalea Path," begins more personally, and immediately rivets:

> The day you died I went into the dirt,
> Into the lightless hibernaculum
> Where bees, striped black and gold, sleep out the blizzard
> Like hieratic stones, and the ground is hard.

Mourning, of course, exacts its own stark requirements of memory, and if certain bees mimic the dead to survive, burying themselves in the rich heat of earth, they might *answer* the way metaphor *answers* in its mysterious interior equation—and therefore recovery—of things. "What do I remember / that was shaped / as this thing is shaped?" Williams asked. Things equal, they do not stop equaling. And in that swift linkage the imagination comes awake and builds, sometimes moving like the hummingbird's wing, so rapid that it appears to us motionless.

That motionless—I think Plath was that motionless, clear about survival in the bee sequence, written the October she and Ted Hughes separated, written out of knowledge of the natural world won in her own solitary way, getting a hive and keeping it in Devon where she stayed on with the children the whole nectar-gathering summer. Such a world, certainly, is a strictly feminine one. The workers are females, as, of course, is the queen. The only males—the drones—are worthless to the colony beyond their grip and prowess at high altitudes during the queen's famous bridal flight. In fact, it was the women in Devon who taught Plath the art of keeping bees. Although her neighbor, Charlie Pollard, would instruct her some and even give her one of his cast-off hives, it was her midwife, Winifred Davies, whom she relied upon for sensible advice that summer into fall, and the "blue-coated woman" from British Guiana whom she met at that first bee meeting. "Today, guess what, we've become *beekeepers!*" she wrote home that June in the manic, expansive tone she habitually used in letters to her mother. But it was true; no longer merely the beekeeper's daughter, Plath would keep bees herself. "Now bees land on my flowers," she told Elizabeth Compton Sigmund, a Devon friend, about the flowers she had painted on her hive.

Late that October, she would go to London to read and be interviewed for the BBC by Peter Orr. Although choosing not to read any of her poems about them, she spoke of the bees and the enormous value of her midwife's instruction. "I'm fascinated by this, this mastery of the practical . . . ," she told him. "I must say, I feel as a poet one lives a bit on air. . . ."

It's tempting, that air. It's how one courts transcendence. So we write—as she did—mostly lyric poems. Plath's bee poems are surely that—lyrics—yet the sequence design does a curious thing: it bestows narrative rigor on the whole scary business, making its own demands for lucidity. And though each poem in the sequence might be weighted, as many critics have assumed, toward the death that would claim her only four months later, because she's worked narratively, toward *story,* we sense hope and recovery: *something this vitally begun is going to will out.*

In the handwritten manuscript, at least, the individual poems are part of a whole, each a numbered section, and though Ted Hughes followed that order, he published them posthumously in *Ariel* as separate pieces. Either way, the shape of the sequence is dramatic, and—no tricks—it proceeds as matter-of-factly as life often does. One goes to a bee meeting for inspiration and information. Step two: one gets a box of bees. If we abstract the rest, their gist becomes as true as this, and as laughable for the reduction. In "Stings" the bees are transferred to the hive, and the queen flies off to mate; in "The Swarm" the colony has doubled and now divides; and in "Wintering" the bees hone in, clustering for heat, venturing out only on warm days to remove their dead, and thus, they live out the cold.

It's not completely ridiculous, I think, to summarize so. Her eye to the clear consecutive facts of the world allowed a leaping-off place, a frame for her personal and metaphorical invention in the poems in exactly the way that for her real narratives—her stories—it did not. "The blunt fact," wrote Ted Hughes in his introduction to her selected prose volume, "killed any power or inclination (in her) to rearrange it, to see it differently." In contrast, in these late poems, the actual bees steadied her, brought her deliciously out of that air on which, she said, poets tend to live, though perhaps that's in part because the details of the colony's life are so profoundly alien. Already the bees must have seemed surreal to her, messengers from the unspeakable inner life.

Two hours now—it was three o'clock, the sun no longer straight up but to my left. We had given up all hope of finding the queen. My companion said, hold it, handing me a slide, one of the hive's extracting frames as heavy as an early-twentieth-century X ray. Hold it to the light, he said, like a surgeon eager to share his bright diagnosis.

It was a comb in my hand, its cells repeating endlessly, perfect and only partly waxed shut, so much of it a lovely gold. Honey, of course, glossy and dazzling, even without the sun behind it.

This was the *after;* the *before* was Plath's:

He and I

> Have a thousand clean cells between us,
> Eight combs of yellow cups,
> And the hive itself a teacup. . . .

It's spring in these lines from "Stings," all possibility, even though—
unseen—the queen is "old / Her wings torn shawls, her long body /
Robbed of its plush—" even though the brood cells from which new
workers and drones and future queens will come to "terrify" and look
like "wormy mahogany." What draws me is the doubt and wonder, an
unlikely combination. And in her fine-nerved phrasing questions mix
with personal flashes, forcing the facts of the colony's life upward into a
human orbit. "I stand in a column," Plath tells us,

> Of winged, unmiraculous women,
> Honey-drudges.
> I am no drudge
> Though for years I have eaten dust
> And dried plates with my dense hair.
>
> And seen my strangeness evaporate,
> Blue dew from dangerous skin.
> Will they hate me,
> These women who only scurry,
> Whose news is the open cherry, the open clover?
>
> It is almost over.
> I am in control.
> Here is my honey-machine,
> It will work without thinking. . . .

The lost queen finally does emerge, and in that we have the heart of
the bee sequence, its climactic revelation. After the entrance and exit
of the so-called "third person," after the high spinning pitch of ques-
tions ("Is she dead, / Is she sleeping? / Where has she been, / With her
lion-red body, her wings of glass?"), we're charged for the simple
triumph of that final stanza, its *now* dropping down with the weight of
stunned discovery.

> Now she is flying
> More terrible than she ever was, red
> Scar in the sky, red comet
> Over the engine that killed her—
> The mausoleum, the wax house.

"The great appeal of *Ariel* and its constellated lyrics," Seamus Heaney has written, "is the feeling of irresistible givenness. There inheres in this poetry a sense of surprised arrival, of astonished being." But that arrival, in the poem "Stings" at least, was a tedious, hard-earned matter of starts and stops, at first more a creature of autobiography than poetic urgency.

Enter again the "third person." During Mr. Pollard's installation of their new swarm, "Ted had only put a handkerchief over his head where the hat should go in the bee mask," Plath wrote to her mother that June, "and the bees crawled into his hair, and he flew off with a half-a-dozen stings. I didn't get stung at all, and when I went back to the hive later, I was delighted to see bees entering with pollen sacs full and leaving with them empty—at least I *think* that's what they were doing."

In Plath's final rendering of "Stings," written four months later in October, the incident, however detailed, is reduced to episode, a kind of dismissal in her summary. Her fascination remains with the bees and the subsequent images of self she borrows from their passionate activity. Translated from prose to poem, the "third person" "has nothing to do with the bee seller or with me—" Plath writes. "Now he is gone."

> In eight great bounds, a great scapegoat.
> Here is his slipper, here is another
> And here the square of white linen
> He wore instead of a hat.
> He was sweet,
>
> The sweat of his efforts a rain
> Tugging the world to fruit.
> The bees found him out,
> Molding onto his lips like lies,
> Complicating his features.
>
> They thought death was worth it, but I
> Have a self to recover, a queen. . . .

In the first version of this poem begun two months earlier in August, the intent is narrower; the piece completely circles this "third person"—he is the magnetic figure, another "maestro of the bees," as Plath remembered her father in an earlier poem, though this time the heroic shine is drastically altered. It begins:

> What honey in you summons these animalcules?
> What fear? It has set them zinging.

Zinging & zinging on envious strings, & you are the center.
They are assailing your brain like numbers,
They are in your hair.

Under the white handkerchief you wore instead of a hat.
They are making a cat's cradle, they are suicidal.
Their death-pegs stud your gloves, it is no use running.
The black veil molds to your lips:
They think they must kiss you, they think death is worth it. . . .

Last winter, when I came upon this handwritten draft in the Smith College manuscript collection, that initial line stopped me; I felt, for the first time, the deep quiet in the room. "What honey in you summons these animalcules? / What fear?" I read again. But "summons" is scribbled above her original choice, "attracts," which is energetically crossed out. *Attracts,* the word is wide and safe, nearing straight description. But *summons*—it's as focused as desire, helpless as dream. I stared at the exacting transformation, this change of "attracts" right before me into the terrible, almost wordless *summons.* I stood there over the manuscript; strangers walked by me, all cast shadows on the page. I recalled a conversation with a friend, our shared annoyance with Plath's impulse to jerk everything toward melodrama, this habit of enlarging by compressing, of intensifying into nightmare for release.

I looked back to the line; the change was definitive, utterly characteristic of both the worst of Plath, and the best. *Summons*—amazing to me how one word upped the ante, made everything instantly strange and interior, impossible to stop. I felt witness to that click, right there, a visible shift, this quickening from major to minor key so close to that moment of "astonished being" that Heaney speaks of. In the last year of her life, Plath wrote a brief childhood memoir, and in that account recalled being read a poem of Matthew Arnold's—"Forsaken Merman"—when she was very small:

I saw gooseflesh on my skin. I did not know what made it. I was not cold. Had a ghost passed over me? No, it was the poetry. A spark flew off Arnold and shook me, like a chill. I wanted to cry; I felt very odd. I had fallen into a new way of being happy.

Happiness then, some brief definitions: "Like this," my companion was saying, the hives behind us now as we walked toward the car. "I held my arms up like this"—and still in gloves and bee mask, he stood radiant, embracing the fall air. I had asked about swarming; his face came alive through the veil. "In May, or early June," he told me. "And one time, I was right here when they started, thousands pouring out, all at once." I imagined them passing over him, a dark cloud of bees, all frantic purpose upward until he was a small, motionless figure way below, his arms still open, letting them go. "The bees have got so far, seventy feet high!" wrote Plath in her poem "The Swarm," euphoric and at eye level with her own rising bees: "Russia, Poland and Germany! / The mild hills, the same old magenta / Fields shrunk to a penny / Spun into a river, the river crossed. . . ." So years and places drop away in the associative flash of such flight, here—Europe's ancient miseries, its deliberate smiling tyrants. What ghost passes over us when we write? "A flying hedgehog," she called the raging colony, "all prickles. . . ."

Plath had a plan for *Ariel,* a map for its long chill and peculiar joy. As Grace Schulman has written, so many of its poems were works "of praise," howbeit "a fearful praise." According to Ted Hughes, Plath herself marked its boundaries with two words: *love* to begin ("Love set you going like a fat gold watch" from "Morning Song" about her newborn daughter) and *spring,* from the final line of "Wintering," to end the book. So the bee sequence would go last, a design Hughes put aside when publishing the collection to finish instead with the inscrutable stark double take of poems written later, "Edge" and "Words." In retrospect, given the fact of her suicide, Hughes's order illustrates, gives reason perhaps, but as both Marjorie Perloff and Linda Wagner have argued, it dishonors intent, and with that, the real triumph of the book.

Plath's own shape for the collection was a hopeful one, but admittedly, the active turn toward spring—at least in the last poem of her sequence—seems to have come as a surprise to her. That poem, "Wintering," is, of course, steadied throughout by domestic detail and necessity. The hive has to be set for winter, the bees fed watered sugar, the honey extracted and put in cellar jars ("next to the last tenant's rancid jam," she tells us, "and the bottles of empty glitters—Sir So-and-So's gin"). The bees themselves in the poem behave as operatically as they do in life, clustering for warmth, removing their dead from the combs, evicting, without a pause, the live males, the drones—"the blunt, clumsy stumblers, the boors," Plath calls them—who now add nothing to the colony's welfare. This purposeful female world hones in to survive, a fact no doubt not lost on the poet, estranged at this point from the marriage that sustained her for six years. "Winter is for women—" she writes in haunting summary. "The woman, still at her knitting, / at the cradle of Spanish walnut, / her body a bulb in the cold and too dumb to think."

But that expansive leap toward spring in the final stanza stuns, breaks through this static sorrow. And if we can believe the several manuscript drafts that still exist, moving eerily as time-lapse camera work, it was authentic liberation from her dirgelike habit.

> Will the hive survive, will the gladiolas
> Succeed in banking their fires
> To enter another year?
> What will they taste of, the Christmas roses?—

In all versions, including the last, this much stands whole. It is with the stanza's last two lines that she struggled. Draft one:

> What will they taste of, the Christmas roses?
> Snow water? Corpses?

To this she added, "A Sweet spring?" but crossed it out. "Spring?"— left intact. "Impossible spring?" crossed out. "What sort of spring?"— crossed out. "O God, let them taste of spring" crossed out. By the third draft, things had moved into typescript, and the final line into frozen, fully tragic images:

> Snow water? Corpses? A glass wing?

But even here, though "Snow water" and "Corpses" remain, the "glass wing" has several lines through it, and handwritten then, at wild angles, are all her spinning options, her stop-start movement toward the right transcendent gesture that will end the poem: "A gold bee, flying?"—crossed out. "Resurrected"—crossed out. "Bee-song?"—crossed out. "Or a bee flying"—crossed out. Everything, in short, crossed out until, in a jubilant cursive—"The bees are flying. They taste the spring."

One great leap remains; the whole stanza is dismissed with an elegant wavy line, and typed beneath is the full published version—with one crucial correction. Plath's oppressive standstill litany—"Snow water? Corpses?"—is violently crossed out, that final line completely given over to the bees and their dizzy upward release:

> Will the hive survive, will the gladiolas
> Succeed in banking their fires
> To enter another year?
> What will they taste of, the Christmas roses?
> The bees are flying. They taste the spring.

All the way home in the car, I could still hear them in my head, their low-grade buzzing, indifferent to whatever joy or grief we make of their sound, in poems or out of them. And for the rest of the day, I couldn't shake the memory of something. Slowly it came back to me, the way dreams do, in flashes.

I remembered waiting in a car, alone, having gone with a friend to pick up her son from his violin lesson. To my right, and down into a meadow, I saw three stacks of white boxes, three hives. The boy was still playing; I could hear the sweet barbed threat of it, that edgy quarreling sound he made, and sometimes a note held so high it disappeared. I kept my ear there, in a trance, a kind of manageable beauty. Even so, something in the meadow drew me; my eye kept returning to it, some busy darkness I could only imagine. For several minutes the boy played. One side of things, and then the other. Unlike Plath, I couldn't begin to balance it.

REFERENCES

Compton, Elizabeth Sigmund. "Sylvia in Devon: 1962." *Sylvia Plath: The Woman and the Work.* Ed. Edward Buttcher. London: P. Owen, 1979.

Heaney, Seamus. "The Indefatigable Hoof-taps: Sylvia Plath." *The Government of the Tongue: Selected Prose 1978–1987.* New York: Farrar, Straus and Giroux, 1989.

Hughes, Ted. "Notes on the Poems." *The Collected Poems of Sylvia Plath.* New York: Harper and Row, 1981.

Orr, Peter. "An Interview with Sylvia Plath," a recording made for the British Broadcasting Corporation, October 1962. Issued from Credo Records, Cambridge, Mass., under the recording title "Plath Reads Plath," 1975. The Credo recording was made under the auspices of the British Council and the Woodberry Poetry Room, Harvard College Library.

Perloff, Marjorie. "The Two Ariels: The (Re)Making of the Sylvia Plath Canon." *American Poetry Review* (Nov/Dec 1984): 10–11.

Plath, Otto. *Bumblebees and their Ways.* New York: MacMillan, 1934.

Plath, Sylvia. Drafts of the Bee Sequence from the *Ariel* Collection of the Manuscript Collection of Sylvia Plath, Rare Book Room, William Allan Neilson Library, Smith College, Northampton, Mass. My thanks to Ruth Mortimer, curator, and the staff of the Rare Book Room, and to Olwyn Hughes, literary executor of the estate of Sylvia Plath, for the permission to examine this unpublished material and to quote from it here.

———. *The Collected Poems of Sylvia Plath.* Ed. Ted Hughes. New York: Harper and Row, 1981.

———. *Johnny Panic and the Bible of Dreams: Short Stories, Prose and Diary Excerpts.* Ed. Ted Hughes. New York: Harper and Row, 1977.

———. *Letters Home.* Ed. Aurelia Schober Plath. London: Faber and Faber, 1975.

Rilke, Rainer Maria. "The First Elegy." *The Duino Elegies.* Trans. by Stephen Garmey and Jay Wilson. New York: Harper and Row, 1977.

Schulman, Grace. "Sylvia Plath and Yaddo." *Ariel Ascending: Writings about Sylvia Plath.* Ed. Paul Alexander. New York: Harper and Row, 1985.

Wagner, Linda W. "Introduction." *Sylvia Plath, the Critical Heritage.* Ed. Linda W. Wagner. London: Routledge, 1988.

Williams, William Carlos. "Asphodel, that Greeny Flower." *The Selected Poems of William Carlos Williams,* Book 1. New York: New Directions, 1969.

Special thanks to William J. Fischang, Department of Entomology at Purdue University, for his time and expertise concerning bees and their habits, particularly for his generosity in showing me the university's field site. Additional entomological sources consulted for this essay include the following volumes: Langstroth, Dadant, et al., *The Hive and the Honey Bee,* edited by Dadant and Sons (Hamilton, Ill.: Dadant and Sons, 1978); Eva Crane, *The Archaeology of Beekeeping* (Ithaca, N.Y.: Cornell University Press, 1985); R. O. B. Manley, *Beekeeping in Britain* (London: Faber and Faber, 1948).

CARL DENNIS

The Voice of Authority

In a skeptical age like ours we are likely to praise our poets more for
their doubts than for their assurances. Suspicious of prophets, we want
our poets to show us that they don't claim to know all things, that they
know that all efforts to tell the truth are more likely to be expressions of
the particular needs of the truth-seeker than revelations of the real na-
ture of the world. What we find to be true, we all tend to agree, is what
is most helpful in promoting the conditions that best serve our interests.
And even if we define these interests in large and generous ways, not in
small and mean ones, we want to be reminded not to claim as true for
others what in fact is true only for ourselves and for people like us.

Poetry is particularly suited to this task because it does not try to deny
its subjective origins. The voices of poetry are particular, the speeches
of particular characters in particular situations, and the meaning of what
is said is never intended to be completely separable from its context. In
narrative and dramatic poetry the context is immediately apparent in
terms of plot, setting, and character. In poems spoken in the first person
by an "I" not always easy to distinguish from the writer, the kind of
poem most commonly written today, the context may be less obvious;
but some particular occasion is almost always suggested, and the
speaker's mood is clearly implied. We read such a poem to make contact
not so much with some objective truth but with a particular mind
trying to know what is true for it, a contact more immediate than the
kind we are likely to get in fiction and drama. And if a poet claims to be
totally objective and favors abstract, categorical pronouncements, we
are likely to find his work unconvincing.

But our demand that poets admit their subjective focus coexists
with a counterdemand, one that I think is more basic for serious
readers of poetry: that poets try to make sense of experience. Though
the truth of the poet is particular, good poets believe that their con-
cerns are representative, that they can make efforts to clarify life in
ways that others can find useful. If we are all ultimately ignorant,
ignorance has many degrees. Unless poets convince us that they are
trying to tell the truth, we are not likely to find their poems worth
reading. Like serious writers of argumentative prose, serious poets
have to examine their opinions with care and resist the natural biases

Denver Quarterly 23,3/4 (Winter/Spring 1989): 137–56.

of their temperaments by deliberate acts of self-distancing. In this regard a great narrative poet like Homer can serve as a model for the writer of a first-person poem with a subjective focus. As a Greek, Homer may naturally favor the side of his ancestors, the Achaeans, in the Trojan War, but as a poet he does his best to treat the Trojan heroes with sympathy. And though his loyalties are to the fighting and dying mortals, not to the immortal Olympians, he does his best to imagine how the war might look from an immortal perspective, so that he is both involved and removed from the action. We cannot say that Homer's treatment of the war is true to some absolute reality, only that he has done justice to the material he has chosen, that he has explored it with a richness that makes his poem still moving long after the particular audience for which it was written, whatever its biases, has long ceased to exist. He still convinces us that what he is saying is true and important. His poem still has authority.

Because of the smaller compass of the first-person poem, its authority usually results less from the slow building up of particular perceptions than from the direct presenting of a character we can trust. In terms of traditional rhetoric, we can say that the argument of the first-person poem is primarily an ethical argument, based on the *ethos* or moral qualities exhibited by the speaker, and only secondarily an appeal to particular evidence. To examine the source of authority in such poems, then, is to examine the qualities we can expect to find in speakers who are convincing. No two speakers, to be sure, are exactly alike; and for most practical criticism it is more useful to concentrate on what distinguishes one speaker from another, including speakers created by the same writer, than to ask what all convincing speakers share. The larger question is harder to answer conclusively because it is fundamentally a question about quality. Still it's useful to remind ourselves that even in skeptical times the distinction between good and bad poetry, the traditional critical issue, can't be avoided.

What attributes must a speaker display if his words are to have authority? For me, three are fundamental—passion, discrimination, and inclusiveness. That is, the speaker must show, first, that he cares about what he is saying; second, that he has reached his position not by ignoring opposed positions but by considering them and finding them wanting; and third that he sees the connections between the subject immediately at hand and other issues. Taking them in turn, I want to discuss some of the ways these qualities are embodied in poetic form.

To seem passionate the speaker must give the impression that his words express a deep-seated conviction, that he stands behind what he is saying. If he is to convince us that what he is saying is true for us, his first task is to convince us it is true for him. To my mind, we are made to feel the speaker's engagement primarily through rhythm, if we define the term broadly to include not only the formal or informal pattern of stressed and unstressed syllables but all that is involved in thinking in lines as well as in sentences. Used well, rhythm makes us feel the presence of a speaker behind the words. Even a poem of two lines may provide enough space for a poet sensitive to the stress and pauses of his syntax to create a voice of deep conviction. Consider this couplet that Ben Jonson uses as a preface for his book of epigrams:

> Pray thee, take care, that tak'st my book in hand
> To read it well, that is, to understand.

These lines are an appeal for Jonson's book to be read with careful attention. To be effective they have to suggest that they themselves deserve careful attention. In this they succeed, despite their plainness, partly because their meaning keeps expanding. What opens as a plea shifts suddenly, in the second foot, to cautionary advice and then, in the second line, to formal instruction as the poet defines what reading well really means. In quick succession the speaker is suitor, enjoiner, and moral instructor. What needs to be noticed here is how much our sense of the speaker's presence is dependent on the prosody, on the handling of rhythm and syntax. The poem opens abruptly with a spondee, "Pray thee," not with the expected iamb of the heroic couplet, and the abruptness suggests that the speaker has dispensed with the language of formal petition for plain directness. The line is then disrupted even more emphatically by the unexpected spondee of the second foot, "take care," which underscores the shift from plea to warning, and our sense of the poem's irregularity is deepened by the enjambment of the first line, which keeps the meaning of the advice suspended to the middle of the second line. The strong break here emphatically isolates the crucial definition that concludes the poem, and the caesura within this final half-line gives so much weight to the final word, "understand," that the reader is forced to reconsider its meaning. Someone, we feel, is talking to us here, someone not interested in writing a formal couplet but in using the form to say something of importance. How crucial a part the prosody plays in establishing the speaker's emphatic presence becomes clear if we rewrite the poem to make the syntax and rhythms more regular:

> Who'er thou art that tak'st my book in hand
> Take care to read it well and understand.

By removing the spondees and the caesurae we have lost the speaker. The singsong iambs give us no personal emphasis. The rhythm seems dictated entirely by the form, not by the pressure of the poet's concern. What tone we can hear seems neutral, almost flippant. We are being asked to care about a book by a speaker who displays none of the concern that Jonson's syntax substantiates.

Developing a passionate syntax was important for Jonson because he wanted to move his poetry beyond the private concerns of the Elizabethan love lyric to concentrate on issues of general social concern. To be as convincing an authority on public morals as on the state of his own heart, he tried to bring into his poetry the presence of a concrete, individual voice that he found in Roman writers like Horace and Martial. In this effort he has served as a model for many poets, in his time and ours, Yeats perhaps most notably, who reaches in some of his late poems for the largest generalizations while managing to maintain a passionate presence. Consider the familiar opening couplets of "The Second Coming," which have as their subject nothing less than the breakdown of Western civilization:

> Turning and turning in the widening gyre
> The falcon cannot hear the falconer.
> Things fall apart; the center cannot hold.
> Mere anarchy is loosed upon the world,
> The blood-dimmed tide is loosed, and everywhere
> The ceremony of innocence is drowned,
> The best lack all conviction, while the worst
> Are full of passionate intensity.

Doubtless part of the power of these lines resides in the suggestiveness of the images—the wheeling falcon, whose own natural energies are no longer in control of the master, as if the traditional disciplines of culture are no longer effective; the man-made object that begins to crumble at the edges under the stress of outward pressure; the blood-colored sea loosed upon civilization like a wild animal. But to see how much the intensity of these lines is in great part a function of their rhythm, we have only to rewrite the passage in regular iambic pentameter:

> The falcon turns and turns in a wider gyre.
> He cannot hear the cry of the falconer.
> The center of the cosmos cannot hold.
> Mere anarchy is let loose on the world.
> The tide that's dimmed by blood is loosed
> The ritual of innocence is drowned.
> The best have lost their firm convictions.
> The worst are full of fierce intensity.

Because of Yeats's variations from the iambic, his speaker seems much more responsive than the speaker of the rewrite to the implications of what is actually being described. The falcon of his first line moves much more quickly and wildly, the stresses more emphatic because more separated by unstressed syllables. The falling apart of the objects he describes is underscored by the median break of the line. His anarchy, in line 4, is "loosed" more emphatically as we rush so quickly over the unstressed syllables that a foot seems to drop away. His "blood-dimmed tide" gets the weight of three bunched stresses to suggest its power. His weak-willed "best" are allowed only part of a line, not a whole line that would balance the worst, and the stresses in the last line on the words "passionate" and "intensity" are so heavy on the first stressed syllables that the second stresses are muted. The emphatic rhythms of Yeats's speaker make clear the passionate nature of his response to the magnitude of the collapse he is witnessing, and this passion is crucial in qualifying the dichotomy of the final lines. The "worst" are not the only ones capable of passionate intensity after all. But the speaker of the rewrite describes the collapse in so quiet and plodding a monotone that we have to conclude that he either does not believe what he is saying or is emotionally torpid.

The important role played by rhythm in making a poem convincing may give pause to those who believe that a poet should be seriously engaged in clarifying experience. It may suggest, at first at least, that a poem is less a matter of truth-telling than of manipulating the reader. The poet seems a master of illusion, a showman who uses the smoke and mirrors of technique to make weak arguments appear stronger. We might respond to this objection the way the Sophists responded to Socrates' criticism that they taught the art of persuasion and not the art of seeking the truth: namely, that rhetoric is a tool, and the fact that it may be misused by liars should not keep truth-tellers from using it to make the truth convincing. But a deeper problem with the objection is that it seems to be based on a false opposition between style and content. Rhythm is not an adornment of a statement but one of its elements. It shapes it, giving it focus and clarity. It endows it with a specific weight that helps define its value. The falcons of Yeats's poem are not dressed-up versions of the falcons in the rewrite. They are different creatures, inherently more graceful and powerful, and their inability to hear the falconer has therefore much deeper implications. And the speaker of Yeats's poem is not a more energetic version of the speaker in the rewrite. He represents a different sensibility, one capable of responding with the feeling that the situation demands. The issue here is that of decorum. Yeats's rhythms are appropriate to their subject. The rhythms of the rewrite are not. They deny the importance of what the poem claims to be important. Their flaw may be called the flaw of bathos or unintended deflation, in contrast to the opposite flaw of overwriting or inflation, in which the rhythms of a poem are more charged and portentous than the subject requires. In either case the truth of the material has been violated.

If the speaker can convince us that he means what he says, that he is speaking from passionate conviction, not glibly or half-heartedly, he still won't be convincing unless we trust his judgment. We call a speaker judicious or discriminating if we feel that the opinions he expresses are reached after considering alternative opinions. Without this quality, the passionate voice will sound naive. So in Jonson's preface, the speaker's plea for understanding works on a distinction between ordinary casual reading and a deeper kind of engagement. The speaker in Yeats's poem is much more emotionally aroused, and he does not contrast his vision of the age to other visions. He simply presents images of the breakdown in a way that makes them seem directly witnessed and so uncontrovertable. And yet we feel the speaker is discriminating because even as he witnesses the collapse he is detached enough to view it not as a unique event but as the out-growth of possibilities latent in the preceding order. The falcon that used to fly still flies and the falconer still calls, but now they can no longer make contact. The center, which has always been able to hold the edges, still makes the effort, but now it fails. The tide has always been dimmed by blood, waiting to drown innocence, and now it's free to do so. The best and worst have always been with us, though now the best have lost their self-confidence and the worst have strengthened theirs. In suggesting how the seeds of disorder live within civilization, the lines make clear how fragile every order must be and so broaden the implications of the vision.

The most dramatic way to confront opposed positions is to have the speaker directly address an opponent and argue him or her into concession. This is the strategy that John Donne uses to give new life to the Renaissance love poem. His idealistic poems make claims for the importance of love that are more radical than the traditional poem of plea and complaint, but his speakers can't be patronized as self-absorbed because they confront those who would disparage love and argue them down. So in "The Canonization," in a tone that is by turns angry, mocking, riddling, and pedantic, the speaker turns on an auditor who has accused love of being a childish pastime and exposes the emptiness of the worldly life the auditor is committed to. But argumentative structure needn't involve an imagined auditor. It is present to some extent whenever a speaker defines his position through contrast with another, a mode that is central to many poems we may not regard as obviously dramatic. We think of Emily Dickinson's speaker, for example, as essentially private, the voice of inner joy and agonies; but one of the traits that makes this voice distinctive is her willingness to defend her circumscription, to make it clear that she turns from the public world not to escape its pressures but to concern herself with life on a deeper and more challenging level:

To fight aloud, is very brave—
But *gallanter,* I know
Who charge within the bosom
The Cavalry of Woe—

Who win, and nations do not see—
Who fall—and none observe—
Whose dying eyes, no Country
Regards with patriot love—

We trust, in plumed procession
For such, the Angels go—
Rank after Rank, with even feet—
And Uniforms of Snow.

The speaker here not only asserts that inner struggles entail more courage than outer ones but also indirectly attacks the values the world lives by. She borrows military metaphors to endow the inner life with glory, but finally suggests that they are part of a world of public causes and rewards that cannot do justice to the deeper significance of individual success and failure. Even the heaven imagined by the group mind fails to be spiritual. Its angels are all company angels, and so can give only cold comfort to a soul scarred by solitary trials. Through a bold argument indirectly stated, the speaker affirms the reality of the invisible world and the fictitiousness of the visible one.

In poets who avoid this kind of direct opposition, it may sometimes be hard to find any position that is being repudiated. An imagistic poem by Williams, for example, which attempts to seize a passing moment before it vanishes, seems to share very little with Dickinson's challenging assertions. But even here, other modes of seeing may be indirectly criticized. Consider "Proletarian Portrait":

A big young bareheaded woman
in an apron

Her hair slicked back standing
on the street

One stockinged foot toeing
the sidewalk

Her shoe in her hand. Looking
intently into it

She pulls out the paper insole
to find the nail

That has been hurting her

This poem is a snapshot of an ordinary, passing moment saved from oblivion by the camera of the poet. The scene is worth remembering, presumably because of the woman's healthy vigor and lack of self-consciousness. She has an earthy energy and nonchalance. But the title of the poem encourages us to widen the context of the description by contrasting the hardiness and innocence of the servant girl with the delicacy and sophistication of a lady who might be more typically presented in the genre of the portrait. The point here is not to replace the aristocratic notions of beauty by the proletarian, but to suggest that our notions of beauty have to be large enough to find it on the street as well as in protected interiors. The young servant looking for a nail in her shoe is a far cry from the princess who proves her noble blood by being able to feel a pea through seven mattresses. But she has her own grace as she toes the sidewalk, and in curing her own pain she suggests she is far more equipped than the hypersensitive princess of fairy tale for the ordinary world. The poems works, then, without any overt discriminations, but indirectly pits one aesthetic against another.

The most difficult challenge in American poetry to the notion that the authority of the poet depends in part on an ability to anticipate opposed positions is probably the accomplishment of some of the more expansive poems in *Leaves of Grass*. Whitman's speaker in "Song of Myself," for example, writes as if he is looking at the world for the first time and celebrates all he sees through a vivid listing, not by arguing. But behind the speaker's praise of the relentlessly common-place and homely lies a judgment about the practice of his contemporary poets that suffers, in his eyes, from too narrow a notion of the beautiful:

> And limitless are leaves stiff or drooping in the fields,
> And brown ants in the little wells beneath them,
> And mossy scabs of the worm fence, heap' stones, elder, mullein, and
>   poke-weed.

It's easy to praise sunsets and daffodils. It's hard to praise ants and weeds and mossy scabs. Until included here, they had in fact been excluded from poetry in English. We can't, to be sure, call Whitman a poet of opposition in any ordinary sense. The stylistic device that we think of as peculiarly his, the catalogue, is meant to suggest not only the rich variety of the world and the uniqueness of each particular but the ultimate equality of all things. Each fact is equally complete and "limitless." But this assertion of equality involves a critique of traditional systems of value, a critique that periodically surfaces through the juxtaposing of lives that social convention would regard as radically different.

> The bride unrumples her white dress, the minute hand of
> the clock moves slowly.
> The opium-eater reclines with rigid head and just-open'd
> lips,
> The prostitute draggles her shawl, her bonnet bobs on her
> tipsy and pimpled neck,
> The crowd laugh at her blackguard oaths, the men jeer and
> wink to each other,
> (Miserable! I do not laugh at your oaths nor jeer you;)
> The President holding a cabinet council is surrounded by
> the great Secretaries,
> On the piazza walk three matrons stately and friendly with
> twined arms,
> The crew of the fish-smack pack repeated layers of halibut
> in the hold. . . .

In deliberately linking bride, prostitute, stately matrons, President, and crew of the fish-smack, the speaker aggressively juxtaposes his leveling values with those of traditional hierarchies. The speaker wins authority by making clear he is fully aware of what his view of the world repudiates.

In all these examples of critical response, the opposed position is external to the speaker, and the speaker's authority is enhanced by showing us that he has been able to anticipate objections. But in many poems the objection is internal and the poem can be viewed as a dialogue between two parts of the self. We may think of this kind of poetry as particularly common since the Romantics, an expression of the shift from Augustan, pragmatic poetics focused on the audience, to Romantic, expressive poetics focused on the poet; but the genre reaches back to the beginnings of lyric poetry. When Catullus writes, "*Odi et amo,*" I hate and I love, he is already working in a tradition of erotic ambivalence. And early Christian poems about the war between sin and virtue are as direct a model as any Romantic poem for a poem like Yeats's "Dialogue of Self and Soul." What is new about the Romantic poem of inner dialogue is that the opposed voices are presented sequentially as different stages in the speaker's development. The poems are structured as narratives, not as arguments, and often, as in Coleridge's Conversation Poems, the narrative is not placed in the past but enacted in the present as the poet moves by a process of association from one state to another, typically from ignorance to insight and uneasiness to rest. The speaker's concluding state has the authority that comes from being the end product of a dialectical process that involves a rich complex of feelings.

The Romantic narrative of psychic change is based on a faith in the mind's own healing powers, a faith not always evident in modern versions of the form, where the change is more likely to be simply a movement toward a deeper understanding of the subject at hand. Lowell's "Alfred Corning Clark" is a good example of the genre:

> You read the *New York Times*
> every day at recess,
> but in its dry
> obituary, a list
> of your wives, nothing is news,
> except the ninety-five
> thousand dollar engagement ring
> you gave the sixth.
> Poor rich boy,
> you were unseasonably adult
> at taking your time
> and died at forty-five.
> Poor Al Clark,
> behind your enlarged,
> hardly recognizable photograph,
> I feel the pain.
> You were alive. You are dead.
> You wore bow-ties and dark
> blue coats, and sucked
> wintergreen or cinnamon lifesavers
> to sweeten your breath.
> There must be something—
> some one to praise
> your triumphant diffidence,
> your refusal of
> the intelligence
> that pulsed in the sensitive,
> pale concavities of your forehead.
> You never worked,
> and were third in the form.
> I owe you something—
>
> I was befogged,
> and you were too bored,
> quick and cool to laugh.

You are dear to me, Alfred;
our reluctant souls united
in our unconventional
illegal games of chess
on the St. Mark's quadrangle
You usually won—
motionless
as a lizard in the sun.

The speaker has chosen a difficult subject for an elegy. Clark's life was uninspiring, if not tawdry, and his association with the poet neither long nor deep. Though the poem opens with a dismissal of the sensationalistic perspective of the *Times,* the poet's own attitude to Clark is initially patronizing, summarizing the early waste of Clark's life with the witty and distant "you were unseasonably adult / at taking your time." But the poet soon makes it clear that he wants to be as sympathetic as he can, and much of the interest of the poem lies in its dramatizing the poet's moving from detachment to involvement, a process whose stages are marked by the shifting of names, from the formal full name of the title to the witty type-casting of "Poor rich boy," to the tender and particular "Poor Al Clark," to the intimate "Alfred." The first movement past irony comes with the recognition that Clark's death involves the loss of possibility that any death entails: "You were alive. You are dead." The next, more difficult step, as the poet tries to fix the particulars of appearance he still remembers clearly, is to find some quality in Clark to praise. The virtues singled out are based on negations, not really virtues at all, but they have a positive meaning for the speaker, whose childhood solitude was comforted by the presence of Clark's example of eccentric independence and nonchalance. The closing figure of the motionless lizard basking in the sun is not honorific in any traditional way, but it entails a respect for Clark's self-chosen separateness that underscores the distance the poet has moved from the patronizing irony with which he begins.

Those who adopt an expressive view of poetry are likely to find poems of inner dialogue more authoritative than poems in which the speaker confronts others. Quarreling with others, we may say with Yeats, is rhetoric; quarreling with oneself is poetry. But not every confrontation with others can be reduced to mere quarreling, and not all conversations with ourselves are worth listening to. The writer of the poem of inner conflict has to be on guard against too private a treatment of his subject, against assuming his audience will be interested in what in fact is of interest only to him. An awareness of this mistake leads us to the third demand we make on the authoritative voice, the demand for inclusiveness. If the poet chooses a personal subject he has to connect it to more than personal issues. He may prefer to write about a moth in his backyard rather than a white whale terrorizing ships on the high seas, but he has to find ways to make the moth important to his audience.

Does Lowell avoid the problem of smallness in "Alfred Corning Clark"? Not entirely. The poem does dramatize the poet's increasing sympathy, but in the process it moves away from Clark's adult life to the small part of his childhood that the poet remembers. The "poor rich boy" who dies at forty-five is not integrated with the cool, detached chess player. He is merely set aside as irrelevant to the poet's real concern, commemorating the chess-player's influence on the young poet. It is not Clark that is "dear" to the poet after all, only the "Alfred" that Clark once was, and only because Clark helped the poet inadvertently in a time of need. The poet is grateful for the help, but not grateful enough to try making sense of Clark's life as a whole. If the Times's response to Clark is superficial, the poet's response, then, is partial and self-centered. The concluding figure is especially troubling. We think of metaphor as one of a writer's primary tools in reaching out beyond his subject or of binding the disparate elements of a subject together. But this figure, instead of integrating Clark's life, insists on its disunity. What could be farther from the rich boy desperately seeking affection than the lizard at ease with itself, basking in the sun? And why, we wonder, isn't the poet interested in exploring the discrepancy?

In fairness to Lowell we should keep in mind that his best poems move out from private loss to embrace the largest issues. "For the Union Dead," which begins as personal retrospection about the poet's boyhood daydreams at the Boston Aquarium, turns into a bitter indictment of contemporary American culture from a large, historical perspective. But for a poem to possess inclusiveness the movement need not be so obvious or so grand. All the poems we have dealt with here turn outward to some extent to engage their audience. Jonson's preface to his epigrams appeals directly for attention with the proud claim that his book will teach its readers something important. Whitman's cosmic bard celebrates the self by celebrating the world. The images used by Yeats's poet at the opening of "The Second Coming" keep the range of reference as wide as possible so that the collapse described does not seem grounded in any particular loss to the speaker, or to his family, or even to his country, but in a more fundamental historical reality. And the speaker of Emily Dickinson's poem on the superior courage of the inner struggle does not ground her argument in an appeal to her private experience. She speaks for everyone in a voice that is movingly impersonal, as if she has moved beyond private pain to a long-considered wisdom about the human condition.

Though inclusiveness involves, in its most basic form, avoiding too narrow or too private a treatment of the subject, in its more ambitious form it entails attempting to connect a wide range of apparently unrelated elements. The inclusive speaker presents himself as a seeker of unity amid diversity, and so gives expression to what the Romantics might call the synthesizing power of the imagination. The nearest examples of poets inspired by this kind of ambition are the great moderns, Yeats, Pound, and Eliot, who attempt to bring to bear on the moment a large, historical perspective that involves evaluating the entire sweep of Western culture. Their example, however, no longer seems to exert a deep influence. The moderns tended to be system builders, and system building has become suspect because so many of the particular horrors of the twentieth century seem attributable to the efforts of authoritarian ideologies to impose their single visions on the world. It may be unfair to allow a hatred of dogmatic political ideology to infect our respect for ambitious art, whose authority is earned and not imposed, and whose influence works toward widening our sympathies, not narrowing them. But the ease with which nations betrayed the values of their art has suggested to many that the influence and authority of art are not dependable, and art that makes grand claims for its own importance is particularly suspect. Humility has its excesses, however, as well as ambition, and a distrust of system building need not lead to a distrust of inclusiveness, though it may lead to more tentative and provisional conclusions. Poets should be able to write about all that interests them, and if their interests do not engage them deeply and widely in contemporary life, their poetry is likely to be thin. In traditional poetry the range of interests is expressed through a range of genres—epic, satire, epistle, epigram, georgic, pastoral, ode, and song. Though cultural change has undermined some of the assumptions that made these genres work, the communal impulses behind them are still alive, and all should find refuge within an enlarged version of the first-person poem.

One kind of inclusiveness common now is the rendering of the flow of ordinary life as opposed to reaching for a privileged moment of revelation. The speaker of this kind of poem has no grand mission or message. He is not burdened with any frustrated longings for the ideal that would interfere with his responsiveness to the present. In the *Lunch Poems* of Frank O'Hara, one of the best and most influential examples of the genre, where the present involves the vivid and constantly shifting street life of New York City, the poet, out for a casual stroll at lunch, is content to record his meandering impressions. His attitude is essentially aesthetic. The life around him is a shifting show, a show that includes him as a participant, stirring up within him a shifting flow of responses, and his one task is to be as open as he can to the various facts of his experience. In his inclusiveness O'Hara's speaker is a son of Whitman's, but the facts he includes are not like Whitman's, limitless and holy. They are relentlessly commonplace, however graceful or comic or fresh, and the poems do not suggest that they can be changed more to our liking. How troubled we should feel by this essentially passive role for the poet, this denial of transforming power, is an issue that O'Hara himself addresses in one of his best-known poems, "The Day Lady Died."

It is 12:20 in New York a Friday
three days after Bastille day, yes
it is 1959 and I go get a shoeshine
because I will get off the 4:19 in Easthampton
at 7:15 and then go straight to dinner
and I don't know the people who will feed me

I walk up the muggy street beginning to sun
and have a hamburger and a malted and buy
an ugly NEW WORLD WRITING to see what the poets
in Ghana are doing these days
                                        I go on to the bank
and Miss Stillwagon (first name Linda I once heard)
doesn't even look up my balance for once in her life
and in the GOLDEN GRIFFIN I get a little Verlaine
for Patsy with drawings by Bonnard although I do
think of Hesiod, trans. Richmond Lattimore or
Brendan Behan's new play or *Le Balcon* or *Les Nègres*
of Genet, but I don't, I stick with Verlaine
after practically going to sleep with quandariness

and for Mike I just stroll into the PARK LANE
Liquor Store and ask for a bottle of Strega and
then go back where I came from to 6th Avenue
and the tobacconist in the Ziegfeld Theatre and
casually ask for a carton of Gauloises and a carton
of Picayunes, and a NEW YORK POST with her face on it

and I am sweating a lot by now and thinking of
leaning on the john door in the 5 SPOT
while she whispered a song along the keyboard
to Mal Waldron and everyone and I stopped breathing

As an elegy for Billie Holiday, the poem calls attention to itself because only the last four lines are concerned with the speaker's response to the singer's death. The first twenty-five lines describe a casual afternoon of eating, banking, and buying presents for friends, emphatically unportentous activities that the poet seems to be enjoying. But the last four lines break the casual and comic mood. What might be ordinary sweating on a muggy day merges into the sweat of shock, and the speaker is pulled by his recollection out of the casual flow of the present into a state of breathless stillness that is produced by Holiday's singing. Holiday's death, then, makes an ordinary day, "three days after Bastille day," a momentous one, just as her art has made past occasions momentous. What makes the poem self-referential is the contrast it draws between Holiday's art, which resists the flow of ordinary life, and the speaker's listing of events, which seems to give the flow predominance. The difference is underscored by the powerful effects of Holiday's singing on her audience. For a moment her listeners become one, and this community, which includes the poet, makes the poet's efforts during the day to find connections seem pathetically inadequate. He has to make do with a dinner whose providers are unknown to him, with the trust of his bank teller, with the community of fellow writers met in an anthology. And though his careful gift buying suggests that he cares about the particular tastes of his friends, he gives no indication that these individual friendships, important as they may be to him, are part of some larger whole. O'Hara's poem, then, provides a space for two kinds of art to meet, but it does not exemplify the kind of power that the speaker most admires.

A poet who turns from passive models of inclusiveness to active ones, who believes that impressions that reflect the moment need to be augmented by desires and possibilities that challenge the moment, has to be careful to avoid the kind of stridency and intolerance for which O'Hara's poetry serves as an antidote. Even if one is not tempted to system building or the brooding nostalgia for a lost culture, a critical stance runs the risk of imposing a theme on the world in a manner that is too exclusive, that shrinks the world somewhat to make it comprehensible. To remain open, we may have to learn to resist from a position of uncertainty rather than countering a benighted certainty with an enlightened one. We can take as our model here Melville's Ishmael in *Moby Dick,* a quester who is willing to rest in doubt, as opposed to Ahab, who purchases his power of resistance at the cost of excluding all that does not support his single vision. Resisting Ahab's aggressive movement toward one goal, we may have to become, with Ishmael, masters of digression. The need for openness is especially clear when we recognize that the poetry of resistance will inevitably have a political dimension. To imagine alternatives to the life of the moment involves a critique of the existing conduct of public life, and the poet has to avoid thinking as a spokesman for any particular program or party. To be inclusive he has to be an explorer, not an expounder, and has to create his audience rather than presume one to be ready and waiting.

If the writer can achieve an individual voice that is open and critical, that can give the largest stage to private subjects and private resonance to public issues, his poem will produce an exhilaration that more modest poems cannot easily achieve, the pleasure of contact with a personality not intimidated by the world around it. In American poetry Whitman's expansive bard is a model for this kind of authority, a man at home everywhere, whose "elbows rest in sea gaps," whose "palms cover continents." American poets today may feel less at home on the planet, but it isn't hard to think of several whose work often expresses large social and political concerns—Adrienne Rich, Robert Bly, Louis Simpson, C. K. Williams, Robert Hass, and Robert Pinsky, to name a few. But as a gesture of inclusiveness here I want to choose an example from contemporary Eastern Europe, whose literature is now an inspiration to many American writers. Living under oppressive governments has impelled their poets and novelists to focus much of their energies on political issues. Oppression, of course, is no guarantee of good poetry. It offers, in fact, the temptation of a rhetorical pose that makes good poetry impossible, the temptation toward the melodrama that casts political life as a struggle between powerless virtue and empowered evil. One of the remarkable things about the best of these poets is how they work to avoid this posture, how they create speakers who try to take responsibility for as much as they can, to be not merely witnesses but participants, a part of the world they present, a part of the problem and a part of the cure, and how they test their imagination by constructing liberating alternatives to the present, rebuilding lost cities or imagining futures that challenge and complete the moment rather than merely reflect it. Consider this poem by the young Polish poet Adam Zagajewski:

THE GENERATION
to the memory of helmut kajzar

We walked very slowly down the concrete
slabs near the Olympic Stadium
in Berlin, where the black star
of Jesse Owens had flamed in that prehistoric
time, and the German air
had screamed. I wanted to laugh,
I couldn't believe you could walk
so slowly in the place he had run so fast;
to walk in one direction, but to look
in another, like the figures in Egyptian
reliefs. And yet we were walking that
way, bound with the light string
of friendship.
Two kinds of deaths circle about us.
One puts our whole group to sleep,

takes all of us, the whole herd.
Later it makes long speeches to substantiate
the sentence. The other one is wild, illiterate,
it catches us alone, strayed,
we animals, we bodies, we the pain,
we careless and uneducated.
We worship both of them in two religions
broken by schism. That scar
divided us sometimes when I had
forgotten: we have two deaths,
and one life.
Don't look back when you hear
my whisper. In the huge crowd of Greeks,
Egyptians, and Jews, in that fertile
generation turned to ashes, you walk straight
ahead, as then, unhurried,
alone.
The walls are not tight, windows open
at night to the rain, to the songs of stars
muffled by distance. But
every moment lasts eternally, becomes
a point, a haven, an envelope of emotion.
Every thought is a light coin which
rolls, in its shy secretive
being, into a song, into a painting. Every joy,
even the nonexistent one, leaves a transparent trace. Frost
kisses the pane because it can't get into the room.
This is how a new country arises,
built by us as if by mere chance,
constructed for the future, going down, in tunnels,
the bright shadow of the first country, an unfinished
house.

The poem gives public resonance to a friendship by placing it in increasingly wider historical contexts. These contexts threaten the friendship as well as enlarge it because they suggest that the friends are shaped in part by historical forces they can't control, forces that bear on each of them differently. As Poles, both are drawn to the Olympic Stadium in Berlin as a shrine of the defeat of the Nazi theories of German superiority. But the poet is distant enough from the past to find some comedy in his friend's total absorption. Their different attitudes relate to differences between Jewish and Christian history. The "scar" of schism divides the two when the poet forgets that they experience the meaning of death differently, the Jew as a part of his communal history, the Christian as a private event:

> That scar
> divided us sometimes when I had
> forgotten: we have two deaths,
> and one life.

If the poem had ended here it would simply have given historical amplification to the limitations imposed on friendship. But at this point the speaker makes a bold leap. He tries to establish a posthumous relation with Kajzar that helps assert the power of the individual to resist contingency. Addressing Kajzar in the present tense, he encourages his friend to function as a model of affirmation of future possibilities. Because the dead Kajzar is in fact no longer in control of his life's meaning, we have to see the poet's exhortation to his friend as an exhortation to himself to resist the temptation to see the forces of history as beyond human control. Unlike Jesse Owens, Kajzar needs help to become a hero, and the poet tries to provide it by a series of bold generalizations that insist on human freedom:

> The walls are not tight, windows open
> at night to the rain, to the songs of stars
> muffled by distance. But
> every moment lasts eternally, becomes
> a point, a haven, an envelope of emotion. . . .

These lines, and the string of assertions that follows them, are risky because they are not grounded on any facts we can point to in the poem. But their strain is perhaps deliberate. The speaker is trying to outline the creed of a new gospel, speaking as a kind of oracle shadowy pronouncements about a "new country" that is as yet unembodied, that is always prospective. All that supports it in the poem is the speaker's feelings for his friend, and this seems enough of a platform for the speaker's imagination to build its vision.

In moving from a rueful acceptance of limits to faith in the possibility of a "new country," Zagajewski's poem may be read as a challenge to those of us in America who have accepted too casually the notion that the central fact of modern political life is the powerlessness of the individual. If this notion can be resisted in Eastern Europe, surely it can be resisted here where the failures of our leaders reflect the failed insight of the people who elected them. America has always existed as two countries, the unembodied ideal that casts its "bright shadow," and the embodied fact. The painful discrepancy between the two may tempt us at times to narrow the range of our identifications so that the country's failure may not be felt as our own. But the qualities we ask of the voice of authority should work against this narrowing. They all involve the will to resist withdrawal from the world. When we ask that the voice be passionate, we ask that it commit itself to the importance of its subject rather than protect itself from failure or foolishness by not taking itself or its subject seriously. When we ask that the voice be discriminating, we ask that it reach its conclusions in dialogue with others (or with itself conceived as an other) rather than in some unchallenged, self-admiring solitude. When we ask the voice to be inclusive, we ask it to consider all things within its range of interests, to find nothing for which it is not willing to assume at least some responsibility. The voice of authority is communal, not speaking for a community but directed toward the making of communities, beginning with the community of speaker and reader. It may be more difficult now for us to reach our audience than it was in traditional cultures in which poetry was able to confine itself to traditional materials. But a poet like Homer is still read because he did not define his audience too narrowly, and we can't be sure now to what extent Homer spoke for his culture and to what extent he helped create his culture by using the old stories in a new way. For all we know, Homer had as much work to do in making his community of readers as Odysseus had in reestablishing his home after an absence of twenty years. We should remember that the first time the *Odyssey* is told occurs near the end of the epic when Odysseus and Penelope, on the first night together, tell each other all that happened during their separation. Stories are all they have to bridge the gap, and all that makes the stories effective is the willingness of the listener to believe. We can't expect such devoted listeners, but we can hope to win a hearing if our speakers make the effort to reach out.

ALAN WILLIAMSON

Falling off the World

Poetry and Innerness

Trasumanar significar per verba / non si poria, says Dante on his ascent into Paradise. "To get beyond the human cannot be signified / through words." And yet, a large part of the effort of lyric poetry has been to deal with those moments—Wordsworth calls them "fallings from us, vanishings"—when an eruption of our inner life takes us out of the shared social world, partly because that world has no terms by which to acknowledge such moments. Poetry can do pioneer work at the margins of the sayable, where the genres that belong entirely to communal experience—the sermon, the political tract, the popular song, and even storytelling insofar as it derives from the group in the tavern or around the village well—are not allowed to go.

I take my title from Elizabeth Bishop's "In the Waiting Room." It is a poem about an experience of the unsayable, a kind of vertigo, that comes on a small child who is trying to sort out the mystery of identity and connection, who she is and how far she is defined by the world outside. Left alone in a dentist's waiting room, "too shy" to look at the adults sitting around her, she takes refuge in an issue of the *National Geographic.* The world of the poem, at this point, is the flat world of fact—"grown-up people" are not very different from the clothes that define them, "arctics and overcoats," which in turn are not very different from "lamps and magazines." The facts in the magazines, on the other hand, are mysteries and powers, somehow connected to the child though nothing in the world could seem more strange: the powers of material being, a volcano "spilling over / in rivulets of fire"; what people have done to children ("Babies with pointed heads / wound round and round with string") and to other adults ("'Long Pig,' the caption said"); the adult instinctual body already waiting in her own genes ("those awful hanging breasts"). This sense of a connection she doesn't quite want is brought to focus when she hears her Aunt Consuelo cry out in the dentist's chair. Though the child—being a lonely, parentless, and therefore skeptical child—can form her own critical judgment ("even then I knew she

---

Adapted from an essay entitled "Rilke, Love and Solitude," *Michigan Quarterly Review* 32, 3 (Spring/Summer 1993): 386–403.

was / a foolish, timid woman"), the resemblance of "family voice" is so strong that she hears the cry as *"me: / my voice, in my mouth."* And this plunges her into an almost indescribable state of discovery and panic.

What she discovers, I think, is paradoxical and double: that she is one and only one person, and that this makes her exactly the same as everyone else. It is a discovery that Sartre, in his study of Baudelaire, calls the "empty" or "purely formal" aspect of our experience of individual uniqueness. But this awareness, far from leading to a comforting sense of commonality, produces an ultimate estrangement from herself and everything else, which takes shape as a physical sensation, as if she were falling out of space and time. She tries to get back into the fact-world, and cannot:

> I said to myself: three days
> and you'll be seven years old.
> I was saying it to stop
> the sensation of falling off
> the round, turning world
> into cold, blue-black space.
> But I felt: you are an *I,*
> you are an *Elizabeth,*
> you are one of *them.*
> *Why* should you be one, too?

She seems to know, at that very moment, that this is one of the defining experiences of her life:

> I knew that nothing stranger
> had ever happened, that nothing
> stranger could ever happen.
> Why should I be my aunt,
> or me, or anyone?
> What similarities—
> boots, hands, the family voice
> I felt in my throat, or even
> the *National Geographic*
> and those awful hanging breasts—
> held us all together
> or made us all just one?
> How—I didn't know any
> word for it—how "unlikely" . . .
> How had I come to be here,
> like them, and overhear

> a cry of pain that could have
> got loud and worse but hadn't?

Her physical vertigo is the exact equivalent of her spiritual puzzle-ment. Why should we be "here" at exactly one place and exactly one time? What in us could possibly find that strange? What other "likeli-hood" do we know that could make the very conditions of our being seem "unlikely"? Probably every religion, and every system of psy-chology, would have a different way of talking about such experi-ences. Object-relations theory would stress Bishop's essentially moth-erless childhood, as making both solitude and dependency peculiarly terrifying. Buddhism, on the other hand, would see the beginnings of a real discovery: that our selfhood is empty, but that we are also something else, call it a not-self. Sartrean existentialism would fall somewhere in between.

But what I want to stress is how this experience, however one interprets it, is the beginning of Bishop's career as a poet:

> How—I didn't know any
> word for it—how "unlikely" . . .

By including her child-struggle with language, Bishop suggests that the entire process leading up to the poem "In the Waiting Room" is an effort to resolve that struggle. And here, I think, she speaks for other writers as well. For many of us, the moment when we experienced something we could not share with our outer world, because our outer world had given us no "word" to acknowledge it, was the moment that impelled us toward poetry. And poetry was a struggle with the given language, to make it give us better words than "un-likely" for what had fallen out of this world's likelihood.

But if there is, as I believe, a deep connection between lyric poetry and innerness, there is a prevalent contemporary aesthetic that is deeply distrustful of that connection; that feels it is wrong and dangerous for poetry to turn away from the social world. This aesthetic began, per-haps, with Wendell Berry's 1975 essay "The Specialization of Poetry"; it has certainly been audible at Warren Wilson in recent years. The code word for this distrust is "solipsistic"—though how any attempt to translate the unsayable into the "dialect of the tribe" can be "solipsistic" is a little beyond me. Distrust falls not only on modernist obscurity, or the preoccupation of certain "confessional" poets with the details of their own lives, but on any tendency to value the inner world at the expense of the shared world, the social and political world. There is even the suspicion—influenced perhaps by the neo-Marxist "literary theory" now popular in English departments—that such valuation is a cover for, or at least deeply compatible with, antidemocratic social values. •

The positive side of this aesthetic is a high valuation of narrative. Narrative, it is felt, brings together the outer and inner perspectives on experience, allowing us a full latitude of interpretation. Bishop's poem would actually get very high marks in this aesthetic, because it hews so rigorously to narrative, and to a believable speaking voice. It gives us the full human context—all the data—so that the object-relations theorist is free to follow out certain overtones, and the Buddhist others.

I suppose this aesthetic troubles me most when it shifts from describing different methods of presenting experience to entertaining prejudices about experience itself: when I feel that being prone to experiences of innerness is in some way *wrong*. That if you are a healthy, sufficiently physical person you don't have, or don't want to have, sensations of falling out of your body. That reality is primarily social and political, and to say it isn't brands one a crypto-conservative. Or, perhaps most troubling of all, that if your daily way of experiencing life is made to seem meager by an inward, or an artistic, vision of a fuller way, you are—as Robert Hass argues in his essay "Looking for Rilke"—somehow making a choice in favor of "death," that can be opposed to a choice of "life."

Obviously, these are matters of one's experience of living, and therefore in some ultimate sense unarguable. But I think the prevalent distrust of innerness arises from literary-historical reasons beyond any personal ones. Those of us now in our forties grew up at a time when fashion was turning away from an autobiographical realism, like Bishop's or Robert Lowell's, that presented strangeness in its full, contingent context. In that shift of fashion, the outer world—unless it was a pristine wilderness with a few Indians wandering through—was likely to be called "the dead world" (to quote Robert Bly). And poetry began not only to treat experiences of falling off the world as all-important, but to suggest that they remain essentially incommunicable.

Consider W. S. Merwin's "Air," a deservedly famous poem of that period. It is a lovely, very musical piece, but what it argues is that the outer world is so unspeakably remote that the poet's innerness, unlike Bishop's, will never find a better word than "unlikely":

> Naturally it is night.
> Under the overturned lute with its
> One string I am going my way
> Which has a strange sound.
>
> This way the dust, that way the dust.
> I listen to both sides
> But I keep right on.

In this night—the "natural" condition—the poet's "way" has only its one "strange sound," like a musical instrument with only "one string." It is "strange" because there is nothing to measure it by, nothing to respond. The world's divisions and differences are sterile, two "dusts," "two deserts"; at best it is the great resonating belly of the "overturned lute." It is, I think, symptomatic of this poem's extreme alienation that it cannot take any detail of its landscape from lived experience, but only from literary convention: those twice-removed Victorian redactions of the Middle Ages through which a Child Roland wanders with his troubadour's song and his quest. The mood of the poem often seems to be one of cynicism or bewildered resignation; if it is an account of spiritual journey it presents only its negative side, of criticism and purgation:

> This must be what I wanted to be doing,
> Walking at night between the two deserts,
> Singing.

Such "surrealism"—as it was called at the time, a little inaccurately—seems to suggest that the inner world *must* devalue and exclude the outer world, even if that leaves it only an almost wordless "Singing." "Silence" is "the owner of the smile."

I don't intend to talk here about why this kind of negative spirituality became so overwhelmingly fashionable. The critic Paul Breslin wrote an excellent article about that, called "How to Read the New Contemporary Poem," at a time when such poems were still new; and I've explored some of the reasons in *Introspection and Contemporary Poetry*. What I want to emphasize here is that there has been a mood swing back, which has produced not only a wealth of very fine narrative and quasi-narrative poetry, intensely curious about the outer world, but also an understandable suspicion that inwardness itself is the enemy. But this historical moment needs to be reminded that Merwin's poem is not typical for all time. That a poem can be deeply invested in the importance and value of interiority, and still be concerned with how we live the life we have in common. And that while narrative is a profound and powerful way of conducting this mediation, it is not the only way. Surrealistic imagery can serve a mediating function without producing a poetry of alienated innerness, as it does in Tomas Tranströmer's great poem "The Gallery." It is a poem about the self that is visible and the self that is not visible, and how we must deal with both in our approaches to other people. Here is the poem's ending:

> It happens rarely
> that one of us really *sees* the other:

a person shows himself for an instant
as in a photograph but clearer
and in the background
something which is bigger than his shadow.

He's standing full-length before a mountain.
It's more a snail's shell than a mountain.
It's more a house than a snail's shell.
It's not a house but has many rooms.
It's indistinct but overwhelming.
He grows out of it, it out of him.
It's his life, it's his labyrinth.

I should mention that prior to these lines this poem has used narrative fragments very powerfully in delineating the problem. But it is the surreal terms that draw a kind of outline around its unsayable core, the elusive nature of the inner self, and how it is constructed out of, but at the same time constructs, our actions.

Philosophical discourse can also be a way of mediating. And I want to spend the rest of this essay on what seems to me the greatest of all discursive poems about the problem of innerness, Rilke's *Duino Elegies* (I quote throughout from Stephen Mitchell's translations). I am going to concentrate on the theme of love in the first four elegies, partly because one needs some kind of specific focus to discuss the *Elegies* at all in this short a space; but also because that theme has become a veritable lightning rod for the distrust of inwardness in poetry. We are reminded that Rilke left his wife only two weeks after their daughter was born, claiming it was better for both of their artistic careers; that he refused to go to that same daughter's wedding, because it would interfere with his writing; that he expressed a repeated and, in Hass's phrase, "tiresome" preference for unrequited over requited love.

I have to say that, for me, Rilke gives a deeper account of why love, and living with another person, are difficult, than any other poet I know. What he sees, with peculiar clarity, is that although, or because, love is an intense encounter with the outside, the feelings it stirs—the longing, the terror of losing one's self, the strangeness—go far beyond the individual beloved or even the conscious self; they go back into the prehistory of the psyche. Yet, in the moment, we can never draw those distinctions clearly:

> . . . we never know
> the actual, vital contour of our own
> emotions—just what forms them from outside.

And if we want to feel secure in love, we cannot help dreading that further dimension a little, both in ourselves and in the other person, as if it were a rival:

> . . . Where can you find a place
> to keep her, with all the huge strange thoughts inside you
> going and coming and often staying all night.

In the Fourth Elegy, Rilke will put the same insight more harshly, though very hauntingly:

> . . . Aren't lovers
> always arriving at each other's boundaries?—
> although they promised vastness, hunting, home.

When we fall in love we expect infinite adventure, expansion, newness, and at the same time to be infinitely accepted and familiar—at "home." Impossible, and contradictory, expectations—and when they come up against the quirks and limits of any particular beloved, we are likely to feel as if we had bumped into a solid oak door when we thought we were walking into a grassy field. It is in this mood, I think, that Rilke comes to the notorious remarks about requited love:

> . . . Sing
> of women abandoned and desolate (you envy them, almost)
> who could love so much more purely than those who were gratified.

For the unrequited lover doesn't have to be disappointed in those "boundaries"; her love (it is always *her*), because, like the mystic's, it no longer wants anything, can become what the mystic's is, a pure assent to the other person's existence.

Not, I think, a contemptible thing to have thought or felt. But it would be a mistake to take it as Rilke's last word on the subject. For the *Elegies* are, to use an overused word, a "process"; the movements of thought pose the terms for later movements, rather than resting in one place forever. Those who would suggest that Rilke undervalues physical love, "the possibility of union with the other in their bodies," as Hass puts it in his essay, must contend with the Second Elegy, which, though skeptical, contains one of the most brilliant descriptions ever written of the metaphysics of lovemaking:

> You, though, who in the other's passion
> grow until, overwhelmed, he begs you:
> "No *more* . . ."; you who beneath his hands
> swell with abundance, like autumn grapes;

you who may disappear because the other has wholly
emerged: I am asking *you* about us. I know,
you touch so blissfully because the caress preserves,
because the place you so tenderly cover
does not vanish; because underneath it
you feel pure duration. So you promise eternity, almost,
from the embrace.

Rilke knew, very vividly, how the caress, the being "tenderly cov-
ered," makes the body, and the self in the body, exist as it has never
existed before. It creates *Dauern,* "duration," the Bergsonian moment
that is like "eternity" because it is experienced without division, with-
out clock-measurement. The loved self becomes a complete self, an
inexhaustible "abundance, like autumn grapes"; or it may actually take
pleasure in its own disappearance, "because the other has wholly
emerged" into the same utter, self-sufficient goodness.

But it is the very fluidity of the self, which love momentarily heals,
that makes love so fleeting and risky. What can exist more completely
can also exist less completely. The moment will come—many mo-
ments will come—when one lover is completely present, but the other
is, even if ever so slightly, somewhere else:

> . . . When you lift yourselves up
> to each other's mouth and your lips join, drink against drink:
> oh how strangely each drinker seeps away from his action.

And what, then, becomes of the infinite hope?

Why do we have this innerness, this ontological complexity, that
prevents us from taking even our happiness simply? It is to Rilke's great
credit, I think, that (in an odd way, like Elizabeth Bishop) he explores
this question on the psychological plane as well as on the plane of
existential philosophy. Rilke's friend and former lover, Lou Andreas-
Salomé, had become a disciple of Freud. In 1913, at a psychoanalytic
conference, she introduced Rilke to Freud, who had just published
Totem and Taboo. Out of that conjunction, later the same year, came
Rilke's revisionist-Freudian history of the psyche, the Third Elegy.

Here, Rilke writes for once from the male point of view, and begins
with the mother. It was in the relationship to the mother that we first
experienced a world that seemed to be completely in harmony with
our identities, completely expressive:

> Ah, where are the years when you shielded him just by placing
> your slender form between him and the surging abyss?
> How much you hid from him then. The room that filled with
>   suspicion

at night: you made it harmless; and out of the refuge of your heart
you mixed a more human space in with his night-space.
And you set down the lamp, not in that darkness, but in
your own nearer presence, and it glowed at him like a friend.
There wasn't a creak that your smile could not explain,
as though you had long known just when the floor would do
　　　that. . . .

But we paid a price for that security. "Mother, *you* made him small,"
Rilke says, with a telling ambiguity. And if there is an element that is
not completely explored in the elegy it is the fear of the mother's
power, and the shame at smallness—these emotions made the boy,
later, fear the very thing he wishes to recover, a symbiosis with a
woman.

In any case, the early symbiosis could not last, and what interferes
with it is precisely the boy-child's desire for the mother herself:

> And he himself, as he lay there, relieved, with the sweetness
> of the gentle world you made for him dissolving beneath
> his drowsy eyelids, into the foretaste of sleep—:
> he *seemed* protected. . . . But inside: who could ward off,
> who could divert, the floods of origin inside him?

The "floods of origin," here, are clearly sexual floods ("that hidden
guilty river-god of the blood")—both the flood from which the child
has so recently taken his origin, and the flood of his desire to originate.
Guilty desire is, in this myth, the origin of innerness. The world of
dreams, a world that cannot be spoken of, separates from the daily
world, and becomes itself an object of desire:

> . . . How he submitted—. Loved.
> Loved his interior world, his interior wilderness,
> that primal forest inside him, where among decayed treetrunks
> his heart stood, light-green. Loved. Left it, went through
> his own roots and out, into the powerful source
> where his little birth had already been outlived.

But, strangely, the inner world seems already to have been there,
waiting to be discovered—like a rain forest of dead trees on which
the new growth rises. Here Rilke begins to sound more like Jung
than like Freud—the collective unconscious waiting in everyone,
which the newly created individual unconscious reawakens. But we
must remember that *Totem and Taboo* was the book in which Freud's
ideas were most like Jung's; in which he argued that the Oedipus
complex was so compelling because a primal father had actually been

murdered by his sons, at the beginning of human consciousness. That is why the child, in Rilke, discovers the "ravines / where Horror lay, still glutted with his fathers." That is why "Terror" is entwined with his experience of sexual discovery, "like an accomplice"; and why he must in some sense "love" that terror—it is a part of him from the beginning.

It is, then, an immensely populated psyche that we bring to adult love. How can that not cause a great deal of trouble? We will confuse the new beloved with all its characters:

> . . . Dear girl,
> this: that we loved, inside us, not One who would someday appear,
> but
> seething multitudes; not just a single child,
> but also the fathers lying in our depths
> like fallen mountains; also the dried-up riverbeds
> of ancient mothers. . . .

Furthermore, these characters, in the unconscious, remain very much active agents, with a will of their own. Won't the never-forgotten mother be jealous of the girl who supplants her? Isn't male desire bound to seem brutal, even to the man himself? After all, it descends from the primal father and his murderous sons. And what, too, of the child-self, with its never quite fulfilled longing?

> . . . What passions
> welled up inside him from departed beings. What
> women hated you there. How many dark
> sinister men you aroused in his young veins. Dead
> children reached out to touch you. . . .

From this discovery the elegy comes to its immensely moving peroration. A balance must somehow be struck; for the psyche to be healed, the outer world must become as real as the inner one. And the beloved can do this for the lover, by her grace of living in the daily world, which establishes her solidity, her individuality. (It is the same task, essentially, that Rilke assigns to the artist in a later elegy.)

> . . . Oh gently, gently,
> let him see you performing, with love, some confident daily task,—
> lead him close to the garden, give him what outweighs
> the heaviest night. . . .

Here, as in the *Elegies* as a whole, Rilke comes to value the outer world as much as, if not more than, the inner one. The image is of a balance shifting from one side to the other: "counterweight," *Übergewicht*.

But this too, it must be said, is not the *Elegies'* last word on the subject. In later passages—fueled by further failures to break out of his own patterns—Rilke again insists that love cannot solve the problem of existence; cannot take the place of spiritual quest. Still, one wishes that the end of the Third Elegy—with its tentative but overwhelming hope—were half as well known to the general reader of Rilke as the praise of unrequited lovers, Gaspara Stampa, the Portuguese Nun, and the like.

What is the moral of all this? The moral, I suppose, is that the war between outerness and innerness is perennial in human experience, and one of the great wellsprings of poetry. Perhaps it is not absolutely perennial; perhaps in earlier societies, where the rational ego was not as developed, and the unconscious was projected for everyone in myth and ritual, it was not as clearly felt. But we do not live in such a society, and it is wasteful to spend more than a certain amount of our time lamenting that fact.

We live in a double world, and poetry responds to that in many ways. Some poems try, as it were, to cut the Gordian knot. At one extreme is Merwin's poem, which refuses even to be interested in outerness. At the other extreme is the poem—we can all supply titles and authors—in which the poet congratulates himself or herself on preferring the particular to the abstract; on loving this world so much. To me, both extremes are less interesting than what falls between, because I sense in them an element of pose; but I suppose they must seem sincere to some people, or such poems wouldn't get written. In between, there are probably as many records of mediation, or of tension and pain, as there are varieties of temperament. The real moral is that we must approach that variety with curiosity and tolerance; that we think about what kind of animal we are sniffing up to, before we fall back on our particular decade's programmatic or ideological sense of what poetry "should" or "should not" be doing. As William Blake said, "One Law for the Lion & Ox is Oppression."

PART TWO *Ancient Salt*

All that is personal soon rots; it must be packed in ice or salt. . . .
Talk to me of originality and I will turn on you with rage. I am a
crowd, I am a lonely man, I am nothing. Ancient salt is the best
packing.

—William Butler Yeats,
"A General Introduction to My Work"

RENATE WOOD

Poetry and the Self
Reflections on the Discovery of the Self in Early
Greek Lyrics

Every time we sit down to write a poem we set out to discover, to
define and redefine the Self or some aspect of it, this essential, yet to
some extent invisible and therefore open territory of our personhood.
Like a good metaphor, the Self is open-ended: concrete as the
stimulus-receiving capacity of our senses and yet infinitely rich in its
suggestive-imaginative attributes. We find it reflected in our specific
way of seeing the world and in the language we choose to interpret
and communicate our experience. I am not thinking only of our pri-
vate Self; there is also a public Self, the Self of the culture we live in or
come from and know intimately. As a member of a community, the
Self is also a political element; in fact the Self as we know it today was
first discovered in the Western world when the Greek city-state devel-
oped and introduced a new sense of community and plurality, in
which individuals could observe themselves in others and note the
differences. But first of all body and soul, these complementary ele-
ments of the Self, had to be identified, each in its own right and
together as a whole.

It is an amazing moment, when the body first emerges from the
abstractions of the primitive mind and achieves a natural presence.
This was brought home to me a few years ago in an exhibit on the
human figure in early Greek art. I remember the shock, after looking
at the pottery of the geometric period—Homer's time—with its styl-
ized figures filled in with dark paint-like shadows against a light back-
ground, when suddenly, toward the end of this period, a pottery shard
displayed a figure merely outlined by a dark brush stroke, which left
the body flesh-colored and for the first time completed with detail:
brows, eyes, a beard, wrists, knees, and ankles. It seemed to me at this
moment that the body was born and with it a first glimpse of an
emerging Self. And this body was not part of a decorative design of
stylized figures lined up in a circle around the belly or lip of the pot,
but was part of a scene and part of a story: Odysseus and a companion
lifting a spear to blind the Cyclops Polyphemus.

No wonder that when Homer refers to the human body, for which
he still had no name in the sense we do, he often uses the word *chros,*

which means "skin as surface" or "the outer border of man." *Chros* is not skin or body in anatomical terms but the outer edge of the human body, as if it were a territory with a border around it. Once this territory was discovered, the soul that inhabited it emerged through face and gesture and word to make complete this unit of body and mind we call the Self.

In the catalog of the same exhibit, the introduction by the Greek minister of culture speaks of "ageless youths, the eternity of the Odyssey in their breasts, the lyrics of Sappho on their breath. . . . From the past to the present they have come. . . . Naked, clothed only in their own Self."[1] The drama of the language aside, it is true that nakedness, the celebration of the beautiful body, is closely connected with the discovery of the Self. From the early sixth century—Sappho's time—Greek athletes performed in the nude, and their athletic achievements were also a celebration of the body, a pride and confidence in the body, shocking even to the pagan Romans, but essential to the Greek sense of wholeness: spirit and body were one. As Kenneth Clark puts it, "nothing that related to the whole man could be isolated or evaded," and he compares this "conquest of an inhibition that oppresses all but the most downward people" to "a denial of original sin."[2] Perhaps it is no accident that the discovery of the Self in the West concurs with this denial, which was suppressed again during the Christian Middle Ages until it briefly reemerged during the Renaissance.

But painting and sculpture cannot tell the more intimate story of how body and soul became one in the way that language can. This emerging union became evident two thousand five hundred years ago in the work of the Greek lyric poets Archilochus, Sappho, Anacreon, and others, who followed Homer and preceded the era of tragedy, which could not begin before the Self had been discovered. Only speech can reflect the movements of the mind in the struggle with daily existence, in lament and celebration, and the moments of acute awareness of what it means to be alive. Without any comforting illusions about an afterlife, since being a shade in Hades could only be dreaded, the Greeks like few others celebrated the physical world, the body, and the present. "Now, today, I shall sing beautifully for / my friends' pleasure," says Sappho, and also: "As for him who finds / fault, may silliness / and sorrow take him."[3] In his more caustic way Archilochus states, "What breaks me / young friend, / is tasteless desire, / dead iambics, / boring dinners."[4]

Studying this literature made me for the first time appreciate what it took to discover the Self. It increased in me the wonder of having a Self. Fragile, confused, and always to be rediscovered and redefined though it may be, I had also taken it for granted and at times even considered it as something suspect. I became more conscious of the responsibility to preserve this Self in an age of mass society and mass media, a Self that is as much part of me as it is of you. Perhaps rather than to *preserve* I felt it was the task of our poems to *serve* it with all the honesty and passion we have.

The history of the Self in the West is a relatively new one. Anthony Storr points out that

> the idea that individual self-development is an important pursuit is a comparatively recent one in human history; and the idea that the arts are vehicles of self-expression or can serve the purpose of self-development is still more recent. At the dawn of history, the arts were strictly functional for the community, not for the individual artist.[5]

The work of the Paleolithic artists was an incantation, a belief in the power of their image, which would insure them the desired "mastery over the object."[6] In western Europe names of individual painters began to appear with their works only by the middle of the thirteenth century. But even then, it was not the individuality of the subjects that mattered but their rank in society, which seemed to be a clearly visible identity, while the rest of the person was still hidden under a veil. Collin Morris claims that "it is not possible to be certain, with any portrait before 1200, that it is in our sense a personal study."[7] It was in Italy with the rediscovery of antiquity that the consciousness of individuality first evolved during the late fourteenth and throughout the fifteenth century. From the Renaissance onward, the notion of a person as a separate and unique entity developed rapidly through the Reformation and Luther's emphasis on individual conscience, through Calvinism and the invention of a Protestant work ethic, which encouraged the acquisition of wealth as compensation for an individual's perseverance and toil, up to our present-day absorption of the individual into a mass society. Here the Self is threatened by an alienation from any sense of community sustained by a continuing tradition and therefore also from a viable sense of its own identity.

The modern meaning of the word *self* as "a permanent subject of successive and varying states of consciousness"—according to the *Oxford English Dictionary*—was not established until 1674. At about the same time *self* was introduced into the language as part of a group of compounds, the source of which was mostly the literature of theology and philosophy. Examples are:

> self-sufficient (1598), self-knowledge (1613), self-made (1615), self-seeker (1632), selfish (1640), self-examination (1647), selfhood (1649), . . . self-conscious (1687).[8]

The word *individual,* as Peter Abbs has pointed out, originally signi-
fied "indivisible" and in connection with the Trinity or a married
couple indicated something that cannot be parted. Abbs describes the
gradual shift in the meaning as follows:

> The gradual inversion of meaning for the word *individual,* moving
> from the indivisible and collective to the divisible and distinctive,
> carries quietly within itself the historical development of self-
> consciousness, testifies to that complex dynamic of change which
> separated the person from the world making him self-conscious and
> self-aware, that change in structure of feeling which during the
> Renaissance shifted from a sense of unconscious fusion with the
> world towards a state of conscious individuation.[9]

This "shift" for which the Renaissance and its artists have been cele-
brated was, of course, as the word *Renaissance* indicates, a rebirth of a
discovery made approximately two thousand years earlier. It is this
"shift" and the early Greek poets' contribution in bringing it about
that has captivated the minds of many scholars of antiquity, among
them Bruno Snell, whose book *The Discovery of the Mind: The Greek
Origins of European Thought*[10] has become a widely recognized and
often debated addition to the canon. Much of what I have to say in the
following is based upon this source.

By the time of the early Greek lyricists, in the two hundred years
that followed Homer, the notions of body and soul had evolved to
such a degree that they had become complementary parts of a person
who, though the gods were still generally revered as the providers of
personal fates, began to speak as an individual. The monodies (songs
for solo voice accompanied by lyre or flute) of Archilochus, Sappho,
Anacreon, and others contain songs of praise to gods and men, espe-
cially wedding songs and eulogies, but these poets also speak about
themselves in ways similar to those we use today.

Archilochus, a mercenary soldier of the first half of the seventh
century B.C., is not a monodic poet proper, because he used the flute as
an accompaniment. This practice, at a time dominated by choral lyrics
and the lyre as the traditional instrument, was still considered im-
proper or vulgar. His voice is colloquial, sometimes cynical, but also
often straight from the heart. Sappho, from an aristocratic family on
Lesbos, who around 600 B.C. spent some time in exile on Sicily, and
Anacreon, born around 572 B.C. in Asia Minor and for years court
poet of the tyrant of Samos, both wrote monodic lyrics proper, accom-
panied by the lyre. The work of these lyricists covers about two
hundred years and has come to us only in fragments, some of them
found in the rubble of archaeological sites, some in passages quoted by

later writers, and others from shreds of Egyptian mummy wrappings, for which unwanted papyrus was torn into long strips, mutilating the poems by separating the beginning, middle, and end of the lines. The poems of Anacreon created a following of epigones popular at the Renaissance courts of western Europe. For a long time his work overshadowed that of Sappho, which, because it openly acknowledged her love for women, was not tolerated by the Church. Of her seven books only a pitiful remnant of poems and fragments exists today.

These three poets and a few others discover in their poems that not all men are striving for the same goals and that they differ in their desires. They discover also that what is intensely felt outweighs external pomp, and all of them, in many variations, speak about the troubles of their lives and become aware of the alternating pattern of distress and reprieve imposed by the gods, which has to be endured but which, if understood, also provides comfort. One of the areas affected most by this discovery is their love poetry. Here Sappho is the first, with her "bittersweet Eros," to hint at ambiguity as a condition of the soul and at memory as something that can be jointly owned by separated lovers.

All of these discoveries, which charge the imagery of the lyricists with a vibrant personal intensity, may not seem to us as amazing as they were then. We can only appreciate them properly if we understand how hidden the Self still was at Homer's time and what it took for these poets, all of whom knew Homer's work and were instructed by it, to move in the new direction they chose. At the time of the lyricists, the act of seeing had come to be understood in a different way than in Homer's time, when many details of nature could still not be "named" because they were not "seen" as neutral objects with specific properties. Moreover, the lyric poets had learned to perceive the human body as one unit and the soul as its singular and vital complement, concepts not yet available to Homer in the way we understand them today.

In Homer's work, dated roughly in the eighth, possibly into the early seventh century B.C., abstractions are still in their beginnings, but his language is rich in words for immediate sense perceptions. What interested Homer's contemporaries were "the palpable aspects, the external qualifications, of the act of seeing" rather than "the essential function itself, the operation common to every glance."[11] Consequently, Homer uses many verbs—Snell mentions nine—each defining a specific type of vision: there is, for example, a verb denoting "to see" in the sense of having a threatening impression of an object, and another, which denotes "to see something bright," and still another, which means "to look with a glance that incites terror," and so on. It is the beheld object and the sentiment associated with the sight that give each word its peculiar quality. There is no word simply representing the function of sight, which leads Snell to conclude that "as far as [Homer's contemporaries] were concerned it didn't exist."[12]

By the time of the lyric poets the act of seeing was understood as a function independent of the object beheld, and two words, similar to what we have in "to see" and "to look," survived the abundance of verbs Homer depended on. Other areas of the language opened up, because the observed objects now owned specific properties, which previously could not be clearly separated from the process of seeing. Shapes, textures, colors, and motions were described in new ways and received their "names," as did the human body and through it the dimensions of soul and mind.

Max Treu[13] points out that the Greek poets of Sappho's time began to use attributes they had observed in plant life for the human body: there is a new attention to surfaces, and an abundance of epithets for the tactile emerges. There is a fascination with the elastic quality of the human body, and also with its swelling and dwindling properties. There is a new acute awareness of becoming instead of being, which has an impact on the sense of time. An epithet previously used for the surface of water is now applied to the skin, and the expression of a face becomes detailed and transparent to emotion. For the first time heaviness and lightness are not just physical properties but become attributes of emotion. When Sappho says, "The heart turns heavy with misfortune," a physical property becomes an emotional one. For Homer, man is heavy through the weight of weapons, through injury, sleep, wine, or wet clothes; intensity is not expressed through this word. The only adjective he uses symbolically is "golden." Probably because of Homer's particular notion of seeing as a function, in which color must have been perceived as a texture of the process of seeing rather than an attribute of the object seen, his work remains relatively colorless. The poplar leaves are called glittering, not green; red appears only once in the cheek piece of a horse's harness, and blood is always called black. At the time of the early lyricists color begins to play a role not just in connection with landscape but also with a new sense of the body. The colors of cheeks, eyes, hair, and garments become important, and it is Sappho who for the first time calls the grass green. For the first time, too, the body receives a shadow. While for Homer the shadow had been the darkness in the streets after sundown, Archilochus is the first to mention the shadow of a girl's hair on her shoulder.

Already in the second century B.C., Aristarchus, the Alexandrian scholar and interpreter of Homer, pointed out that in the *Iliad* and the *Odyssey* the word *soma,* which later came to denote "body," never refers to a living being. *Soma* for Homer is the corpse. Again Homer employs many different words to signify what we would call the

(1)   (2)

Figures 1 and 2. From Bruno Snell, *The Discovery of the Mind: The Greek Origins of European Thought*. Trans. T. G. Rosenmeyer (New York: Harper and Row, 1960), 7.

living human body. For example, he uses *demas,* which means "in structure" or "in shape" and which can be applied only in the context of being small or large or in pointing out the resemblance to someone. Frequently instead of "body" we find the word "limbs," by which Homer means "the limbs as moved by joints" or "the limbs in their muscular strength." Another way to refer to the body is to use *chros,* which signifies "skin as surface" or "the outer border of man." It is used in the context of "he washed his body" or "he placed his armor about his body" and is not to be confused with skin as part of the anatomy, which is *derma.*

If one looks at the representation of the human body in early Greek art, it is evident, as Snell demonstrates in figures 1 and 2, that it was seen not as a unit but an assemblage of various independent parts. Figures 1 and 2 represent, respectively, a contemporary child's drawing of a man and a figure from a vase of the geometric period. Our children usually draw the torso as a compact center of the body, while the geometric design of Homer's time emphasizes the length of the limbs, the spindly joints, and the bulging of the muscles. The wasplike waist and the triangular chest prevent any sense of compactness of a trunk. The focus is on the vigorous and nimble use of the limbs, as Homer's language for the body reflects: "fleet legs," "knees in speedy motion," "sinewy arms." Snell concludes: "It is in these limbs, immediately evident as they are to his eyes, that he locates the secret of life."[14] And I quote him further:

> The phenomenon is the same as with the verbs denoting sight; in the latter, the activity is at first understood in terms of its conspicuous modes, of the various attitudes and sentiments connected with it, and it is a long time before speech begins to address itself to the essential function of this activity. It seems, then, as if language aims progressively to express the essence of an act, but is at first unable to comprehend it, because it is a function, and as such neither

tangibly apparent nor associated with certain unambiguous emotions. As soon, however, as it is recognized and has a name, it has come into existence, and the knowledge of its existence quickly becomes common property.[15]

As soon as the hidden unity of the body was recognized, the word *soma* took on the meaning of the living human body. From here it was only a step to the individual soul that inhabited it.

Homer does not have words corresponding directly to ours for the "mind" or the "soul." Instead, for the concepts that those two words encompass for us, he mainly uses the three words *psyche, thymos,* and *noos.* All three represent organs of the mind, which were imagined as analogous to organs of the body. The word *psyche,* for example, is related to the Greek *psuchein,* to breathe, and is considered a semi-organ for breathing. In this sense it is also the force that keeps a human being alive and, by extension, something like consciousness. It can be lost in battle where it leaves the dying through the mouth or a wound to fly off to Hades. *Thymos* is perceived to be "the generator of motion and agitation."[16] Though it leaves after death it does not continue as a shade in Hades, but being an organ of motion and emotion it is the source of joy, love, and sympathy. It is often translated as "heart," the seat of emotion in our sense, though sometimes it also functions as knowledge and will. Finally *noos* is a kind of "mental eye," which amounts to something like intelligence and individual thought.

Though the lyric poets still use Homer's words for the organs of mind and soul, they no longer think of them as analogous to physical organs, but as abstractions ar at least semi-abstractions with logical and psychological attributes. When Archilochus, in a poem, addresses his *thymos,* he talks to his heart in the way that we have done ever since.

During the period from Homer to the fifth century, *soma* and *psyche* emerged, probably coupled as complementary terms, to acquire the new meanings of "body" and "soul." Snell attempts to describe this complex process:

The word denoting the eschatological soul was put to a new use, to designate soul as a whole, and the word for corpse came to be employed for the living body; the reason for this must be that the element which provided man during his living days with emotions, perceptions and thoughts was believed to survive in the psyche. Presumably people felt that animate man had within him a spiritual or intellectual portion, though they were unable to define this element by one term sufficiently accurate or inclusive. As a matter of fact, this is the state of affairs which we shall meet among the early Greek writers of poetry. And it may be inferred that, because the eschatological psyche had been correlated with the soma of the dead, the new psyche, the "soul" demanding a new body to suit it, caused the term *soma* to be extended so that it was ultimately used also for the living body. But whatever the details of the evolution, the distinction between body and soul represents a "discovery" which so impressed people's minds that it was thereafter accepted as self-evident in spite of the fact that the relation between body and soul, and the nature of the soul itself, continued to be the topic of lively speculation.[17]

By the time of Heracleitus (between 540 and 480 B.C.), the term *psyche* had been established as the soul inhabiting the living human body, an inner dimension no longer associated with any specific physical organs. When he says, "You could not find the ends of the soul though you traveled every way, so deep is its *logos*," he refers to a perception of depth unknown to Homer. It had come to Heracleitus from the lyric poets, who began to see the intensely felt as more compelling than external appearance and to discover the soul as an inner realm with its own dynamics. "Deep" in this context, according to Snell, is "more than an ordinary metaphor; it is almost as if speech were by this means trying to break through its confines, to trespass on a forbidden field of adventure."[18] It seems to me that one cannot applaud these discoveries of the early lyricists without becoming aware of a beginning process, during which body and soul separated into something physical and nonphysical, a process that eventually would sever the essential bond between the two, casting the body into a dubious and subservient role. But for the lyric poets, the bond between the two still existed; in fact it is the body and its vulnerability that first give them access to the depth of the soul and a new sense of Self.

Together with the dimension of "depth" comes a new sense of the soul's intensity. Homer understands quantity, but not intensity. He uses terms like "much-pondering" and "much-thinking"; for him, as Snell puts it, "the intensive coincides with the extensive"[19]: if a man has experienced much and often, he will have acquired intensive knowledge. But "intensive" for Homer has to do with accumulation and not with increased "tension" or depth, just as he is unable to perceive feelings as torn. He expresses the conflict between a man and one of his organs when he says, "he was willing but his *thymos* was not," but it is not a conflict within the same organ; in other words, he doesn't understand the notion of being genuinely divided in one's feelings as Sappho expresses it in her "bittersweet Eros." It is also Sappho's time that coins a new expression, the equivalent of our "I am conscious of," though it literally says "I share knowledge with myself," *sunoida emantō*. The root of *sunoida* indicates the idea of "together" that is still present in the Latin-based word "conscious."[20]

Finally now there is an imaginary space in which consciousness is gathered into a sense of personhood, which can say "I" similarly to the way we do today.

It is this "I" that begins to recognize the differences between men and their various goals in a way not yet recognized in the *Iliad*. When Archilochus moves from the line of the *Odyssey*, "For different men take delight in different actions" to his own line, "Each man has his heart cheered in his own way," the difference may be slight, but the focus is now on the individual:

> Such a mind, Glaucus son of Leptines, do mortal men have
> as Zeus may usher in each day, and they think their
> thoughts in accord with their daily transactions.

Even though the gods, as in Homer's world, still fashion the events of each day and each mind, there is also space for an emerging Self and its own qualities.

A poem by Sappho, restored from a badly damaged Egyptian manuscript, lets the speaker boldly express her own preference in the face of all others:

> Some say cavalry and others claim
> infantry or a fleet of long oars
> is the supreme sight on the black earth.
> I say it is
>
> the one you love. And easily proved.
> Didn't Helen—who far surpassed all
> mortals in beauty—desert the best
> of men, her king,
>
> and sail off to Troy and forget
> her daughter and dear kinsmen? Merely
> the Kyprian's gaze made her bend and led
> her from her path;
>
> these things remind me now
> of Anactoria who is far,
> and I
> for one
> would rather see her warm supple step
> and the sparkle of her face—than watch all the
> dazzling chariots and armored
> > hoplites of Lydia.[21]

Horses, soldiers, and ships do not sway the speaker from her conviction that "the supreme sight" on earth "is the one you love." An emotional value outweighs the obvious and visible signs of power and pomp, and it is the memory of two physical attributes of the loved person, Anactoria's "supple step" and "the sparkle of her face" (or eyes), which conveys the charge of emotion. The spell of love that led Helen astray is replaced by the speaker's own spell of memory and longing.

While Homer and Archilochus grant that there are differences in people's desires, Sappho evaluates those differences and is the first to state that wealth and military might cannot match the power of what is deeply felt. But Archilochus as a soldier discovers this divergence of values in his own way:

> I do not like a tall general, striding forth on his long
> legs; who prides himself on his locks, and shaves his chin
> like a fop. Let him be a small man, perhaps even bow-legged,
> as long as he stands firm on his feet, full of heart.

To unmask the pomp of power and success as an enfeebling vanity is to take another step in the process of weighing the relationship between inner and outer values. Here attributes of the body are used to reveal the deceiving relationship between character and appearance. Another example is Anacreon's witty ridicule of the nouveau riche Artemon:

> Once he went about in filthy clothes and waspy hair,
> with wooden rings on his ears, and wore around his ribs
> an unwashed hairy oxhide from an old miserable shield.
> Our con-man pimped a living from bakery girls and whores,
> and got his neck bound to a whipping block where the leather
> made raw meat of his back—and best, he rode the wheel
> so that hairs could be torn from his beard and scalp.
>
> But now the good Artemon rides like a generous lord
> in an excellent coach or litter; he wears gold earrings
> and carries a special ivory parasol like a grand lady.[22]

No matter the difference in these voices, all these poets are aware of an inner dimension more essential than the often misleading outer disguise. They are acutely sensitized to the difference between being and appearance.

There are other poems by Archilochus, in which he draws from his life as a mercenary soldier, where meager rations, drinking while on watch aboard a ship, and the harshness of war reflect the frustrations and sorrows of daily existence. His love poems as well, with acute realism, all emphasize the sufferings of love. From Homer, Archilochus was familiar not only with the celebration of love and its pleasures in association with festive banquets, drinking, and dancing, but also with hints of its dark side in the magic of Aphrodite's girdle containing "love, desire and cunning chatter which rob even the wise of their sense." Archilochus now focuses on this side:

> Such a desire was entwined in my heart
> and shed a thick mist over my eyes, stealing the
> subtle wits from my breast.

While for Homer "the mist poured over the eyes" indicated death or unconsciousness, Archilochus develops it into a symptom of unhappy love. In the pangs of desire the body experiences a kind of psychological death, and the focus shifts from the god-given sufferings of life to a suffering caused by one's own body, within one's own person. Sappho, who was familiar with Archilochus's work, wrote a love poem in which she describes her physical symptoms in similar ways:

> That man appears to me equal to the gods who sits before you,
> and by your side hears your sweet speech and your charming
> laughter which has put wings on the heart in my breast.
> When I look at you but once, my speech ceases to obey me.
> My tongue is broken, a subtle fire creeps under my skin,
> my eyes see nothing, and my ears begin to ring. Sweat pours
> down over my limbs, a trembling seizes me from head to toe,
> I am paler than grass, and I appear close to death. But one
> can endure all. . . .

The focus of the poem is on the symptoms of the body, which are caused by desire and reflect its deathlike spell. There is a triangle of people involved: the girl who speaks and whom the poet loves, the man who listens to the girl and sits near her, and the poet who observes all, but mostly herself. Jealousy, though perhaps part of this scene, is not what the poem dwells on. The focus is on the speaker's mind—the phrases "appears to me" and "I appear" occur at the opening and closing—and what goes on there is expressed through images of the body. The "sweet speech" and "charming laughter" of the girl are contrasted with the speaker's failing senses: the loss of normal perception, the loss of control over the body, the apparent death of the body and yet the awareness of still being alive in some extension of the body that "can endure all." While the people in this poem are all static, it is the speaker's body that acts out a great drama of the soul, the subject of which is desire. And this inner dimension is not god-given but rather an extension of the body, owned by the Self in its enduring and suffering. As a contrast, the man who sits near the girl and listens is, in Sappho's eyes, "equal to the gods" because he doesn't suffer but seems to remain in control, immune to the invasion of desire that threatens the boundaries of her body and awakens her to those of the soul.

Following Hesiod, who had already applied the traditional image of sleep as the "looser of limbs" in connection with Eros, Archilochus uses it to describe his own experience of desire and passes it on to Sappho who develops it further:

> Once more Eros, the looser of limbs, drives me about,
> a bitter-sweet creature which puts me at a loss.

The reference to limbs here still echoes Homer's perception of the body, and for Sappho as for Archilochus, love is still not an emotion but an event provoked by the gods. But her interpretation of this event as "bittersweet," her feeling of inner division and powerlessness, are her own. While Anacreon's line, "I love and love not; I rave, nor do I rave," describes the lover's struggle of having to combine two opposing forces in one body, Sappho expresses the same paradox in her more poignant phrasing of the "bittersweet" Eros (*glukupikron:* literally "sweetbitter") and with it invents a way to acknowledge the ambiguity of emotion unknown to the epic and the poets before her. When the beloved girl in Sappho's presence gives her attention to the man at her side, the sweetness seems to ensue from the girl's "sweet speech" and "charming laughter," which "has put wings" on Sappho's heart, while at the same time she suffers the "bitterness" from feeling the dissolution of her own body. The "wings on her heart" and the feeling of being "close to death" collide. Desire splits the soul: Eros means longing and lack.

Eros, never mentioned by Homer, is a discovery of the lyricists, and his influence is associated with an invasion of the body and a painful loss of control. "Looser of limbs," also translated as "melter of limbs," is just one of many metaphors for his dissolving powers, as Anne Carson has pointed out:

> Alongside melting we might cite metaphors of piercing, crushing, bridling, stinging, biting, grating, cropping, poisoning, singeing and grinding to a powder, all of which are used of Eros by the poets, giving a cumulative impression of intense concern for the integrity and control of one's own body. The lover learns as he loses it to value the bounded entity of himself.[23]

It is passion and unrequited love that awaken the mind to itself in moments when normally accepted values do not seem to count, when frustrated desire isolates the individual and forces the soul, like an awareness of an "enduring," hidden, inner body, to confront itself.

Snell's proposition that the "obstruction" of desire (Eros) as described in the lyric love poetry first leads to the discovery of the mind and the still uncharted territory of the soul is debated but by now mostly accepted among scholars. For poets, it is an exciting and intriguing thesis, particularly hard to resist if one perceives the soul as an extension of the body and not as a separate entity, as Snell sometimes seems to do. Moreover, another argument, not considered by Snell, has been raised to support his thesis. "Is it a matter of coincidence," Anne Carson asks in *Eros, the Bittersweet,* "that the poets who invented Eros, making him a divinity and a literary obsession, were also the first authors in our tradition to leave us their erotic poems in written form?"[24] The time of the early lyricists was a period in which the shift from an oral to a literate culture was taking place, "perhaps the most dramatic of the innovations with which the seventh- and sixth-century Greeks had to cope."[25] In a literate society, in the act of reading or committing words to written form, the natural immediate contact of the senses with the physical world is necessarily inhibited and the body—perceived now in new ways—suffers from an unaccustomed deprivation. It has to turn into itself. Is it possible that the lyricists' experience of Eros was triggered or influenced by the strains of the new literate tradition with its enforced isolation? Definitely their breaking away from traditional phrasing and the personal traits of their voices reflect a new era.

The almost amazed awareness of their own vulnerability is voiced by these poets not only in their love poems but also in their description of the constant upheavals of life. With this awareness now has come the realization that the alternating moments of joy and suffering, god-given as they are, form a recognized, natural pattern, and that understanding this pattern ensures comfort. Already Archilochus states this clearly:

> Heart, my heart, convulsed with helpless troubles, rise
> up, defend yourself against the foe, meet them with
> truculent breast. With firm stance receive the enemy's
> onslaught, and neither rejoice openly if the victory is
> yours, nor crouch at home and wail if you lose. But when
> life brings joy, rejoice, and when it brings suffering,
> do not grieve overmuch. *Understand the rhythm of life*
> which controls man.

> (emphasis mine)

Sappho expresses the same idea in a poem that, according to Snell, is her only completely preserved one:

> On your dappled throne, eternal
> Aphrodite, cunning daughter of Zeus,
> I beg you, Lady, don't crush me
> with love's pain
>
> but *come to me now,* if *ever before*
> *you heard* my remote cry, and yielded,
> slipping from your father's gold
> house, and came,
>
> yoking birds to your chariot.
> Beautiful sudden sparrows took you
> from heaven through the middle sky,
> whipping wings,
>
> down to the dark earth. Blessed,
> with a smile on your deathless lips,
> you asked what was wrong now,
> why did I call you,
>
> what did my mad heart want to
> happen. "Sappho, whom shall I get
> to love you? Who is turning
> against you?
>
> Let her run away, soon she'll be
> after you. Scorn your gifts, soon she'll
> bribe you. Not love, she'll love you,
> even unwillingly."
>
> So come to me *once again* and free me
> from blunt agony. Labor
> and fill my heart with its fire,
> and be my ally. [26]

(emphasis mine)

The effectiveness of the poem is in its use of tense. The comfort received in the past is described in the motion of the goddess's descent from the golden house to the black earth and the tenderness of her gestures and words. It is the goddess's soothing voice that reminds the speaker of the constant alternating pulse between lack and fulfillment, and so through the memory of the divine voice the speaker appears to comfort herself. Therefore the last requests in the poem, "free me from blunt agony" and "be my ally," seem already halfway granted. It is easy to suspect that the poem implies not only the ebb and flow of external events but also of the mysterious tide of the soul.

After Sappho, Anacreon's love poems develop this fluctuation in the flow of life into a formula, and the word *again (dēute)*, indicating the repetition and unpredictability of lack and fulfillment, forms the opening of many of his poems:

> *Again* golden-haired Love throws me his purple ball and
> calls me to play with a bright-sandalled child; but the
> girl—she comes from glorious Lesbos—ridicules my
> hair—alas it is white—and gapes after another.
>
> (emphasis mine)

There is a moment in the *Odyssey* that seems to prepare for this insight into the changing rhythm of life now generally accepted by the lyric poets. When Odysseus returns home in disguise on the night before his great revenge on Penelope's suitors, he is enraged by the maids passing him to spend the night as usual with his enemies. He wonders whether he should dispense with his disguise and kill them all right away, or whether he should restrain himself and leave them alone for another night. While his heart "barks" within him, he tells himself, "Endure my heart; you once bore a baser thing, when the Cyclops devoured your comrades. But still you endured till your guile found a way." He checks his resentment by remembering a previous incident that had been even worse. The psychological pattern is essentially the same as in the lyric poems, but for Odysseus the recurrent pattern of reprieve and stress is not yet an accepted fact and he cannot rest until Athena comes to soothe him.

Homer understands the excitation of soul and mind essentially as a symptom of one of his spiritual organs (*psyche, thymos,* or *noos*), which function in the same way as any of his other organs. Therefore self-control or the ability to achieve inner peace remains outside of his reach. When Archilochus addresses his *thymos,* he no longer thinks of it as part of the anatomy, but as a dimension of the soul, just as for us the heart has been a spiritual or emotional entity for centuries. This development is true for the lyric poets in general, except that they have not coined different words for their findings and rely still on Homer's vocabulary. But Archilochus uses phrases unknown to Homer, which reflect the new direction the lyricists have taken. When he calls his *thymos* "stirred up with suffering" or says of his general that he is "full of heart," the original organs have become metaphors for an emotional state. Sappho and Anacreon go beyond Archilochus when they recognize the ambiguity inherent in emotion, which does not arise from the conflict between two separate spiritual organs but is the tug and pull of one and the same. Finally it is Sappho who also confirms that longing can conjure up shared memories, which offer comfort, or can with an imaginary leap bridge and transcend distances.

An incomplete poem by Sappho tells of a girl called Arignota, who has moved to Sardis, the capital of Lydia, and of another girl, Atthis, whom Arignota loved and who has stayed behind with Sappho. While Sappho imagines Arignota's life "among Lydian women," she poignantly evokes her longing for her friends left behind on Lesbos:

> Even in Sardis
> Anactoria will think often of us
>
> of the life we shared here, when you seemed
> the Goddess incarnate
> to her and your singing pleased her best
>
> Now among Lydian women she in her
> turn stands first as the red-
> fingered moon rising at sunset takes
>
> precedence over stars around her;
> her light spreads equally
> on the salt sea and fields thick with bloom
>
> Delicious dew pours down to freshen
> roses, delicate thyme
> and blossoming sweet clover; she wanders
>
> aimlessly, thinking of gentle
> Atthis, her heart hanging
> heavy with longing in her little breast
>
> She shouts aloud, Come! we know it;
> thousand-eared night repeats that cry
> across the sea shining between us[27]

As Snell points out, the first sentence says literally "often she has her mind here from the direction of Sardis," indicating that the mind can move independently from the body and that memory can bridge physical distances in a way even a loud voice cannot. This type of phrasing would have been beyond the reach of Homer, for whom the mind was still solidly anchored in the body and its organs. When Odysseus longs to return from the island of Calypso, Homer says:

> But Odysseus longs to see the smoke rising from his land,
> and then to die.

As touching as Homer's lines are, longing for him is still focused on specific unfulfilled goals and not, as in Sappho's poem, on an exploration of the emotion and the means to bridge the distance and create a sense of momentary union or comfort through the memory of the past. In the banquet lyrics of the same time, which celebrate the friendship and love between men, the union of souls over drink and song, a similar solidarity of the minds is expressed, but not with the tenderness and subtlety of Sappho's lines.

The bond of shared experience is not only the subject of the love poems, it is also, in another sense, part of these poets' apprehension of audience. In spite of signs of an emerging Self, or maybe because of it, the Greek lyricists almost always address their poems to "another," whether god, man, or community. They do not experience themselves as isolated individuals in our sense, but as part of a vitally felt community where feelings and thoughts are shared and confirmed by others.

The work of the early Greek lyricists is intimately connected with the emergence of the *polis,* the city-state, and the sense of being citizens under the same law. Here the individual lived in close contact with others and yet had specific rights that—at least in the private sphere and to some degree in public—allowed him to dissent, to establish his own preference. The lyric writers give the clearest picture of this emerging new Self, this integrated whole of a body inhabited by a soul, which begins to chart its own territory. Homer's perception of body and soul, as expressed in the vocabulary available to him, does not yet delineate the attributes of the soul, which were prefigured by the lyricists and outlined by Heracleitus. Snell sums up these attributes as "*tension,* which included both intensity and depth, *spontaneity,* and *solidarity* or *joint possession.*"[28] Once the lyric writers had grasped the simultaneity of positive and negative charges concerning one and the same object, they were able to establish the ambiguity of emotion and with it *tension.* And once these poets had discovered that possession of the soul could be shared as communal property, the notion of *solidarity* entered the language. Finally, when these writers analyzed the misery of unrequited love, they became aware of the *spontaneity* of the soul, for the sufferings of love seemed to originate inside their own bodies and not in the fates assigned by the gods.

Snell's analysis of the lyricists' achievements focuses more on areas of mind and soul and less on the body, the soul's complementary part of the Self. The fact that he does not acknowledge Sappho as lesbian and interprets her erotic language as part of her mentor's role in guiding and tutoring daughters of the aristocracy shows that he tends to read the physical and sensual imagery as a sublimated expression of the soul. He generally tends in his interpretation to separate body and soul strictly into opposites according to our Western Christian and Cartesian tradition, as if the achievement of these poets rested on their discovery of the soul as something independent from the body and essentially nonphysical. Surely the beginning of this separation was then on its way, but it was still balanced by the Greek appreciation of the body, in whose beauty they celebrated the reflection of the divine. As we have become more aware of the close connection between *psyche* and *soma* in this century, it seems that the polarity between them is gradually being diminished, but only after the body had threatened to become a soulless and dispensible entity.

Although it may seem that I am straying from my subject, I want to relate these ideas to a more recent development in the history of the Self, the repercussions of which are still with us. John Carey in his T. S. Eliot Memorial Lecture "Revolted by the Masses"[29] gives a poignant picture of this development when he analyzes the response of writers and intellectuals early in this century to the sudden population explosion and the spread of education among the urban masses created by the Industrial Revolution. It is interesting to juxtapose this response with the Greek lyricists' discoveries and to realize the threat that the appearance of "the masses" posed to Self, body, and soul, as we had understood them until then.

When Ortega y Gasset published his book *The Revolt of the Masses* in 1931, he outlined the population increase in Europe, which from the sixth century up to 1800 had remained under 180 million and then in a sudden explosion had reached 460 million by 1914. Ortega speaks of "a gigantic mass of humanity," a threat to civilization and culture, which can only exist among a minority of the "best." With the emergence of the masses, the political process had changed and the new "hyperdemocracy" had become an instrument to serve the masses and erase the individual. Already before Ortega, Nietzsche in his *Will to Power* had proclaimed that "a declaration of war on the masses by higher men is needed." "Everywhere," he said, "the mediocre are combining to make themselves master" and the consequence of this will be "the tyranny of the least and dumbest."

According to John Carey, Nietzsche is one of the earliest products of mass culture, because it created him "as its antagonist," and in this role his influence on the intellectuals of his time was tremendous. But there were also others who, before him or at the same time, reacted with disdain to the new phenomenon of the mass. Already Ibsen's *The Enemy of the People* (1882) had taken the side of the eccentric individual against the venal masses, and Flaubert, in 1871, had expressed his disgust with the mob: "I believe the mob, the mass will always be despicable. . . . One could not elevate the masses even if one tried."

John Carey draws a line between the nineteenth-century "mob" and the twentieth-century "mass." The difference is literacy, promoted by The Education Act of 1871 in England, which was met by many intellectuals and writers with suspicion and premonition. G. B. Shaw commented on the newly created reading masses as "readers who had never before bought books, nor could they have read them if they had." The following explosion of journalism and newspapers was the cause of further hostility among the intellectuals, and T. S. Eliot, referring to the impact of mass publications, called their readers "a complacent, prejudiced and unthinking mass."

This contempt for the newly literate masses and the shallowness and vulgarity of the literature that sprung up to meet their demands drove intellectuals and writers apart from the general reading public. Writers began to perceive themselves as isolated and ignored, at best as members of a small elite trying to carry on an ever less appreciated cultural mission. At the same time, the word *high-brow* was coined to express the disdain felt by the masses toward the intellectual elite. But what seems most distressing is that the masses, whose physical presence had inundated and "degraded" all the public places, appear in the eyes of contemporary writers as people devoid of souls. Now that the body of the man in the street had become a replaceable and almost disposable commonplace, the soul also had lost its base.

Already Thomas Hardy had called the crowds "mentally unquickened, mechanical, soulless" and the privileged and educated few "living, throbbing, vital." More and more the soulless masses were depicted as something dead or close to dead. While the Greeks had imagined with dread the bodiless souls crowding the underworld, now the mass of soulless bodies crowding the cities began to haunt the imagination. Eliot's *The Waste Land* offers a poignant example:

> A crowd flowed over London Bridge, so many,
> I had not thought death had undone so many.

The soulless bodies of the masses and the bodiless souls of the Greek underworld are both doomed. But the latter at least had lived once as a vital whole of body and soul, while the former were thought to be excluded from life altogether, bodies reduced to mechanical robots.

D. H. Lawrence, who also was struck by this association between the masses and their deathlike existence, became almost obsessed with the idea: "The mass of mankind is soulless. . . . Most people are dead, scurrying and talking in the sleep of death." He even goes so far as to contemplate the disposal of all the unfortunates at the fringes of society, a logical step, as Carey points out, since "if most people are dead already, then their elimination . . . will not involve any real fatal-ity."[30] In a chilling letter from 1908, Lawrence describes how he envi-sions this process:

> If I had my way, I would build a lethal chamber as big as the Crystal Palace, with a military band playing softly, and a Cinematograph working brightly; then I'd go out in the back streets and main streets and bring them all in, all the sick, the halt, and the maimed; I would lead them gently, and they would smile me a weary thanks; and the band would softly bubble out the "Hallelujah Chorus."

Lawrence fantasized, however, not only about an extinction of the masses but also about his own, in order to free the earth from its pestlike human invasion. "I think it would be good to die," he writes to E. M. Forster in 1916, "because death would be a clean land with no people in it; not even the people of myself." It is eerie to contemplate what happened less than thirty years later; obviously no mass extinc-tion can leave a "clean land" behind.

In 1934 Aldous Huxley referred to the newly created literate masses as "an immense class of what I may call the New Stupid." And guided by this attitude European writers and intellectuals seemed resolved to become guardians of a literature and culture that was designed to exclude the masses. John Carey sees the creation of modernism and the avant-garde as part of this effort, an effort which on the one hand denied the masses a soul, a full participation in the inner dimensions of human life, and on the other "failed to acknowledge that the mass does not exist. . . . We cannot see the mass. Crowds can be seen; but the mass is a metaphor for the crowd in its metaphysical aspect—the sum of all possible crowds, and . . . has the advantage, from the viewpoint of individual self-assertion of turning other people into a conglomerate."[31] If we remember that the introduction of alphabetic literacy among the early Greeks is believed to have contributed to the discovery of Eros and his dissolution of the body in conjunction with the first glimpses of the Self, it is interesting to note that now again with the spread of literacy among the previously uneducated masses the boundaries of the body had to be redefined. "Mass" became a metaphor for the lack of soul or Self, of individual intellectual and spiritual presence. What Carey unmasks is the psychological twist through which writers and intellectuals in the early part of this cen-tury, alarmed by the threat to the Self through tremendous social changes, attempted to rescue it by assuring themselves of *their* indi-viduality, while denying it to others. This was the climate that helped prepare for the horror that was to come.

Primo Levi in his autobiographical book *Survival in Auschwitz* says:

. . . we have learnt that our personality is fragile, that it is much more in danger than our life; and the old wise men, instead of warning us "remember that you must die," would have done much better to remind us of this greater danger that threatens us. If from inside the Lager, a message could have seeped out to free men, it would have been this: take care not to suffer in your own houses what is inflicted on us here.[32]

Curiously, at the same time that the bond between body and soul seemed to be dissolving, it also began to be rediscovered with the emergence of a new psychology. "Psychology did not begin to develop," Maurice Merleau-Ponty has pointed out, "until the day it gave up the distinction between mind and body, when it abandoned the two correlative methods of interior observation and physiological psychology."[33] And as we have become more aware of the close connection between *psyche* and *soma,* it seems that their polarity, which had dominated our perception, is slowly being diminished, and even in contemporary poetry the attention to the body seems to reinforce it as the indispensible complement of the soul and necessary part of the Self that it is. Recent titles such as Sharon Olds's *The Gold Cell,* Stephen Dobyns's *Body Traffic,* or C. K. Williams's *Flesh and Blood* reflect this tendency. It is also evident in recent attempts to describe the creative process, such as Stanley Burnshaw's *The Seamless Web,* which analyzes artistic endeavor from the viewpoint of "the body makes the minde,"[34] and in new definitions of body and soul as in the provocative writings of Norman O. Brown and James Hillman.

It took the early Greek poets' achievements to help establish the Self. Today again we may be at a crossroads: having become mass-people ourselves, at home with daily newspapers, TV screens, and an explosion of mass-produced information, perhaps our task lies in discovering and preserving the Self within the crowds, making visible those faces among the faces, of which each of us is only one.

NOTES

1. *The Human Figure in Early Greek Art* (Athens and Washington, D. C.: Greek Ministry of Culture/National Gallery of Art, 1988), 9.

2. Kenneth Clark, *The Nude: A Study in Ideal Form* (Princeton: Princeton University Press, Bollingen Series, 1990), 24.

3. Mary Barnard, *Sappho: A New Translation* (Berkeley: University of California Press, 1975), numbers 1 and 2.

4. Guy Davenport, *Carmina Archilochi: The Fragments of Archilochos* (Berkeley: University of California Press, 1964), 29 [#70].

5. Anthony Storr, *Solitude: A Return to the Self* (New York: Ballantine Books, 1988), 75.

6. Ibid., 76.

7. Collin Morris, *The Discovery of the Individual 1050–1200* (London: London SPCK, 1972), 88.

8. Peter Abbs, "The Development of Autobiography in Western Culture: From Augustine to Rousseau" (thesis, University of Sussex, 1986), 130.

9. Ibid., 131–32.

10. Bruno Snell, *The Discovery of the Mind: The Greek Origins of European Thought,* translated by T. G. Rosenmeyer (New York: Harper and Row, 1960). Unless otherwise indicated, Homer and all Greek lyricists are quoted from this source as translated by T. G. Rosenmeyer. For the purposes of this essay these more literal translations were often essential, even though they do not always reflect the rhythmical and colloquial patterns of speech effectively and take an unconventional approach to line breaks. Where the argument did not depend on these more literal translations, I have used those by Willis Barnstone and Mary Barnard, as indicated in the notes.

11. Ibid., 4.

12. Ibid., 5.

13. Max Treu, *Von Homer zur Lyrik: Wandlungen des griechischen Weltbildes im Spiegel der Sprache* (Munich: C. H. Beck'sche Verlagsbuchhandlung, 1968), 171 and passim.

14. Snell, 8.

15. Ibid., 7.

16. Ibid., 9.

17. Ibid., 16–17.

18. Ibid., 18.

19. Ibid.

20. Julian Jaynes, *The Origin of Consciousness in the Breakdown of the Bicameral Mind* (Boston: Houghton-Mifflin Co., 1982), 285.

21. Willis Barnstone, *Sappho and the Greek Lyric Poets,* translated and annotated by Willis Barnstone (New York: Schocken Books, 1988), 66 [#124].

22. Ibid., 124 [#329].

23. Anne Carson, *Eros, the Bittersweet: An Essay* (Princeton: Princeton University Press, 1986), 40–41.

24. Ibid., 41.

25. Ibid., 42.

26. Barnstone, 72 [#147].

27. Barnard, number 40.

28. Snell, 69.

29. John Carey, "Revolted by the Masses," 1989 T. S. Eliot Memorial Lecture, University of Kent; reprinted in the *Times Literary Supplement,* Jan. 12–18, 1990. I am indebted to this source for the brief citations from Ortega y Gasset, Nietzsche, Flaubert, Shaw, Eliot, Hardy, Lawrence, and Huxley.

30. Ibid., 44.

31. Ibid., 45.

32. Primo Levi, *Survival in Auschwitz* (New York: Collier Books, Mac-Millan, 1961), 49.

33. Maurice Merleau-Ponty, *Sense and Non-Sense,* translated, with a preface, by Hubert L. Dreyfus and Patricia Allen Dreyfus (Evanston, Ill.: Northwestern University Press, 1964), 53.

34. Stanley Burnshaw, *The Seamless Web* (New York: George Braziller, 1970), 10, quoting John Donne.

ALLEN GROSSMAN

Orpheus/Philomela *~ nightingale*

Subjection and Mastery in the Founding Stories of
Poetic Production and in the Logic of Our Practice

I am going to discuss the founding stories of literary—and in particu-
lar *poetic*—practice, as if any occasion of making (each moment when
we write) were already foretold. I choose to talk about the founding
stories inside which our practice is enacted in order to contribute to
our power as poetic makers, as literary workers, because power flows
from knowledge of the prophecy—from the ability to hear the story
as it is known in the source, and having heard the story to work with it
out of knowledge of it, and by working with it out of knowledge of it
to turn subjection (the state of being in which our writing is already
written) into mastery (what we call "originality"), that is writing both
from knowledge of the origins and against it.

Western civilization (our given set of life-forms of which we are
either the subjects or the masters) is singularly discontinuous. Western
religion, for example, was interrupted and then overpowered and
changed by Judaeo-Christianity, and is therefore a split tradition with a
dominant, manifest aspect or face and also a suppressed, unmanifest,
darker and older countenance always below, bespeaking another source
and another world. But the founding stories, or paradigms, by which
we construct our poetic practice (and indeed our management of repre-
sentation in general) are by contrast continuous and ride through time,
are patient, are the principles of knowability of all else. The story about
Orpheus and the story about Philomela (the nightingale) are paradigms
of poetic knowledge in our civilization that precede, are maintained
within, and follow after (survive beyond, as some think) the split life-
forms of Western religion—in the same way and for the same reason
that representation as such is ubiquitous and prior to all particular figura-
tions of the world. Study of the founding stories, or paradigms, is
fundamental to learning about writing with the intention to write. And
only in the practice of the art—the making of the poem—can the mean-
ing of the founding story of the practice be known, and the cultural
implications of its reproduction be assessed. The poetic maker is both
the beneficiary *and the judge* of the logic of the practice.

TriQuarterly 77 (Winter 1989–90): 229–48.

I

Consider the fifth poem of the first sequence of Rilke's *Sonnets for Orpheus:*

> Set up no stone to his memory.
> Just let the rose bloom each year for his sake.
> For it is Orpheus. His metamorphosis
> in this one and in this. We should not trouble
>
> about other names. Once and for all
> it's Orpheus when there's singing. He comes and goes.
> Is it not much already if at times
> he overstays for a few days the bowl of roses?
>
> O how he has to vanish for you to grasp it!
> Though he himself take fright at vanishing.
> Even while his word transcends the being-here,
>
> he's there already where you do not follow.
> The lyre's lattice does not snare his hands.
> And he obeys, while yet he oversteps.

For the West the name (Orpheus) signifies the person who signifies by poetic making, *poesis,* and all speaking about Orpheus is speaking about the origin and logic of speaking in the poetic way.

> . . . Once and for all
> it's Orpheus when there's singing . . .

The story about Orpheus is a story that founds the poetic work as a human work (an origin story of poetic practice) not because it is, as it were, a boundless *subject* for poems, but because it is the story that is always enacted when poetry becomes the action of the person—"it's Orpheus when there's singing." In effect, the Orpheus story encodes a powerful logic (this before that, this because of that, *this and not that*), both of the civilizational function of the poetic kind of the artistic form of words (the structure of the human world that the structures of poetry reproduce), and of the form of life that poetic power produces in the poet, the subject of that power. The story about Orpheus is continuously present in our tradition because it reproduces the invariant, or paradigmatic *logic* of the poet as a civilizational agent, a maker of the social order of the human community; and it presents invariably the story of the *subjection* of the maker who intends and brings to pass the structure of a human world (like Virgil's Rome, or Milton's Commonwealth, or Yeats's Ireland, or Whitman's or Crane's America), which is founded in and reproduced through the (Orphic) structure of the song. The unmistakable trace or stain of the narrative logic of the story about the poetic maker (Hart Crane calls it the "bright logic")— who is always present in the making of civilization (and who is therefore always *present,* as Rilke says) and whose subjection is required to effect his purposes—is the name Orpheus itself, which is etymologically derived from Greek *orphanos* (our orphan) and signifies the person who is set the task of constructing a human world by singing *because* the givenness of the world (the inevitability of any relationship) is lost.

> Orpheus with his Lute made Trees,
> And the Mountaine tops that freeze,
> Bow themselves when he did sing.
> To his Musicke, Plants and Flowers
> Ever sprung; as Sunne and Showers,
> There had made a lasting Spring.
> Everything that heard him play,
> Even the Billowes of the Sea,
> Hung their heads, and then lay by.
> In sweet Musicke in such Art,
> Killing care, and griefe of heart,
> Fall asleep, or hearing die.

The Orpheus story that the Jacobean singer as maker sings about the orphaned singer (who by singing makes a world out of nature that accommodates human desire) is unmistakably gendered male. The subjection of nature that we hear at the beginning of this poem ("Trees . . . And the Mountaine tops . . . Bow themselves"), and the exclusion that we hear in the killing and death at the end—the exclusion of care and grief—become the other story: the woman's story of the nightingale Philomela whose song in fact Orpheus, wandering in his bereavement after the loss of Eurydike (as Virgil tells us), hears and is not consoled.

Month in, month out, seven whole months, men say beneath a skeyey cliff by lonely Strymon's shore [Orpheus] wept, and deep in icy caverns, unfolding this his tale, charming tigers, and making the oaks attend his strain; even as the nightingale, mourning beneath the poplar's shade, bewails the loss of her brood, that a churlish ploughman hath espied and torn unfledged from the nest: but she weeps all night long and, perched on a spray, renews her piteous strain, filling the region with sad laments.

Philomela's song (the nightingale's song) is omnipresent in history in the same way that pain is omnipresent in history (and therefore mythographically older than Orphic logic, because always already there even for Orpheus in his pain), and is the female gendered response to the Orpheus song, defining the limits of the mastery of Orpheus's song and defining also the reality Orpheus's song subjects, figured as rape and infanticide. We hear Philomela's song in the seventh stanza of Keats's "Ode to a Nightingale" as the high requiem omnipresent in history and constituting the unity of history:

> Thou was not born for death, immortal Bird!
> No hungry generations tread thee down;
> The voice I hear this passing night was heard
> In ancient days by emperor and clown:
> Perhaps the self-same song that found a path
> Through the sad heart of Ruth, when, sick for home,
> She stood in tears amid the alien corn;
> The same that oft-times hath
> Charmed magic casements, opening on the foam
> Of perilous seas, in faery lands forlorn.

This invariable song ("self-same," "The same that oft-times") produced as a single word *forlorn* is the *other* invariable song counter to the Orpheus song. It is Medea's song, Antigone's song, Sappho's song, Ophelia's song, Dickinson's song, Plath's song; but its word *forlorn,* though produced (as I argue) by the omnipresence of the civilizational Orpheus song, is also kindred (in the strange kinship of interrupted kinship) to that of Orpheus/*orphanos*—for both these originary stories of poetic practice are about the overcoming of blocked communication—communication blocked in the social world, the overcoming of which blockage generates the poetry that completes the relationship another way *insofar as poetry can.*

Thus far I have spoken of the Orpheus story, gendered male, as constituting the omnipresent logic of civilizational order in the West; and I have spoken of the Philomela story, gendered female, as constituting the omnipresent logic of pain. I have observed that these two stories constitute (also) the originary narratives of the production of poetry (indeed of literary production in general in the West), and I have observed that each story (each logic, if there are two) seems both prior to and derived from the other. I will explain and amplify these matters. I wish, however, to dwell for a moment on the fact (as I understand the matter, and have already suggested) that these two stories or story systems function as *paradigm stories,* or ideal narrative patterns. By "paradigm stories" I mean stories that are transmitted across time and reproduced *invariably* by reason of their self-sameness, inside which self-sameness there is a logic (the deeply encoded features of the story that make it recognizable and reproducible across time) that bears upon poetic practice—yours and mine. Orpheus is always a civilizational hero who *therefore* loses Eurydike and *as a consequence* sings with greater power. ("Once and for all / It's Orpheus when there's singing.") Philomela is always violated, infanticidal and in pain, as a result of which her song becomes, as Keats reminds us, a principle of universality in history. As poets, and writers, we are committed to poetic practice. The reason for my presentation of the myths and paradigms of that practice is to articulate its logic and to give an account of the implication of that logic for our practice— which has in any case been put severely in question elsewhere in the culture. At the end of this essay I will introduce a myth of our practice and make some inferences about our situation.

II

But first I want to frame these stories by a larger structure of concern that contains them and is stated by them. What concerns me is the following: looking from the scene of our practice back at the paradigms—Orpheus and Philomela—we observe that all the founding stories of poetic discourse, the originary myths of the generation of song, are violent. This violence—indeed atrocity—so deeply encoded in the poetic logic of Western civilization can be specified: it arises primarily within a life-and-death struggle, or warfare (generally, gods on one side and humankind on the other), between sponsors of competing descriptions of the human fact, the person who is the subject of art. Thus, the practice of art is urgent and dangerous, and (because the warfare is both external and internal to the mind of the maker) alienating. What is at stake in the competition for the power of description of human being is the value and status of the person in the cosmos and social order. The champion on the human part is the poet. For this reason, all poetic practice because of its function is situated *in crisis at the edge or boundary of human being altogether,* where the resistance of the nonhuman (both inside and outside the person) and its repressive descriptions of human being is opposed by the poet-singer, the master of that voice of wonder that acknowledges the whole beauty of humankind. For example, at *Iliad,* book II, line 594, we read in the "catalogue of ships," in the course of the account of the cities whose warriors were under the leadership of Nestor, of a place called Dorion and a poet called Thamyrus:

> Dorion where the Muses
> Encountering Thamyrus the Thracian stopped him from singing
> As he came from Oichalia and Oichalian Eurytos;

For he boasted that he would surpass, if the very Muses,
Daughters of Zeus who holds the Aegis, were singing against him
And these in their anger struck him maimed, and the voice of wonder
They took away, and made him a singer without memory. . . .

In the case of Thamyrus, the human challenge to the description of the human state of affairs sponsored by the high god (the Muses are daughters of Zeus) is punished by the violent taking away of the poet's voice, the voice of wonder. This disabling of the poet is effected by the canceling of poetic mind, a retributive violence suggestive of our post-modern predicament in poetic education—*the taking back of deep mem-ory*. For the Muses (daughters of Memory on their mother's side) are Memory itself, conformed to the various genres of the poetic art. Thamyrus is an experimenter with the deep freedom—the "free verse," as it were—of human self-description. He seeks freedom from the tyranny of Zeus—the freedom of self-constructed, self-witnessing description (and therefore constitution) of humanity. This Thamyrus does by turning memory against its source (the Muses, daughters of Memory). In his case, the effort to produce a dominant description sponsored by poetic humanity—a free song—results in the withdraw-ing of all song, the taking away of the voice of wonder, the poetic voice. This is the violence, structured as warfare between describers, of which I speak.

You will remember that Marsyas, a musician who invented a new form of music for the oboe, challenged Apollo and was flayed—lost his human image over a question of artistic structure. Linus, another ancient singer about whom stories were told, was a brother of Or-pheus. Herakles, whom Linus was tutoring, killed him with a blow of the lyre, but was exonerated on a plea of self-defense. Again, we see how dangerous in our civilization the true practice of poetic art is, and how it is implicitly and inevitably a challenge to the hierarchies that maintain the universe.

Further, the example of Marsyas, who lost the skin of his physical body, which constituted his recognizability as human, his body as the picture of the self, requires that we note how the same atrocious sanctions bear upon both poetic production and sexual reproduction of the person—the synergetic authorship of the woman's body and the mother's glance. The male paradigmatic singer most like Orpheus is Amphion, who by his singing built the material walls of Thebes. The violence that is required by the logic of the paradigm is, in Amphion's case, displaced—for he is said to have become husband of Niobe, in whose story as told by Homer (*Iliad,* book IX) we find the gen-derically feminine—the woman's, the Philomela—form of the para-digm of making, its deep material form, the reproduction of the hu-man image as a function of the physical body. Not the male Orpheus version (Thamyrus; Linus, Orpheus's brother; Amphion; Musaeus, Orpheus's son), but the woman's version, the nightingale version:

> For even Niobe, she of the lovely tresses, remembered
> To eat, whose twelve children were destroyed in the palace
> Six daughters and six sons in the pride of their youth whom Apollo
> Killed with arrows from his silver bow, being angered
> With Niobe, and Artemis killed the daughters
> Because Niobe likened herself to Leto of the fair coloring
> And said Leto had borne only two, she herself had borne many;
> But the two, though they were only two, destroyed all those
> Nine days long they lay in their blood, nor was there anyone
> To bury them, for the son of Kronos made stone out of
> The people; but on the tenth day the Uranian gods buried them.
> But she remembered to eat when she was worn out with weeping
> And now somewhere among the rocks in the lonely mountains
> In Sipylos, where they say is the resting place of the goddesses
> Who are nymphs, and dance beside the waters of Acheloios,
> There, stone still, she broods on the sorrows the gods gave her.

The image of Niobe—her statue that is her body, "stone still," the image of the greatest pain endurable without the loss of human form, the pain of the image—is the inhuman product of the challenge of the form of the person as human, of which the woman is the author, to the form of the person as it is described by the gods.

Thus, there are two violences that the originary stories of poetic production and its logic entail: the violence of image making (as we shall see it patterned in the stories of Orpheus and Philomela) and the violence which that violence opposes. I now return to my account of Orpheus and Philomela, their complementary logic, who are our models or paradigms of the human resource—itself violent—which opposes the inhuman describer.

III

Orpheus was the son of Memory itself, Mnemosyne as mother of the Muses and therefore the divine form of the poetic mind, or the son of one of Memory's daughters, Calliope ("beautiful voice") who presides over the genre of epic that constructs the cosmos and state—whether Hesiod's, or Virgil's, or Milton's, or Hart Crane's. Calliope as mother of a genre commits her son to a genre and therefore a constrained kind of freedom produced but also qualified by the requirements of service to social order. Orpheus, the mortal hero, belongs to the generation of the fathers of the heroes who fought the Trojan War, and the epic project of which he is part is recorded in the *Argonautika* of Appolonius Rhodius (circa 250 B.C.)—the story of the quest for the Golden Fleece. Orpheus is taken aboard the Argo, Jason's ship, as a technician. He has no self. He neither acts nor suffers, but rather performs the tasks his powers *as a poet* enable him to perform.

As poet he is master of rhythm in service of meaning and therefore he sets and regulates the rhythmical activity of the working sailors and the rowers. As the child of cosmic Memory, he knows the order of the universe, and therefore can resolve quarrels that arise on shipboard by singing of the harmonious order of things—a song that conforms the order of the human world to the order of the divine. As poet Orpheus also is master of the music that has mastery over the demonic countersong—the song of the sirens, which bereaves humanity of its image, interrupts the prophetically driven enterprise of the human community, and kills men (*Argonautika,* book IV, lines 900 ff.):

> And ever on watch from their place of prospect with its fair haven, often from many had [the sirens] taken away their sweet return, consuming them with wasting desire; and suddenly to these heroes too they sent forth from their lips a lily-like voice. And [the argonauts] were already about to cast from the ship the hawsers to the shore, had not . . . Orpheus . . . stringing in his hands his Bistonian [Thracian] lyre rung forth a hasty snatch of rippling melody, so that their ears might be filled with the sound of his twanging; and the song overcame the [siren's] voice.

Orpheus, technician of the artifact of the human image, also assures the harmony of marriage by marriage song, brings invisible springs into visibility by materializing the nymphs of the springs, assigns names to places and inducts into mysteries. But all that he does flows from the logic of his poetic function as the cosmic male who regulates the human world by supplying order and destination to the energies and powers of mind and nature in accord with the Great Memory that is his by right of birth and in service of the world that acknowledges Zeus (the principle of "things as they are") as Lord. Indeed, Orpheus becomes associated in historical times with a religion (Orphism)—a sort of ascetic pagan Protestantism—a prominent contribution of which was an account of the origin of human beings that represents them as reconciling an archaic guilty nature (Titanic) with a modern rational nature (Apollinian). This aspect of Orphean tradition (Orpheus as *priscus theologus*) is father of the world constructive mysticisms of the modern poet (Yeats, Eliot, Crane, Merrill, Olson) and in the context of the Orpheus story we can see their function. Thus, Orpheus is omnipresent in the history of poetic making as the archetype of the regulator, the perfect servant of his mother, daughter of

Zeus. Orpheus is memory as language, and specifically language in service of the order of the world.

But the most commonly invoked story about Orpheus tells of his marriage, and the loss of his wife Eurydike to the underworld, where she rules in accord with her name as a wide judging power, *because Orpheus looked back.* This story follows in time the myth of the service of Orpheus to the Argonauts, and finds Orpheus imprisoned in the bitter logic of the paradigm of his discourse, which elucidates his story and puts it in question. Though Orpheus saved the heroes of the Argonautic expedition from wasting desire by the power of his song, he was unable to consummate his own marriage—he who was the master of the marriage song. In general, as the paradigm of the Orphic myth is transmitted from Apollonius to Ovid and Virgil, and through innumerable medieval and Renaissance versions to Milton, Hölderlin, Whitman, Yeats, Rilke, and Blanchot, it becomes increasingly an inquiry into the impotence of the master—his subjection to the violent logic of a story in which he redeems the world but not himself. The order that Orpheus serves is not an order in which he can participate because he enacts the logic of his art and suffers its violence. The voice of the poet in the West is orphaned (Orpheus is an *orphanos*) in the same sense that the *persona* who speaks the poem is not (cannot be) the same as the *person* who writes but rather is an *order of speaking* that serves the human world as Orpheus served the Argonauts. Orpheus is admitted to the underworld by reason of his song, which knows the structure of all things as they are in the Great Mother Memory (Mnemosyne). He may dwell in all the regions of his song and move from mansion to mansion (from Heaven to Hell) in it, but he is forbidden to look back, for *to gaze* in Orpheus's case is to construct experience on his own behalf and that is a violation of the decorum of the *persona*—and thus, by the bitter logic of the paradigm, Eurydike must be lost.

> And now as he retraced his steps he had escaped every mischance, and the regained Eurydike was nearing the upper world, following behind—for that condition had Proserpine ordained—when a sudden frenzy seized Orpheus unwary in his love. . . . He stopped, and on the very verge of light, unmindful, alas! and vanquished in his purpose, on Eurydike, *now his own,* looked back! In that moment all his toil was spent, the ruthless tyrant's pact was broken. . . .
>
> (*Georgics,* IV, ll. 485 ff.)

The motive to look back—memory not being enough—engages Orpheus with the logic of the paradigm like a character in a story who seeks to evade the logic of the narration of which he is a part, seeks to become "real" (actual) and therefore to cease signifying on behalf of the whole. It is in this sense that Christianity identified Orpheus with the crucified Christ, another *orphanos*. Within the bereaving logic of this paradigm, which sets (cosmic) Memory against (individual) experience, the general against the personal, "form super-induced" (in Coleridge's language) against "form self-witnessing," freedom as service (Orphic freedom) against freedom as autonomy, much of our discussion of how poems ought to be written takes place. Orpheus's wordless, backward-looking gaze is an appeal directed toward the outside of language as to the outside of narrative (or art itself) into which he is drawn back by the logic of his nature as discourse. The endless cultural preoccupation in the West with Orpheus's pain reflects the weariness of the masters of language with the labyrinthine paradox of presence through absence that requires the subjection of language's servants, the poets. "Does the imagination dwell the most," Yeats's poet asks, "On a woman won or a woman lost?"

Orpheus's lamentations, after the loss of Eurydike, are the most powerful poems of his making. It is through them (the poems of uncompensated pain) that he charms the animals, builds walls of cities, commands trees to constellate orchards, produces the space of the (collective) human world in which—as orphaned desire—he has no power to dwell. In the end he is torn to pieces by the Thracian women in the inevitable (systemic) violence that befalls the maker, destroying his human form (a form inconsistent with his function)—and he becomes, like the written word or a published poem that constructs the world, a talking head that is slow to die.

IV

When Orpheus in Virgil's account wanders lamenting the loss of Eurydike, he is compared (as we have already observed) in his inconsolability to the *philomela,* which is the nightingale, the lover not of the signified but of the sign.

> Month in, month out, seven whole months, men say beneath a lofty cliff of lonely Strymon's cave he wept, and deep in icy caverns unfolded this his tale, charming the tigers, and making the oaks attend his strain; even as the nightingale mourning beneath the poplars shade, bewails the loss of her brood, that a churlish plowman hath espied and torn unfledged from the nest: but she weeps all night long and perched upon a spray renews her piteous strain, filling the region round with sad laments.

The moment of Orpheus's grief—his lament for desire's dead child, victim of the logic of his world-making song (this always and only before that), the mortal beloved—is the crossing point of the two great paradigm stories of artistic production that I am retelling: Orpheus and Philomela. Orpheus is omnipresent in history (always with us when we write, with us now) as the power of order contributed by Memory (mother of the Muses) without experience, that expels experience (the always-lost Eurydike) and *thereby* reproduces the harmony of the universe through poetry as the productive rhythm of social work. Philomela is omnipresent in history (the "self-same song," as Keats says) as the pain contributed by experience without memory (the sign of it is the "churlish plowman," *durus arator*)—the interruption of order that is figured as rape, infanticide, and final metamorphosis, the loss of the human image. In Virgil's simile the *philomela* functions as the always-at-hand representational vehicle of the grief of the maker.

The Philomela story is simple: there were two sisters, daughters of the Athenian king, Pandion. In accord with the decorum of sisters, the elder is given in marriage first to a barbarian king to whom the father is indebted. The husband's name is Tereus. The elder sister, the married one, in her loneliness sends Tereus to fetch her younger sister for a visit. Tereus is aroused by the beauty of the younger sister, imprisons her among his slaves in a dark wood, rapes her, and cuts out her tongue so she cannot tell her story. At this moment of violation and atrociously blocked communication there arises a founding instance of woman's text—a textile that is an epistle addressed in the older versions of the story by Procne to the wife of her rapist, Philomela: "Procne is among the slaves." In the later versions of the story the beautiful name is assigned (as a kind of metamorphosis) to the mutilated girl and *she* is called Philomela (thus condensing pain upon the beautiful word). The wife of Tereus receives the message, liberates her sister. Together they avenge themselves upon Tereus by killing Tereus's child, the child of the elder sister, and feeding the body to the brutal husband and father. In his rage he pursues the women and all three are turned into birds, Philomela into a nightingale. The fitness of rape as a founding story of poetic discourse (and also of the novel, Richardson's *Clarissa* being both a rape story and a generic exemplar) is widely attested. The woman's counterstory to the male story—the Orpheus story—found poetry not only at the point of pain, but pain resulting from the overwhelming of the will (the power that maintains human form) of the person by the inhuman desire that the human form arouses but cannot regulate. "Philomela is among the slaves." Orpheus is the captive of the *above* (memory prior to experience); Philomela is captive to the *beneath* (experience prior to memory). In each case the most powerful song arises at the moment after loss has become inconsolable and the destination of the individual self irretrievable.

In Orpheus's case "form" is a captivity (memory without experience)—his bitterly paradoxical empowerment. In Philomela's case the captivity is formlessness, the bitterly paradoxical empowerment of experience without memory. Indeed, in many medieval and Renaissance texts she must remind herself (so memory-less is she) of the cause of her pain by leaning upon a thorn as she sings beautifully in the night. It was thus that Keats's poet found her. For her personal history has been abolished in the metamorphosis by which she became a power for the world.

I will draw my examples of Philomela's story from Shakespeare in order to place before you his witness with respect to the logic of the paradigm. In *A Midsummer Night's Dream,* she is invoked to guard the body, the domain of her peculiar care—the night body of the lover (act II, scene ii):

> Philomel with melody,
> Sing in our sweet lullaby;
> Lulla, lulla, lullaby; lulla, lulla, lullaby.
> Never harm
> Nor spell nor charm
> Come our lovely lady nigh.
> So good night, with lullaby.

While Philomela, the raped and mutilated girl, sings, the lovers have permission of their bodies—as when Juliet awakes in bed with Romeo (act III, scene v):

> *Juliet.* Wilt thou be gone? It is not yet near day.
> It was the nightingale, and not the lark
> That pierced the fearful hollow of thine ear.
> Nightly she sings on yon pomegranate tree.
> Believe me, love, it was the nightingale.

In both these cases the Philomela song is invoked in order to obtain its mastery in the contest for the description of the world (against the demonic magician, against the social lark); and the violence of the paradigm mediated by the vicarious suffering of its subject is put in service of the body. The subjection of Philomela becomes the mastery of disorder on behalf of general humanity (the audience of song) through the poem of which her metamorphosis is the sign.

The paradigmatic story supplies the logic of the mastery of disorder in history through the vicarious suffering (the subjection) of the originary masters—Orpheus and Philomela. But when the violence of history exceeds the violence of the paradigm, what then? When the stories of first poets, which anticipate on the world's behalf the atrocious logic of poetic representation, fail to include the pain of history, then history as representation is no longer within the paradigm of representation. This state of affairs, which finds the violence of history in excess of any violence displayed by the logics of art (including poetry), was the concern of Shakespeare in his earliest analysis of the Philomela story. We see already in the speech of Juliet the fading of the power of the paradigm—for the day that will bring death *has really dawned*. But the most radical case in Shakespeare of the invocation and overwhelming of the paradigm occurs in his first tragedy, *Titus Andronicus*. Lavinia, daughter of Titus, is raped and mutilated in the course of dynastic struggle. Her assailants cut out her tongue; but also (because they have read Philomela's story in Ovid) cut off her hands as well so that she cannot weave the textile letter that betrayed the barbarity of Tereus. The man who discovers her says:

> Fair Philomel, why she but lost her tongue
> And in a tedious sampler sewed her mind.
> But, lovely niece, that mean is cut from thee.
> A craftier Tereus, cousin, hast thou met,
> And he hath cut those pretty fingers off
> That could have better sewed than Philomel.

Lavinia with her stumps discovers a schoolboy's books:

Titus.   Lucius, what book is that she tosseth so?
Boy.   Grandsire, 'tis Ovid's *Metamorphoses*.
            My mother gave it me.
Marcus.   For love of her that's gone,
            Perhaps, she culled it from the rest.
Titus.   Soft, so busily she turns the leaves.
            Help her. What would she find? Lavinia, shall I read?
            This is the tragic tale of Philomel,
            And treats of Tereus' treason and his rape. . . .
            Lavinia, wert *thou* thus surprised, sweet girl,
            Ravished and wronged as Philomela was,
            Forced in the ruthless, vast, and gloomy woods?
            See, see. Ay, such a place there is where we did hunt—
            O, had we never, never hunted there!—
            Patterned by that the poet here describes,
            By nature made for murders and for rapes.

Shakespeare represents his characters in a world in which (as in our world) the "patterns" (the paradigm stories) are received by reading. What is bad reading? What is good reading? Here bad reading is exemplified at least three ways: the rapists read to find the "pattern" of the crime they intend and to learn how to escape its consequences. Titus, the father of the raped girl, reads to find the "pattern" and therefore the nature of the crime that has already been committed. (He reads to identify a state of affairs.) But Lavinia reads in the most desperate sense of all. She enacts—becomes—the "pattern" (what I have called the paradigm) and suffers its violent logic of representation in her own person. A few lines later she *writes* in the dust, holding a staff in her mouth and guiding it with her stumps. In Lavinia's case the paradigm fails, because Philomela's story does not prevent Lavinia's terror. It does not effect for her the endless deferral or anticipation of the violent logic of representation that is the productive consequence of vicarious suffering in the space of representation, when the difference between representation and reality is successfully maintained. When the themes of art reproduce crime (the rapists' reading) rather than prevent it (as might have occurred had the story taught the father not to hunt in the "ruthless, vast and gloomy woods")—when, in short, the pattern becomes the fact—the pain of the paradigm becomes the pain of history and the competition for the description of the human world is lost to the energies that do not know human form (the *durus arator*), which clearly include the energies (together with their logic) that construct the human form—because the logic of representation is unendurable by the natural person. When the difference between representation and reality is lost, then we are all with Philomela among the slaves.

As we move from the Philomela of *A Midsummer Night's Dream* to the Philomela of *Titus Andronicus* (backward along the track of the Philomela narrative and backward through the history of Shakespeare's production) we move also from a song that is situated in the difference between art and life (the song sung by "fairies" who signify that difference) to the Philomela enactment of Lavinia in which no such difference can be made. The story Lavinia suffers in her own person is exactly a founding story of representation. Rape founds poetry because it is the radical challenge to the woman's self-characterization as human—the ultimate assault by the violence of the alien describer that drives into existence the counterpower on behalf of the woman's body and name: Philomela's letter and Philomela's song. Because the poetry, gendered female, is driven into existence by the body's pain (pain being the indescribability of the body, the final conquest of the alien describer of which "nuclear warfare" is one dire signifier) we must take care, for example in articulating a constructive program of our art and of our reception of art, not to abolish the difference between the paradigm and the reality even in the interest, as we may conceive, of the body. The poetry that facilitates the peace of the body is not a poetry without violence and alienation; but it is a poetry that by reason of the productive powers of alienation keeps the human image by keeping the difference of the counterstory to history, which is one of our few great allies against the force that would reduce us to the ash of its indifference—"so rudely forced."

Our Anglo-American poetry since Keats and Emily Dickinson

tends toward the female model—the lyric, Philomela kind, the pain story—which engages the contest of describers at the point of threat to individual self-invention. Orpheus, by contrast, the cosmic singer, the male epic-master alienated to the above, the technician of the social order, has become the implicit enemy of our project, especially in his high modern (for example, Yeatsian) character. The moment in the English poetic system that projects the (postmodern) crisis of the Orpheus paradigm is Milton's account in "Lycidas" of the last segment of Orpheus's story: the segment of the Orpheus story that finds him expelled from personal life (and finally from life itself) after the loss of Eurydike, and become the greater singer, the builder of walls, gatherer of orchards, tamer of animals—in effect, not a person but a *persona,* the true poetic voice who arouses feeling but cannot reciprocate the feeling he arouses, and so is torn to pieces by the inflamed women of Thrace, who ratify his death as an individual subject by making of him a singing head. In "Lycidas," Milton's speaker concerns himself with the fact that his drowned friend, a poet, served the institution of poetry but was not rescued by it from the sea, which defeats the image of the person poetry promises to conserve—as if the mistake of the Thracian women who cannot distinguish between *persona* and person were a mistake also of the elegist himself.

> Ay me, I fondly dream,
> Had ye been there!—for what could that have done?
> What could the Muse herself that Orpheus bore,
> The Muse herself, for her enchanting son
> Whom universal nature did lament,
> When by the rout that made the hideous roar
> His gory visage down the stream was sent,
> Down the swift Hebrus to the Lesbian shore?

Here the master, himself, is seen to be subjected; and the subjection of the master must be understood to demonstrate the impotence of the Mastery (the divine sponsors of the art and the institutional order it constructs)—the impotence of *poetry* to overcome the violence of the obliterative counterdescription (the "hideous roar") that has defeated the paradigmatic agent of representation. There is in Milton's poem a strong sense of a poetic culture that produces more violence than it pacifies, as if the logic of representation *were* the logic of history, as indeed might seem to have become the case when Milton's early imagination of revolution passed into the fact of the Commonwealth. The elegiac hero is seen in "Lycidas" to embody the fate of the structure of poetic representation, and thus to entail upon the elegiac speaker the search for a culture of representation that is neither vulnerable to nor complicit with the violence of history. This search seems to me the fundamental motive that drives our experimentation as artists (the search for an *adequate discourse,* which takes the constructive form of a search for the subject in the poem, the *persona,* that can logically speak it), and so structures our thought. Milton's solution to that Orphean logic, which fails at the point of the peril of the agent of representation in history (Henry King, the individual person), is an appeal to an even deeper abstraction of source and order, not Mnemosyne but the "heavenly Muse" Urania—as at the end of "Lycidas" or in book VII of *Paradise Lost* at the beginning:

> . . . Still govern thou my song,
> Urania, and fit audience find, though few.
> But drive far off the barbarous dissonance
> Of Bacchus and his revelers, the race
> Of that wild rout that tore the Thracian bard
> In Rhodope, where woods and rocks had ears
> To rapture, till the savage clamor drowned
> Both harp and voice; nor could the Muse defend
> Her son. So fail not thou who thee implores;
> For thou art heav'nly, she an empty dream.

Milton here recomposes the last stage of Orpheus's story as a defeat of the champion of human representation, in the violent warfare of describers, by "barbarous dissonance" and "savage clamor." Then as a poetic practitioner who intends, as an inherently poetic task, the reconstruction of the sufficient conditions of the representation of persons against the dissonant clamor ("barbarous" and "savage") or the demonic counterpowers who do not know the person, Milton summons by invocation a new source, more powerful for persons, Urania. The action of such invocation or "calling" is fundamental to (indeed, constitutive of) the effective cultural practice of the poet. Insofar as the "sufficient conditions of the representation of the person" can be accounted for in terms of a subject or agent who produces them, they are implicit in the logic of the founding stories of representation that have been the subject of this essay. Insofar as "the sufficient conditions of the representation of the person" are an appeal to, or restoration of, the facts of the world that the poet supplies to the culture he addresses, and insofar as they entail a specific structure of experience, they are the subject of the third essay in this series. In any case, it is upon poetic practice, or practices structured like poetic practice, that the maintenance of the human image depends.

In this essay I have stated (for the purpose of reminding both you and myself) the two paradigms of poetic production inside and between which we do our work as poets—the two stories that register the logic reproduced in our practice. I have laid stress on the generic maleness of the Orphic story, its reference to the "above" and the great memory of the mother muse who takes historical and generic form as epic, on the function of poetry in the Orphic story as social reconciliation, the provision of productive work, the sanctioning of marriage and especially the defeat of the inhuman form of human energies by the ordering music of the lyre as in the overcoming of the sirens. I have also stressed the particular violence figured, for example, as the loss of Eurydike and the dismemberment of Orpheus entailed by the Orphic kind of making of the human world. In discussing the Philomela story, I have laid stress on its genderic femaleness, its reference to the beneath and, in particular, to unregulated energies—experience without memory—which defeat the will toward the humanity of the body. I have stressed also the originary character of the Philomela story as a founding story of poetic reference especially to the body, and the power of poetry that it disposes (for example, in the Shakespearean song "Philomele with melody") toward the protection of the body as in the vulnerability of sleep. In my example from *Titus Andronicus,* I have articulated the terror that the Philomela story anticipates when the originary (and constructive) violence of the paradigm of representation becomes identical with the violence of history at the point of the abandonment of the *regulative function of practice.*

I have framed this discussion within the contest, or warfare, of description—the urgent and always vitally undecided contestation in civilization of the violence of representation against the violence of indifference (figured provisionally as the "hideous roar," or *durus arator*—the hard plowman of history). And I have assumed that representation is ubiquitous, as (and also *because*) language is ubiquitous in civilization and that therefore the entailments of the "bright" logics of representation are continuous and prior to (for example) the logic of religion (the split tradition of world construction to which I referred earlier) and that, therefore, the Orpheus and Philomela paradigms are systematically prior to and thematized within traditional religious cultures in the West. In the domain—thus deeply founded—of poetic discourse, violence is entailed in the founding moment of representation when the flesh is made word, as in the case of the first writing of the woman's text: "Philomela is among the slaves." And the same violence is reproduced whenever person is made *persona* (Orpheus loses Eurydike), natural language is made poetic language (whether metrical or not), whenever little memory (as in the case of Orpheus) is overwhelmed by big Memory, the particular and personal destination of the self by the general and social, or when (as in the case of Philomela) the self-possessed body encounters experience and overcomes it by metamorphosis to the nonhuman principle of song. We are between the productive violence of representation and the destructive violence of history; only art engaged as practice, or something like it, can keep them apart. But the culture in which we live, including poetic culture, has grown weary of the productive violence (in a sense, *the work*) of representation and has tended to identify it for reasons that are not trivial with the violence of history. Only at the point of practice will the matter be clarified, and practice must in my view be governed by vigilant attention to the productive outcomes that Orpheus and Eurydike in their stories serve.

I will conclude with two examples, themselves originary, of the right functioning of the paradigms, by which you can see how the paradigms become part of human practice. The beginning of every historical literary system is seen to be announced by a "calling" of the person to conformity with the paradigm of the project of poetic representation—"a conversion of the mind" and an empowerment by means of representation with respect to origins. The story about Caedmon is drawn from Bede's *History* and gives an account of the Orphic commissioning of the first vernacular poet in the tradition of our language:

> [Caedmon] had lived in the secular habit until he was well advanced in years and had never learned any songs. Hence sometimes at a feast, when for the sake of providing entertainment, it had been decided that they should all sing in turn, when he saw the harp approaching him, he would rise up in the middle of the feasting, go out, and return home.
>
> On one such occasion when he did so, he left the place of feasting and went to the cattle byre, as it was his turn to take charge of them that night. In due time he stretched himself out and went to sleep, whereupon he dreamt that someone stood by him, saluted him, and called him by name: "Caedmon," he said, "sing me something." Caedmon answered, "I cannot sing; that is why I left the feast because I could not sing." Once again the speaker said, "Nevertheless you must sing to me." "What must I sing?" said Caedmon. "Sing," he said, "about the beginning of created things."

The second and final example is a poem by the first world-historical woman poet since Sappho, Emily Dickinson, who witnesses to the commissioning of her mind in the scene of the reading of the nightingale voice of Elizabeth Barrett Browning, a metrical voice that sustains and amplifies time and the world and confers the great counterpower of Philomela's magic that contributes rest to the body:

> I think I was enchanted
> When first a sombre Girl—
> I read that Foreign Lady—
> The Dark—felt beautiful—

And whether it was noon at night—
Or only Heaven—at Noon—
For very Lunacy of light
I had not power to tell—

The Bees—became as Butterflies—
The Butterflies—as Swans—
Approached—and spurned the narrow Grass—
And just the meanest Tunes

That Nature murmured to herself
To keep herself in Cheer—
I took for Giants—practising
Titanic Opera—

The days—to Mighty Metres stept—
The Homeliest—adorned
As if unto a Jubilee
'Twere suddenly confirmed—

I could not have defined the change—
Conversion of the Mind
Like Sanctifying in the Soul
Is witnessed—not explained—

'Twas a Divine Insanity—
The Danger to be Sane
Should I again experience—
'Tis Antidote to turn—

To Tomes of solid Witchcraft—
Magicians be asleep—
But Magic—hath an Element
Like Deity—to keep—

ELEANOR WILNER

The Medusa Connection

An awkward stumbling on the brink of speech. Think of the penguin. The penguin of the present age who cannot fly, but whose long ago ancestor could. Watching the penguin careen toward the brink, then slide with a glorious ease into the water, it seems natural to wonder: does evolution reverse itself? Can one lose an evolutionary advantage, regress, as it were, to an earlier form? Built into these questions is a culture's long bias in favor of flight; its desire to disembody itself, to rise, to measure value and virtue by height and to weigh perfection by loss of gravitational mass. As if attachment to earth were an insult to spirit. Looking, then, through the lens of an old bias, the penguin's move from wings to fins seems a regression, a devolution.

There is another cultural bias that drives that presumption—that time is linear, like a highway on which it is possible to move ahead or go back—ideas of progress and reversion being two sides of the same coin. And this linear notion has traditionally been joined to a teleology that sees time as a progression toward its own extinction in some divinely ordained freeze-frame bliss, an unchanging state superintended by God and intended for us.

Reversing the maxims of the Right, poverty we may hope to extinguish, but time we shall always have with us. Whether time will always include us is a far more vexed question, a fear for ourselves that certainly feeds the current obsession with species extinction. For nature does not repeat itself, and evolution is like the Heraclitean river in which you can never step twice. The penguin's seeming reversal of evolution is an illusion sponsored by our prior assumptions. In fact, says Victor Scheffer, "in giving up wings capable of flight, penguins did not reverse in their tracks; they simply advanced on a route that took a hairpin curve. The wings of the modern penguins are not atavistic structures but are strong and dependable swimming organs. . . ."[1]

In the world of imagination, similar adaptations seem to be underway. As this essay sets out to track the spontaneous recurrence in our poetry of the ancient figure of the Medusa, it may be well to remember that adaptation is not regression, but a change that continuity requires. As fins were a fresh advantage for the penguin, so, in a parallel imaginative development, new forms that resemble older ones

---

An earlier version appeared in *TriQuarterly* 88 (Fall 1993): 104–32.

may in fact be an adaptation to changed circumstances, carrying us into the fluid medium of real time with an ease that resembles the modern penguin's sudden grace when it enters water.

It has been a long time, culturally speaking, since the "Spirit moved upon the face of the waters" in Genesis, and the world was created by fiat and by division. That recorded the moment, some 1500 to 1200 years B.C.E., when the sky gods, over the deserts of the Middle East and the dry hills of Greece, usurped the old animal powers and established the dominion of detached mind over the older cyclical powers of the earth. Time, henceforth, was to be ruled from above, as by an absentee landlord.

It is possible, with some historical imagination, to reawaken the excitement of that dawn when, in Joseph Campbell's phrasing, "the shining righteous deedsman of autonomous human will" broke through the passes of history, newly mounted on horseback, winged in feelings of mental power—heroes to serve the sky gods of Greece and Palestine who, for all the differences between them, were alike to break the power of the old nature religions, their priesthoods and their determinism, and to celebrate that act through mythic stories of the slaying of dragons or the treading underfoot of the newly demonized snake. The dawn riders of nearly four millennia ago, high on their defeat of the serpents of time whose cyclic coils they had cut with swords both literal and intellectual, could not have anticipated an age as addicted to and appalled by the long-term consequences of their triumph as our own. Nor one in which the dragon slayers of the West have met the dragon worshipers of the East, and have begun, in the crucible of imagination, to forge a new vision.

It is often politically expedient and psychologically seductive to let desire color history, to invoke and idealize in order to set precedent and authorize the emergent against the entrenched. But as figures from deeper strata spontaneously recur in the poetic imagination of our time, they come not to announce the neoprimitive return of the past, but to accomplish the alteration of its meaning in the mind of the present. These chastened and conscious figures, trailing the shrouds of what was once called glory, are both recognizable and fundamentally altered by the work of time.

So, transformed and transformative, Medusa resurfaces, a figure who relocates the sacred in a new sense of order involving a reconnection with natural history, human intellect in a loving relation with the matter of which it is made. For it is not nature as mindless matter that returns, but nature mindful of itself—not the severed head of Orpheus, that bard of nostalgia—but the head of Medusa, not severed but crowning—the word used in obstetrics for the appearance of the infant's head in birth. The head is perceived in this positioning as the emergence of a whole being, a recapitation that delivers from monstrosity the natural imagery of creation and birth from within, and forges a metaphoric link between natural birth and time-ripened, world-engendered spiritual and intellectual rebirth. An animating figure for a poetics of generation, this Medusa is no mere replay of an ancient figure; her contemporary embodiment is shaped by all that has intervened between her death and rebirth:

> She stepped out of the framing circle of the dark.
> We thought, as she approached, to see her
> clearly, but her features only grew more indistinct
> as she drew nearer, like those of statues
> long submerged in water. We couldn't name her,
> she who can't be seen
> except in spaces between wars, brief intervals
> when history relents. . . .[2]

This emergent Medusa is a figure of change whose indistinct features suggest not only the work of time's waters, which undo even stones, but the translucent mask such figures have become for our conscious age—a shifting apparition of emblem and presence. The figure is traditionally connected with the history of Western art through both the wingèd horse Pegasus who sprang from her severed neck and whose hoof opened the Pierian Spring, later haunt of the Muses; and the shield of her slayer Perseus, a prototype for image making, the mirror of art that allowed one to look on the terrible through a displaced image, or reflection, and live. What happens to this figure is not only something that happens in our poetry, but something that is happening *to* it, to our very conception of aesthetic creation. And, by extension, to our conceptions of beauty and of monstrosity—or, put another way, of order and the locus of value.

In fact, it even seems possible to measure by the way the Medusa appeared to them where contemporary poets stand, imaginatively speaking, on a historical continuum of vision; to find existing simultaneously a new vision and traditional paradigms that were adaptive to earlier circumstances but that have survived for a variety of reasons— among them inertia, privilege, terror. Thus a traditional view may coexist with a transitional one and both with a genuinely transformational vision. In addition, there may be hybrid versions, though often with the older ideology dominant. Even where new ruling elites wish to replace older paradigms, the older forms may subvert and reorganize the new. Change is real but much slower than impatient hope leads us to believe. Old emblems die hard.

So let us begin with the original story, mainly the version given by Ovid's *Metamorphoses*. Medusa was the child of the elements, of ocean gods (or some say of Gaea [Earth] and Oceanus), the mortal sister of the Gorgons, whose name meant "Queen." Originally known for her beauty and her lovely, lively hair, she had the misfortune to attract Poseidon, the latest sea god and brother to the new Olympic sky god Zeus, who raped Medusa in the shrine of Athena, armored goddess of wisdom and war, female mind recast by cerebral birth from the head of her father Zeus. It was Athena, angry at the desecration of her shrine, who transformed Medusa into the monstrous female with snakes for tresses, a figure of dread the sight of whom, or whose gaze (both versions are given), turned men to stone.

It should be obvious from the story that it retells the history of migration and invasion and of the overthrow of one religion by another: of the older, elemental gods—those of nature, of human subjugation to the serpent/chthonic powers of the earth and the cycles of seasonal time—by the new immortal gods of Olympus, sky gods of intellect and will, sponsors of the new, and tragic, heroes of human autonomy. It is one of those heroes, Perseus, who hunts Medusa to her lair at the horizon's rim in that darkness where heavenly bodies vanish for rebirth; it is there we find the figure now, at the edge of the known, like a new sun rising so many centuries after these mythically mirrored events, and out of the dark sea of their consequences.

The second part of the story finishes the job of desecration/ transformation through the agency of the hero, Perseus, "child of the sunlight in the tower room,"[3] who, aided by a shield, the gift of Athena (naturally), is able to fix the Medusa's image in its bright mirror, and so behead her without himself being transfixed. Out of her severed trunk—delivered in a perverse, matricidal birth—the airborne Pegasus springs, his hoof opening the springs of artistic inspiration, revealing how this violent separation was felt as creatively energizing to the culture of that time.

Perseus, with Medusa's head secured, goes on to play out the tale's convention (one that would last, moralized and spiritualized, into the Christian era): to slay a sea dragon, rescue a helpless maiden, and thereby inherit a kingdom. Power is the ultimate issue in these myths that mark a change of worlds, and of rulers. And, as the divine analogue to this earthly reordering of powers, Athena took the severed but still dreadful head of Medusa and affixed it to the breastplate of her armor, taking over the ruined powers of her enemy, making nature and the lower world the captured emblem of her own chilly aegis. It is worth noting, though, that it took centuries to complete the demonizing of this older form of the sacred. Though divided and conquered, the figure kept something of the contradictory nature of elemental powers: many classical (and neoclassical) images of the Medusa's head retained her beauty along with her snakes; the legendary founder of Western medicine, the healer Asclepius (himself associated with a snake-entwined staff, surviving as the physician's caduceus), was reputed to have used blood from her right side as a healing medicine, from her left as a poison.

≈

Let the asterisks above indicate the passage of several millennia, and all that has become posthumous. Now it is 1952 and the Medusa reappears in the eye of a changed Perseus, drawn by W. S. Merwin in the tranced world of his first book, *A Mask for Janus,* where "One dreams fixed beasts . . . not blinking . . . exhausted leaves, suspended . . . no breath moving the gray flowers. . . ."[4] In his cryptic "Ode: The Medusa Face," the first-person speaker is a hero for whom "healing," when it is connected with a perfection that rests on the denial of time, has become equivocal: "I cannot tell if stone is upon me / Healing me, clotting time until I stand / dead." He has come to where "tall over the breathless shore this day / Lifts on one equal glare / The crass and curling face." The Medusa's glare is the blinding sheen of sun on water, her face and its crown of snakes identified with the curling lift of ocean itself, the word "crass" a last derisive gesture against the tidal surge of life. Because the wave that hangs here in suspense must soon break and flood that "breathless shore." The perplexed hero is unsure "what shield were faithful found, what weapon?" and even whether in fact "the heart still moves." His immobility is a monumental hesitation ("I stand as in a sloth of stone"), for he is paralyzed not by the Medusa but by a new sense that *what he does to her will happen to him:*

> Amazed, for a maimed piece of one's own death,
> Should that lithe hair stiffen
> Were the shape of her fall.[5]

Another, more open act of identification with the Medusa-as-victim takes place when—late in the 1950s, writing of the city of Florence, of the way nature in Italy is more implicated in human meaning than it is in America, and thinking back to the golden apples of classical mythology, ripening now into real fruit—Robert Lowell wrote:

> The apple was more human there than here,
> but it took a long time for the blinding
> golden rind to mellow.
>
> How vulnerable the horseshoe crabs
> dredging the bottom like flat-irons
> in their antique armor,
> with their swordgrass blackbone tails,
> made for a child to grab
> and throw strangling ashore!

Oh Florence, Florence, patroness
of the lovely tyrannicides!
Where the tower of the Old Palace
pierces the sky
like a hypodermic needle,
Perseus, David and Judith,
lords and ladies of the Blood,
Greek demi-gods of the Cross,
rise sword in hand
above the unshaven,
formless decapitation
of the monsters, tubs of guts,
mortifying chunks for the pack.
Pity the monsters!
Pity the monsters!
Perhaps, one always took the wrong side—
Ah, to have known, to have loved
too many Davids and Judiths!
My heart bleeds black blood for the monster.
I have seen the Gorgon.
The erotic terror
of her helpless, big bosomed body
lay like slop.
Wall-eyed, staring the despot to stone,
her severed head swung
like a lantern in the victor's hand.[6]

Looking up from his observation of (and identification with?) the armored and vulnerable horseshoe crab to the towers and righteous beheaders of Western founding myths, Greek and biblical, Lowell allows that "Perhaps, one always took the wrong side—." On that *perhaps,* the balance of cultural sympathies shifts. "Pity the monsters!" twice repeated, then, the full transfusion of fellow feeling: "My heart bleeds black blood for the monster."

And perhaps most compelling is the simile in the last lines: "her severed head swung / like a lantern in the victor's hand." Indeed, the way the Cellini Perseus holds the head before him invites the reading as lantern but only to one prepared, as was Lowell, and Howard Nemerov in his 1970s poem "Hero with Girl and Gorgon," to perceive this once horrific image as a new source of illumination: "that great head," says Nemerov, "swung by the serpents held / At lantern height before you, lighting your way. . . ."[7]

The Lowell poem is a transitional one in several ways. First, it mixes, in the crabs, qualities of both Medusa and traditional warrior hero. The horseshoe crab, one of the most ancient surviving creatures on the planet, is a sea-dweller that resembles both a head and an Iron Age helmet; it has a swordlike tail (a two-edged blade of weapon and fragility: *swordgrass,* coupled with the oxymoron *blackbone*); and, under its dark armored shell, its squirming legs resemble the hideous headful of Medusan snakes, or the tentacles of the jellyfish bearing her name. The mixture of images of antique armor and vulnerability suggests the futility of old defenses and heroics (it is child's play, says the poem, to defeat such armored creatures), while art records the history of the helplessness of the body and our erotic nature before the swords of the highminded "lords and ladies of the Blood"—the final horrifying images of the body decapitated, made helpless and hideous by division.

The poem records a shift in sympathy, but not yet in power—for the body remains defenseless and "formless" by its separation from the intelligence, a pure victim. The world is still dual and dominated, the erotic life under the foot of the "victor," but the quotation marks have been put, invisibly, around that word, and it is the head of the Gorgon held aloft that becomes the "tyrannicide," "staring the despot to stone." "The eye altering, alters all," said Blake, and it is through her stare and in her light that the poem ends. And if that stare can turn, not men, but "the despot" to stone, then what might it achieve were it turned on those frozen by a despotic history's constricting definitions and murderous actions—those immobilized by the horror of the "righteous" destruction of populations, the carnage of our age when the slaughter of the innocents has become as massive as it is casual. The time of writing here is late in the 1980s:

> . . . As if
> an ancient spell had been read backwards:
> though what we'd seen—the burning cities
> at our backs—had stopped us
> in our tracks, a frozen chorus, colonnade
> of salt, pillars like the wife of Lot,
> the sight of her restored us
> to ourselves. How else explain it? The way
> she walked among us as we lined her path,
> her gaze intent on us till we returned
> her look, and then, like embers caught
> in a sudden draft, our hopes blazed up
> again, the flush of blood crept up
> reviving limbs. . . .[8]

The appearance of this recapitated figure, the attachment of intelligence to the life it is meant to serve, explains the power her gaze has to revive. Here is the reversal of a spell, for language, poetically understood as a way of seeing, can alter being. An ancient scene is here recast. In the old story, the terrain around the Medusa's haunt is dotted with figures of stone, men who had come there to destroy her, and been petrified for their presumption. But here the stone figures are like Lot's wife, those numbed by atrocity, by the burning cities of history—the sky gods made literal by bombers of the air force; the more hideous the crime, the higher the purpose invoked to justify it. Authorized violence is now seen not as what opposes but as what creates the monstrous. And the statues that line the path of this emerging figure make a kind of outdoor horror museum, the horror of a beauty exterior in time—the love of the unchanging revealed for what it is as its spell is "read backwards."

Revival here suggests that living pattern is inextricable from matter, that both exist only in time—and if *pater* lurks within pattern, and *mater* within matter, this is only a symptom of how the ego-driven mind, refusing the generation that eventually brings its own extinction, had genderized nature into the stupidity of a simple dualism. So when Time was shaped into a human moral drama in the Bible, and made a secondary realm both by the ascendance of the Olympians and their dissolve into the abstract, extratemporal ideas of the Platonic reductio, women fell with the old cyclical systems into the abyss of the dreadful. This perpetuated in new and canonized forms the mistake of the earliest religionists who made an identity of a correspondence between earth's cyclical and self-consuming fecundity and woman's child-bearing body. Thus was woman made responsible for the generational forces of morality so insulting to the individual human ego, that newly crowned king, and so stultifying in their cyclical repetition to humanity's creative mutability.

That the figure of the Medusa should return in female guise is a part of that tradition, and needful, no doubt, to its rectification, but as the various exemplars from poetry should make clear, what has been enlivened by her gaze is not gender-specific, nor is the fate of woman different from the fate of man or either from the fate of the Earth. It is one of the ironies of history that the very powers for so long identified with woman should be precisely those that the imagination of our own time—both scientific and artistic—should see as most needful for our survival, and should value most. No wonder the Medusa, as the feminist writer-critic Hélène Cixous imagines her, is laughing.[9] Or that Helen, as she appears in powerful new poems by Yannis Ritsos[10] and C. K. Williams,[11] should be dying. The Ritsos poem is, however, backward looking, mourning the end of a Greek ideal in the shabby precincts of the present, whereas C. K. Williams's poem refuses, courageously, to look away from a dying woman, and, as she becomes fully human, he ennobles the real with the dignity that the union of human feeling and lucid awareness achieves.

The traditional Western notion of beauty was an eternal perfection, above and exterior to time, unchanging. Beauty in the world was but the image of this eternal form; spiritual value grew with distance from living matter. It is the work of our own time's imagination to stop mourning the loss of this ideal and instead to see clearly its effect on the real world, this error that turned the real hideous, and made body count a proof of divine power. The Helen who stands on the high walls of Troy presides over a field of corpses and a burning city; she comes down to our time as a grotesque, the aging Elizabeth Taylor, the simultaneous literalizing and unmasking of the Western myth of beauty. Eavan Boland, the contemporary Irish poet, brings this home in her "Tirade for the Lyric Muse," the muse a woman in the hospital wearing the "smocked mouth" and white bandages of her latest face lift: "You are the victim of a perfect crime. / You have no sense of time, / You never had."[12]

So it is hardly surprising that the Medusa, time's familiar, should reappear not as a hideous figure but as a shimmering avatar of recovery, one who enlivens what had been immobilized—all that froze with her division, that world of generation in which we have our being. Much has been made, in modern comparative *mythopoesis,* of the Fisher King's illness and its wasteland effect on the world. Its corollary might be seen in the effect of the Medusan stare, not just on those who met her gaze, but on the world itself. In the poem "Medusa" by Louise Bogan, the speaker approaches "the house, in a cave of trees," and is stopped by the "stiff bald eyes, the serpents on the forehead" of the visage that appears from inside the house:

> This is a dead scene forever now,
> Nothing will ever stir.
> The end will never brighten it more than this,
> Nor the rain blur.
>
> . . .
>
> And I shall stand here like a shadow
> Under the great balanced day,
> My eyes on the yellow dust, that was lifting in the wind,
> And does not drift away.[13]

The results of the traditional Medusan stare occur here in a way that comments on the anaesthetic transaction taking place. The stasis is one that overtakes the world itself. We do not feel or see anything happening to the speaker. We see only what the person sees, and that is, after all, the point. This is how a head might see the world if it had lost all connection with its living body. What stands here, the "I," is "like a shadow" on an arrested sundial; what is real is only a stop-frame image of particulate matter, conflating what sees with what is seen: "My eyes on the yellow dust." That the lightest of things, "the yellow dust"—with its lively associations of pollen, of the shower of divine gold that impregnated Danaë with Perseus—should refuse to move is an astonishing arrest that halts both past and future. It stops even the wind, the spirit itself in perpetual suspense, a held breath.

But when the action reverses, the living woman finds herself moving in the silence of the Medusa, finding in it the force of her own refused feelings: "I turn your face around! It is my face. / That frozen rage is what I must explore. . . ." So ends "The Muse as Medusa" by May Sarton, an exploration assured from the poem's opening lines:

> I saw you once, Medusa; we were alone,
> I looked you straight in the cold eye, cold.
> I was not punished, was not turned to stone—
> How to believe the legends I am told?

The question suggests that her face-to-face encounter with the Medusa has undermined the traditional fictions "which had power marshaled on [their] side," legends through which we learned to see ourselves. Now the power of possibility replaces authority: "Being, perhaps, allowed to swim my way," she imagines herself as a fish, lively denizen of the most fluid medium—"fluid, it is also full of healing"—that she will identify with "that world of feeling / Where thoughts, those fishes, silent, feed and rove," an animating image that reunifies thought with feeling and appetite. She introduces those lines with these:

> The fish, Medusa, did not come to grief,
> But swims still in a fluid mystery.
>
> Forget the image: your silence is my ocean
> And even now it teems with life. . . .[14]

Sarton equates Medusa's long silence with the oceanic, the realm that Freud feared, and associated with both religious feeling and chaos, the place of terrors for the analytic mind which, unmoored from feeling, feels helplessly tossed in the very medium where the sympathetic intellect swims with such ease. Faced with the riddle of the Sphinx, of our mortal condition, the mind, fearing extinction, tries to deny its own connection to generation. Thus did King Laius, with the oracle's blessing and Queen Jocasta's collusion, have his own son Oedipus put out to die, and thus did Jocasta unconsciously try to take him back to the place where he was conceived. Both actions may be seen as attempts to undo the work of time and reverse the laws of generation, rather than as the Freudians see them, a bitter family romance. Intellect that stays apart cannot play its role as the brilliant, faithful, and disobedient servant that corrects our despotism in the name of our common life—as Kent and the Fool to Lear—but becomes instead its jailer, or worse, its executioner. What began as a protection—in traditional terms, a sword and shield against our own extinction—like the Department of Defense, ends by becoming death's agent, "the fearful armories within."

Amy Clampitt writes of "Athena,"

> . . . cool
> guarantor of the averted look, the guide
> of Perseus, who killed and could not kill
>
> the thing he'd hounded to its source, the dread
> thing-in-itself none can elude. . . .
> . . .—a space to savor
> horror, to pre-enact our own undoing in—
> living, we stare into the mirror of the Gorgon.[15]

It is fascinating that on the cover of Clampitt's book *Archaic Figure* should be a headless, stone, female Kore, in that frozen frontal pose of the archaic statue. For she holds up to nature the traditional hero's shield, without any longer being able to believe in its efficacy. Her poetry speaks of the natural condition in a way that is both detached and filled with disgust and terror at the world of generation. At times it seems almost the work of a Victorian Martian, for what woman who ever bled could describe her sex with so outlandish a prudery as Clampitt does in "Medusa":

> . . . the sex whose periodic
> blossom hangs its ungathered garland
> from the horned clockwork of the moon. . . .

Here are English gardens, biology, and the mechanism of Newtonian physics, but, in this bizarre, unimaginable mixing, not quite accurate about either natural process or mechanistic device. How, for instance, can a blossom, itself a singular member of a garland, do the hanging of any garland, however "ungathered" that garland may be? This imagistic contraption (concealing and congealing menstruation) hangs heavy on the horns of this dilemma, this waning mechanical moon, whose clock it would certainly stop.

In fact, what is most moving and palpable in her "Medusa" poem, related to her horror of "the stinging jellyfish, the tubeworm," and other archaic terrors of the deep (shades of Syliva Plath's "Medusa" with its tentacled marine horror of a mother), are her descriptions of the Medusa's effect as transformer to stone, but this time experienced internally:

> . . . ay, in the very tissue of desire
> lodge viscid barbs that turn the blood to coral,
> the heartbeat to a bed of silicates. What surgeon
> can unthread those multiplicities of cause
> of hurt from its effect; dislodge, spicule by spicule,
> the fearful armories within, unclench the airless
> petrification toward the core, the geode's rigor?[16]

Here is the total victory of the armory and the final triumph of crystalline form, perfection revealed as petrifaction—the heart a stone with a glittering core: "the geode's rigor."

The damages of a detached posture in relation to our own condition have been unmasked through time, so that even in those still adhering to the older habits of mind and being, the images themselves relocate the horror. Increasingly the monstrous has come to seem, not the Medusa or some other avatar of mortality aware of itself, but the violent detachment of head from body. In a poem by Emily Dickinson (#629),[17] the image of celestial immortality has crossed, in the growing modernity of her imagination, with decapitation:

> I watched the Moon around the House
> Until upon a Pane—
> She stopped—A Traveller's privilege—for Rest
> And there upon
>
> I gazed—as at a stranger—
> The Lady in the Town
> Doth think no incivility
> To lift her Glass—upon
>
> But never Stranger justified
> The Curiosity
> Like Mine—for not a Foot—nor Hand
> Nor Formula—had she—
>
> But like a Head—a Guillotine
> Slid carelessly away—
> Did independent, Amber—
> Sustain her in the sky—
>
> Or like a Stemless Flower—
> Upheld in rolling Air
> By finer Gravitations—
> Than bind Philosopher—

No hunger—had she—nor an Inn—
Her toilette—to suffice—
Nor avocation—nor Concern
For little Mysteries

As harass us—like Life—and Death—
And Afterwards—or Nay—
But seemed engrossed to Absolute—
With shining—and the Sky—

The privilege to scrutinize
Was scarce upon my Eyes
When, with a Silver practise—
She vaulted out of Gaze—

And next—I met her on a Cloud—
Myself too far below
To follow her superior Road—
Or its advantage—Blue—

The remarkable self-division of that final stanza tells all: "I met her on a Cloud— / Myself too far below." And here is a head that is uncannily endowed with a physicality usually associated with a body: "She vaulted out of Gaze," and a faculty of sight so invested with being that vision is expressed as encounter: "I met her on a Cloud." The poem associates, for reasons historical, theological, and psychological, the detached head with privilege, height with spirit and freedom, and both with that beautiful essence, the petrified sap of life, amber—"independent, Amber— / Sustain her in the sky," "Engrossed to Absolute" on "her superior Road." Yet the two similes at the poem's center give the clear price of that privilege: ". . . like a Head—a Guillotine / Slid carelessly away . . . [o]r like a Stemless Flower." And all of this takes place, not only on two disjunct levels of what should be a single being, but also through glass, a cold barrier that is clear enough to allow vision but precludes reunion of the realms it divides.

Indeed the mirror of Perseus, over the long centuries, has become a barrier rather than a shield, even as it has grown transparent in its reference. For we now see "the horror on the hero's shield," not as the unspeakable thing from which the hero is protected, but rather as the deed itself, the crime of which he himself is guilty. What is frozen forever in the shield, as Caravaggio's painting[18] of it suggests, is the image of the howling victim, the round black open mouth of Münch's "Der Shrei," the inarticulate animal cry of pain, "as in the glitter of the shield the sword / Cut backward in aversion"[19]—the act that attempts to reverse time revealed, in the fullness of time, for the murderous paradox it is. When we look at the shield now, it is the eyes of the victim that meet our own. The distance has closed, the projection of otherness has returned to its source. Even as the restored Medusa becomes an animating figure in the imagination of our time, so the once protective shield becomes the mirror that freezes the man.

In a sonnet called "Medusa," William Percy retells the story of Perseus's use of the severed head to freeze the king and court in the banquet hall where Perseus's mother Danaë is about to become the King's unwilling bride:

> There is a tale of brow and clotted hair
> Thrust in the window of a banquet room
> Which froze eternally the revellers there,
> The lights full on them in their postured doom:
> The queen still held the carmine to her lips,
> The king's mouth stood wide open for its laugh,
> The jester's rigid leer launched silent quips;
> Only a blind man moved and tapped his staff.
> I cannot guess that physiognomy
> The sight of which could curdle into stone
> The gazer, though pities, horror, terrors I
> Have made encounter of and sometimes known.
> But I knew one who turned to stone with terror
> Of facing quietly a flawless mirror.[20]

Except for that little horror of Latinate diction—"physiognomy"—there is nothing hideous here to see—only a person regarding himself in a mirror whose designation as "flawless" suggests just how accurate the image is. That the horror of self-knowledge at the poem's end should emerge from the older Medusa story suggests just how poorly "the mirror of Perseus" works now that the projection has been recovered, and the gazer recognizes the image as his own. The opening line with its "clotted hair" images not the Medusa but the bloody crime. The line before the sonnet's turn, "Only a blind man moved and tapped his staff," has a startling effect, reminding us, in this frozen world of stone figures, that the problem is one of vision, and the power of an image to transfix is in the eye of the beholder.

Geoffrey Hartman, in *The Unmediated Vision,* speaks of the poet today as the new Perseus who "disdains or has lost Athene's mirror, and goes against the monster with naked eye. Some say that, in consequence, he is petrified; others, that he succeeds but the fountain of Pegasus is . . . bittersweet. . . ."[21] But this keeps the notion that the poet goes against the real, and that it is a monster, represented by a terrible "She" with a head full of sinuous extensions—the flow of time, of unpredictable ramifications, of the nonlinear, of what is intractably alive, of generation itself. The direct look at the Medusa is a way to "see through" the image, this translucent emblem with its own light. And this is a compassionate mind that sees, not by standing apart, but through extension of feelers, what H.D. called "overmind," a translucent, fluid medium into which "thoughts pass and are visible like fish," a visionary state that she likened, not surprisingly, to a jellyfish.[22]

The sense of this marine Medusa, this head with its many arms, as itself a dark source of light is developed in a poem by Denise Levertov called "The Art of the Octopus: Variations on a Found Theme," in which her visionary creature is the opposite of the armored being, associated with the traditional hero and his mentor, Athena. Levertov's more recent poem makes a strong contrast with "The Octopus" by James Merrill, written in the 1950s, which begins: "There are many monsters that a glassen surface / Restrains. And none more sinister than vision asleep in the eye's tight translucence." When his octopus of vision moves in its glass cage, there is a horror in its drifting through "the gloom of the tank," the way "the writher advances in a godlike wreath / Of its own wrath"; he imagines "a hundred blows of a boot-heel" that "shall not quell" it, playing both parts here, the one who tries to stamp it out, the one whose rebellious power it is; then sees it as a dancing Hindu god with its many arms, creating and destroying: "Till on glass rigid with his own seizure / At length the sucking jewels freeze."[23] The glass of art contains the monster of vision, or rather "the eye's tight translucence" makes it monstrous by restraining and fearing it so deeply; the poem ends with an unmasking of the beauty, which is achieved by extreme compression: "sucking jewels," followed by immobilization: "freeze"—an absolute closure. In Levertov's poem, the glass is gone, and the octopus set free through a literal evolutionary shedding of armor that carries the metaphor:

> *When it gave up its protective shell it developed*
> *many skills and virtues.*

> Virtues? Transparently
> it ingests contrast, regarding it humbly
> as joy. Nourished,
> it gives forth peculiar light, a smoky radiance.
> Some see this aura. Some think it poisonous,
> others desire it. Of those who enter
> that bright cloud, some vanish. Others begin
> to grow long, wavering, extra arms, godlike,

so that at last they touch
many things at once, and reach
towards everything; they too begin
the solitary dance.[24]

The dark becomes a source of light as this dancing, feeling mind
ingests contrasts and overcomes old opposites, as what was once
despised comes to seem the "soul unshelled"[25] and takes on the nu-
minous radiance of the sacred. To see the serpentine as both tactile
mind and a formal principle of order, one that moves in time as if in
a fluid medium, is perhaps to suggest one reason why "chaos" mathe-
matics and its images have had such a remarkable lay appeal, particu-
larly to artists. Where systems are dynamic, complex, and nonlinear;
where time itself is a variable of formal beauty; where that beauty
comes of curvilinear symmetries at various scales; where, in time,
turbulence and chaos produce gorgeous order; where reality is so
infinitely responsive that the most subtle variable can produce long-
term changes so enormous that order and predictability are no longer
synonymous—these characteristics accord so thoroughly with the
contemporary experience of creative process that it is difficult not to
see a kind of *Zeitgeist* here, in which aberration, disorder, or mon-
strosity suddenly appear as a new locus of order and beauty, carrying
both the explanatory power and ultimate mystery we associate with
the sacred. What once froze the mind now excites it; as the physicist,
Ronald Fox, put it: "There was a place where you quit looking at [a
problem] because it became non-linear. Now you know how to look
at it and you go back."[26]

In this new Medusan vision, the Muse, the animating figure of art,
becomes, not the elusive ideal, but the inexhaustible and intractably
real. And if there is a moment when the imagination of the West
registers this change, perhaps it is the moment in that immobilized
world whose "charmèd water" was "A still and awful red," when,
from within the traditionally demonic color and realm, and moving
visibly into his ship's own shadow, the upside-down redemptive vi-
sion of Coleridge's mariner takes shape:

> Beyond the shadow of the ship,
> I watched the water-snakes:
> They moved in tracks of shining white
> And when they reared, the elfish light
> Fell off in hoary flakes.
>
> Within the shadow of the ship
> I watched their rich attire:
> Blue, glossy green, and velvet black,

They coiled and swam, and every track
Was a flash of golden fire.

O happy living things! no tongue
Their beauty might declare
A spring of love gushed from my heart,
And I blessed them unaware;
Sure my kind saint took pity on me,
And I blessed them unaware.

The self-same moment I could pray;
And from my neck so free
The Albatross fell off, and sank
Like lead into the sea.[27]

So the winged spirit of the sacred past, reendowed with the weight of
a long-denied materiality, sinks, mercifully, into the sea, and with it
the burden of self-important guilt for our own mortality. Light and
dark covenantal color flash from what coils and swims within the
flood, and the spell that had frozen even the sea is broken. In Cole-
ridge's vision, a new spring opens, far different from the one opened
by the wounding hoof of Pegasus—"forever," says Mary Oliver,
"which has . . . always been, / like a sharp iron hoof, / at the center of
my mind."[28]

The old vision still retains power, though mainly a negative one: to
fix, to nail down. In "Falling Away," a prose piece about a vision too
immobilizing to turn into poetry, Elizabeth Spires tells of her paro-
chial school introduction to "eternity," described by their teacher as
the time it would take the tip of a bird's wing, lightly brushing once in
a century, to wear down to nothing the world's largest mountain
made entirely of rock:

Ever after, I connect hell and eternity not with fire and flames, but
with something cold and unchanging, a snowy tundra overshad-
owed by a huge granite mountain that casts a pall over the land-
scape. Like the North or South Pole in midsummer, the sun would
circle overhead in a crazy loop, day passing into day without inter-
vening night, each object nakedly illuminated, etched sharply in
light and shadow, unable to retreat into night's invisibility. If I were
unlucky, I'd be there one day, for forever, dressed in my white
communion dress, white anklets, and black patent leather shoes.
And there would be others, too, a field of stopped souls who
couldn't move or speak, but who suffered the cold, suffered inac-
tion, without sleep or forgetfulness. Like children playing freeze tag
on a playground, the field of souls would stretch over the horizon

past the vanishing point. The only moving thing a small black spot in the sky, the bird that flew high over our heads once every hundred years when the century flipped over, like the odometer on a speeding car.[29]

This image is a reminder that perpetual motion in an endless day is as static as the stone against which it is pitted. And that in our high speed age, a divided vision—black and white and frozen—can still compel the public world and trouble the private mind, recalling the horrifying terrain of statues around the original lair of the Medusa. Which brings us to pity the monsters we have made of ourselves, to release the winged mind from its errand of illustrating eternity, and free the children at last from their game of freeze tag. Like the penguin, our longevity depends on our mutability. We have come to that hairpin turn.

NOTES

1. Victor Scheffer, *Spires of Form* (Seattle: University of Washington Press, 1983), 116.
2. Eleanor Wilner, "Coda, Overture," *Sarah's Choice* (Chicago: University of Chicago Press, 1989), 3.
3. Howard Nemerov, "Hero with Girl and Gorgon," *The Collected Poems of Howard Nemerov* (Chicago: University of Chicago Press, 1977), 469.
4. W. S. Merwin, "Anabasis," *A Mask for Janus* (1952), in *The First Four Books of Poems* (New York: Atheneum, 1977), 3–4.
5. Merwin, "Ode: The Medusa Face," *The First Four Books of Poems,* 36.
6. Robert Lowell, "Florence," *Selected Poems* (New York: Farrar, Straus and Giroux, 1977), 106–7.
7. Nemerov, 469.
8. Wilner, 3.
9. The reference is to Hélène Cixous's essay on "writing the feminine," "The Laugh of the Medusa," translated from the French by Keith Cohen and Paula Cohen, *Signs: Journal of Women and Culture in Society* 1 (Summer 1976): 875–93.
10. Yannis Ritsos, "Helen," translated from demotic Greek by Peter Green and Beverly Bardsley, *Grand Street* 8, 1 (Autumn 1988): 65–85.
11. C. K. Williams, "Helen," *The American Poetry Review* 21, 1 (January/February 1992): 3–5.
12. Eavan Boland, "Tirade for the Lyric Muse," *The Journey and Other Poems* (Manchester, England: Carcanet, 1987), 55–56.
13. Louise Bogan, "Medusa," *Hero's Way: Contemporary Poems in the Mythic Tradition,* ed. John Alexander (Englewood Cliffs, N.J.: Prentice-Hall, 1971), 70–71.
14. May Sarton, "The Muse as Medusa," *Selected Poems of May Sarton* (New York: W. W. Norton, 1978), 160.

15. Amy Clampitt, "Athena," *Archaic Figure* (New York: Alfred A. Knopf, 1987), 27.

16. Clampitt, "Medusa," *Archaic Figure,* 22.

17. Emily Dickinson, #629, *The Complete Poems of Emily Dickinson,* ed. Thomas H. Johnson (Boston: Little, Brown, and Co., 1960), 310–11.

18. The reference is to Caravaggio's oil on canvas portrait of the Medusa on a parade shield (1600–1601) in the Uffizi in Florence. The terror-stricken face of Medusa, actually that of a young boy with snakes for hair, is caught, wide-eyed and open-mouthed with horror, as if at the moment of beheading. The portrait is a radical departure from tradition in forcing the viewer to confront a terrified Medusa seen as victim.

19. Nemerov, 469.

20. William Alexander Percy, "Medusa," *Hero's Way,* 179.

21. Geoffrey H. Hartman, *The Unmediated Vision* (New Haven: Yale University Press, 1954), 156.

22. H.D., *Notes on Thought and Vision* (San Francisco: City Lights Books, 1982), 19.

23. James Merrill, "The Octopus," *The Contemporary American Poets: American Poetry Since 1940,* ed. Mark Strand (Cleveland: World Publishing, 1969), 207.

24. Denise Levertov, "The Art of the Octopus: Variations on a Found Theme," *Candles in Babylon* (New York: New Directions, 1982), 19–20.

25. Richard Wilbur, "Advice to a Prophet," *New and Collected Poems* (New York: Harvest/HBJ, 1989), 183.

26. Quoted in James Gleick, *Chaos: Making a New Science* (New York: Penguin Books, 1987), 306.

27. Samuel Taylor Coleridge, "The Rime of the Ancient Mariner," *English Romantic Poetry and Prose,* ed. Russell Noyes (New York: Oxford University Press, 1956), 396.

28. Mary Oliver, "One or Two Things," *Dreamwork* (New York: Atlantic Monthly Press, 1986), 51.

29. Elizabeth Spires, "Falling Away," *Annonciade* (New York: Viking, 1989), 38.

❧

The author wishes to convey thanks and appreciation to LeRoy P. Percy, executor of the estate of William Alexander Percy, for permission to reprint the sonnet "Medusa"; and to Farrar, Straus and Giroux for permission to publish the excerpt from the poem "Florence" by Robert Lowell, copyright © 1976 by Robert Lowell.

MICHAEL RYAN

Poetry and the Audience

There's a moment I love in *The Public Enemy,* starring James Cagney. Rocky has come home a hero from the Great War and moved back into the family's coldwater flat with his poor, widowed, good-hearted, Irish mother. Cocky and ambitious but unable to get better than menial jobs, increasingly humiliated, frustrated, and angry, he falls in with what his poor, widowed, good-hearted Irish mother never tires of calling "the wrong crowd," rolling both *r*s heartily in her stage-Irish brogue. She nags him constantly about it, against all odds and the demands of the plot and the producer, until Rocky's patience (which has far exceeded ours) gives out, and he turns to her and snaps, "What do you want me to do, stay at home all day and write *poems?*" At the end of the movie, after we've witnessed his rise and fall in a life of crime, he is machine-gunned on the steps of the cathedral and dies in the arms of his mistreated-but-ever-faithful girfriend. A passerby asks, "Who is this guy anyway?" And she looks up mournfully and answers, "He used to be a big shot." Camera pans back. Music up. Fade out. The end.

When the houselights go on, I have wanted to stand up and ask the audience, "Now wouldn't Rocky have been better off staying at home and writing poems?" But even if the audience did recall Rocky's opinion of poets by the time the movie was over, someone could answer, "No, he wouldn't have been better off. Instead of being machine-gunned he would have starved. Or he would have kept his rotten jobs, suffered poverty and humiliation, and how would he have found time to write anyway? Besides, he would have *never* been a big shot."

But anthropology has shown us many cultures in which poets were "big shots." In primitive tribes, extant and extinct, the poet is usually the central figure, the shaman-healer. Because he is close to the gods, through his "divine madness," he keeps the tribe together by celebrating in his chants and sacred rituals its shared beliefs, ancestry, and cosmology. The tribe depends on the poet for its life.

Unquestionably, the roots of poetry, as well as of dance and drama, are in performances of myth and magic that have a religious purpose

An earlier version appeared in *The American Poetry Review* 17, 2 (March/April 1988): 7–20.

and socially cohesive effect. As Jane Ellen Harrison said in *Ancient Art and Ritual:*

> Art is social in origins. The dance from which the drama rose was a choral dance . . . what the Greeks called a *thiaros*. The word means a bond and a thing of devotion; and reverence, devotion, collective emotion, is social in its very being.

According to Harrison, it's not at all what the individual feels but "what the tribe feels that is sacred." This may be difficult for Rocky, or us, to understand, stuck as we are in the middle of a powerful industrial capitalist culture in which the primacy of self and the ostensibly inalienable rights of the individual are two essential elements of the encompassing myth. The language of myth, through the metaphors of poetry and drama or science and sports, communicates the values the culture says we must adopt to survive. In a primitive society, in which cooperation is required to kill the meat and gather the vegetables, the myths subordinate the individual to the tribe; the individual can't survive outside the tribe and the tribe can't survive individualism. For the Maori, for example, it would in fact be more accurate to say that there is no such thing as an "Individual."

In preliterate societies, even those as late as ancient Greece and Anglo-Saxon England, the poet is an idealogue, historian, theologian, philosopher, TV, newspaper, and shopping mall "multiplex" cinema rolled into one. Maybe putting it in these terms dramatizes what the poet is not in contemporary American culture and the size of the audience he would have if he were.

But industrial capitalism is only one of the more recent forces that have swept across what was originally the poet's territory and pushed him into the lyric corner where he's ignored by the culture at large. The tribe was interested in what the poet had to say because his subject was the tribe. There are still remnants of this in Chaucer, but *The Canterbury Tales* is the first modern poem in England not only because of its interest in the individual in society but also because it was written to be read. In preliterate societies, in which poetry was orally transmitted, a strict mnemonic regularity—whether Anglo-Saxon alliterative accentuals or Homeric dactylic hexameters—was an essential feature of the verse, for the sake of its survival no less than its effect. Authorship was probably neither entirely individual nor collective. *The Iliad* and *The Odyssey* were probably composed over hundreds of years, the work of many bards. Not coincidentally, both poems take every opportunity to praise such bards, and, since they wandered from place to place reciting their tales, hospitality to strangers is put forth in the poems as a major virtue. Odysseus says in book IX of *The Odyssey:*

I think life is at its best when a whole people is in festivity and banqueters in the hall sit next to each other listening to the bard, while the tables by them are laden with wine and meat, and the cupbearer draws wine from the mixing bowl and pours it into the cups. That, I think, is the happiest thing there is.

In the first century A.D. in Ireland, there was a class of learned men, the *file,* who also made it their task in life to preserve ancient stories; the most distinguished kind of *file,* the *ollamh,* was master of 250 major narratives and one hundred minor ones. Yeats refers to this tradition in "Under Ben Bulben," one of his last poems, when he exhorts, "Irish poets, learn your trade." By the time of the *file,* at least in Europe, poetry was a profession; though his position was no longer central, the poet still had an essential and therefore prestigious social role. According to the historian Daniel Boorstin:

Before the printed book, Memory ruled daily life and the occult learning, and fully deserved the name later applied to printing, the "art preservative of all the arts." The Memory of individuals and of communities carried knowledge through time and space. . . . By Memory and in Memory the fruits of education were garnered, preserved and stored.

The *file* were the libraries and the entertainment, the repositories of information and wisdom, and they were largely responsible for what social cohesion there was. Consequently, the identity of the individual poet was nothing in light of the social function of his poetry. A particular narrative survived only if it served that social function, which in turn depended on how engaging and memorable the story was made. The poem was tested on the audience and modified from its response; the same stories were told over and over again, the stories that concerned everyone. They had to contain quite literally enduring qualities, of both narrative and style. As Gilbert Murray says in his wonderful book, *The Classical Tradition in Poetry:* "The manner of the Heroic Age is that of poets who know what they are describing and audiences that know the thing that is being talked about," and this manner is characterized by "temperance and sobriety of invention." The style's subordination to the subject, the author's self-effacement for the sake of the story, is intimately connected to his social role, a role that's as secure as his clear rendering of the thing. It's not as if the possibility of flashy language and self-display never occurred to these poets. In book II of *The Iliad,* we hear of Thamyris the Thracian who boasted of a new-fangled sort of poetry to surpass the Muses: "And they in wrath made him a maimed man, and took away from him his heavenly song and made him forget his harping." If Homer's line is read with the sense of mythic time—*in illo tempore*—it tells us that the egoism of Thamyris means his heavenly song is already lost.

Given the fact that the social role of the poet now bears about as much resemblance to his role in the Heroic Age as contemporary America does to ancient Greece, it's amazing that those enduring qualities we think of as "classical"—the subordination of style to subject, "temperance and sobriety of invention"—have in fact endured into our century. In Pound's dicta they appear as "objectivity—and, again—objectivity," "direct treatment of the thing," his relentless exhortation in his early essays to clarity and precision. Eliot's self-classified "classicism in literature" is certainly behind his "objective correlative" as working method, his sense of the importance and value of tradition, and his core beliefs that "the emotion of art is impersonal" and "permanent literature is always a presentation."

For both Pound and Eliot, these are not merely aesthetic impulses without social implications. But their "classicism" was nothing Homer would have recognized. *The Waste Land* is hardly characterized by "temperance and sobriety of invention." Yeats recorded his initial response to the poem in a 1924 preface dedicated to Lady Gregory: "the other day when I read that strange 'Waste Land' by Mr. T. C. [!] Eliot I thought of your work and Synge's; and he is American born and Englishman bred, and writes but of his own mind." The dislocation Yeats perceived in Eliot's poem he attributed to a dislocation of place, a disconnection from "the soil" that so concerned the Irish Literary Revival. For Yeats, poetry couldn't exist without an actual, defined audience to ground it. But just who that audience was vacillated in Yeats's mind between the peasantry and the aristocracy, from writing "as an Irish writer and with Ireland in my mind" to writing for an elite international "audience, 'fit though few,' which is greater than any nation, for it is made up of chosen persons from all." At other times, he declared that his ideal audience was, respectively, "the town of Sligo," "young men between twenty and thirty," "a few friends [for whom] one always writes," and "a man who does not exist, / a man who is but a dream." Yeats was no doubt, as he said himself, "anarchic as a sparrow," and his invention of his much-discussed "masks" may have come from his difficulty adopting an "essential stance" toward an audience for longer than the moment of a single poem. But Yeats initially faced in Ireland the same problem regarding an audience for his poetry that Eliot and Pound faced in England and Williams and Stevens faced in the United States: there was none. Pound believed a good book of poems could never sell more than five hundred copies; Stevens's first book, *Harmonium,* in fact sold less than one hundred copies; and Williams's early books sold so badly that he entitled one *Al Que Quiere*—"to him who wants it." These poets responded in various ways to this common situation, and each poet's response bears a direct relationship to the poetry he wrote: its style, subjects, structure, tone, even its syntax—in short, its whole character. The poet's idea of his audience (which may or may not be accurate) is fused to his idea of his cultural role (which may or may not be realistic) and thereby influences and sometimes even generates his poetry.

Yeats's vacillations belie the endurance, clarity, and strength of his conviction that the connection between poetry and its audience is inevitable and straightforward: as Yeats became "a smiling public man," his poetry cut closer to the bone. As early as his first book of essays, *Ideas of Good and Evil* (1903), while his work was still under the specialized influences of the fin de siècle cult of Beauty and the mystical Order of the Golden Dawn, Yeats nonetheless wrote: "Does not the greatest poetry always require a people to listen to it?" That is, not only does the poet require an audience, but the poetry requires an audience, so that it does not become "accidental and temporary," abstract, peripheral, precious, cut off from central human concerns—so that the poet does not "write but of his own mind."

Yeats came to this view through visiting the country people with Lady Gregory to collect stories for her volumes of Irish folklore, and through his efforts with her to establish the Abbey Theater and promote an Irish Literary Revival. He wrote in 1906:

> My work in Ireland has continually set this thought before me: "How can I make my work mean something to vigorous and simple men? . . ." I had not wanted to "elevate them" or "educate them," as these words are understood, but to make them understand my vision, and I had not wanted a large audience, certainly not what is called a national audience, but for enough people for what is accidental and temporary to lose itself in the lump. . . . I have always come to this certainty: what moves natural men in the arts is what moves them in life, and that is, intensity of personal life, intonations that show them, in a book or a play, the strength, the essential moment of a man who would be exciting in the market or at the dispensary door.

As he said in "A General Introduction To My Work" over thirty years later, he therefore "tried to make the language of poetry coincide with that of passionate, normal speech" and sought "a powerful, passionate syntax" for "a poetry stripped of rhetoric, like a cry from the heart." (The latter quotation is from his speech to the *Poetry* banquet in 1914.)

Pound would seem to have disagreed with none of Yeats's ideas about poetry. From 1913 to 1916, he spent the winters in Sussex as Yeats's secretary, and for the ten years before that regarded Yeats as indisputably the greatest living poet. Pound wrote to Harriet Monroe in January, 1915, that the language of poetry ought to depart "in no way from speech save by a heightened intensity (ie simplicity)," and there should be "no Tennysonianess of speech; nothing—nothing that you couldn't, in some circumstance, in the stress of some emotion, actually say." Pound's views, coming from Yeats's cottage, are views Yeats had held for some time. Yet no poetry would eventually be more different from Yeats's poetry than Pound's.

In both structure and content, these differences come from their dissimilar notions of the audience. Despite his sentimental attachment to the idea of aristocracy, Yeats believed the vitality of poetry must be drawn from common life—this is why the audience is essential to the poetry, as well as to the poet. For Pound, the opposite is the case:

> The artist is not dependent on the multitude of his listeners. Humanity is the rich effluvium, it is the waste and manure and the soil, and from it grows the tree of the arts. . . .
>
> It is true that the great artist has in the end always, his audience, for the Lord of the universe sends into this world in each generation a few intelligent spirits, and these ultimately manage the rest. But this rest—this rabble, this multitude—does *not* create the great artist. They are aimless and drifting without him. They dare not inspect their own souls.

This is twenty years but only a goose step away from Mussolini's chamber, where Pound was welcomed as the great poet, though, as the story is told, Mussolini had never read a word of Pound's poetry. No doubt he wouldn't have been able to understand it anyway. Pound's essay, entitled "The Audience," appeared in *Poetry* in 1914, written in response to Harriet Monroe's adopting as a motto for the magazine Whitman's line: "To have great poetry there must be great audiences, too." Seeing the motto on the cover every month irked Pound no end, and he lobbied doggedly for its removal. In his view, poetry is a communication, but "a communication between Intelligent Men"—the audience is a tiny elite group who, by means he doesn't articulate, "manage the rest."

This cultural version of right-wing economics becomes the main theme of *The Cantos*. From the beginning, Pound wrote poems not about poetry (as did Stevens) but about the poem's progress and reception in the world. What Yeats feared most about losing contact with "natural men" is surely realized in the structure and subject of *The Cantos,* even if they are also sometimes "passionate speech"—or fragments of it—especially those written while Pound was without his books in the detention camp at Pisa. Art and its degradation in a botched civilization is, of course, the subject Pound was most passionate about. When Pound arrived in England in 1908, the most popular poets were Noyes, Kipling, Watson, and Newbolt. Their newspaper verses exhorted England to more imperial conquests. In the United States, Longfellow's influence was still palpable, the public was buying James Whitcomb Riley (whom Pound, bizarrely, admired), and in the universities a watery academic romanticism prevailed. Pound devoted his fanatic's energy to putting across his idea of the seriousness and cultural value of poetry—in 1919 alone, he published 109 critical articles.

As early as 1913, chastising Harriet Monroe (as usual), Pound wrote: "It is increasingly hard to maintain an interest in 'the american reader.' GORRD! . . . I have no intention of conceding an inch. The public is stupid, and any other opening, from me, would be the rankest hypocrisy." His pessimism, and his arrogance, could only deepen. Ten years later, soliciting contributions to establish an annuity for Eliot so he could quit his job at the bank, Pound began his "Bel Esprit" circular: "There is no organized or coordinated civilization left, only individual scattered survivors. Aristocracy is gone, its function was to select." In yet another ten years, he would write in a letter: "Don't knock Mussolini, at least not until you have weighed up the obstacles and necessities of the time. He will end up with Sigismundo and the men of order. . . ." Sigismundo Malatesta, a quattrocento patron of the arts and egomaniacal tyrant whose use of terror makes Cesare Borgia look like Mother Teresa, became one of the heroes of *The Cantos*.

Pound's moral universe is a curious, ugly place, and his politics are of a piece with his idea of poetry and the audience. The modernist revolution in poetry was a right-wing coup, and many "postmodern" poets who have followed seem to have accepted modernist aesthetic assumptions without considering their political or ethical implications, as if art existed either in a vacuum or in its own high kingdom apart from the rest of human life. The fact that Pound was a Fascist, and that most of the poets of his generation—Yeats, Frost, Stevens, Eliot, Lawrence, and Jeffers—had aristocratic, reactionary, "royalist," or explicitly Fascist affiliations between the wars can't be explained away by "the obstacles and necessities of the time." Even if the sorry quality of work by their counterparts on the Left—Sandburg and Lindsay, for example, both of whom Monroe championed—argues for a certain distance of the modern poet from mass culture, too much distance results in insularity, the academic poetry of the fifties and the genteel poetry of the eighties, in which the linguistic surfaces are glittery, the experience privileged, the subjects agreeable, and the emotions tepid. Of Pound's generation, only Williams was a democrat, and he says in his *Autobiography*: "The great world never very much interested me." Although Williams complained mightily about the public indifference to poetry, his temperament and bang-em-out aesthetics seem to have been luckily suited to his life: "As far as the writing itself is concerned, it takes next to no time at all . . . there is always time to bang out a few pages." Stevens also seems to have been content enough to write his poetry before nine and after five, but only after his first years on his own in New York recorded in his journal as "living a strange, insane kind of life." The others found themselves in conflict with a culture in which until well past middle age they had to struggle to live and write and could not support themselves as poets.

Pound seems to have felt this conflict most intensely, and to have been least able to accept it as a condition of the poet's life in modern society. Here are a few more lines from the "Bel Esprit" circular:

Darkness and confusion as in Middle Ages; no chance of general order or justice; we can only release an individual here and there.

Only thing we can give the artist is leisure to work in. Only way we can get work from him is to assure him this leisure.

. . . Every writer is penalized for not printing EVERYTHING he can sell.

Eliot, in bank, makes 500. Too tired to write, broke down; during convalescence in Switzerland did *Waste Land,* a masterpiece; one of the most important 19 pages in English. Returned to bank, and is again gone to pieces, physically.

Must restart civilization. . . .

Pound believed for his whole life that the world had come to an end, but it must have been astonishing even to his circle of initiates that he thought he could actually "restart civilization" by giving T. S. Eliot time to write poetry. Pound's inflation of the poet's role, his evangelical faith in the word, is the source of intensity, poignancy, and bombast in his work, bombast that in its own way makes the worst of Matthew Arnold seem like dry understatement. It is as if he spent most waking moments and all dreaming ones trying to make the world possible for poetry.

But if Pound and Eliot didn't "restart civilization," they did, for their part, restart poetry. As Williams said bitterly: "*The Waste Land* returned us to the classroom." Williams of course meant his remark figuratively, though in fact the university had since become exile's island, at least in the United States after World War II, when the GI Bill and the country's industrial dominance of the world caused colleges to burgeon overwhelmingly overnight. But poets were never really repatriated after Plato banished them from the State for being liars. For Plato, language must be used in civilized society to communicate rational ideas for orderly purposes, and this—as he knew—is not how it's used in poetry. In poetry, "a god speaks through the mouth of a man," hence poetry is potentially dangerous to a rule of law dependent upon the rational agreement of citizens. The point at which poetry finally lost its social role in England is usually traced to the Industrial

Revolution and the Romantic reaction to it. Since nascent highbrow culture in the United States took all its cues from England until well into the nineteenth century, it's safe to say that, despite the efforts of Emerson and Longfellow, poetry never played a significant role in forming social values in this country. The aesthetic response of the English Romantics to their lack of audience—articulated in letters by Keats, and lectures by Hazlitt—continues to dominate our own poetic assumptions almost two hundred years later. Because, despite the overwhelming changes since that time in the texture of daily life, the discoveries of science, and the evolution of habits and values and ways we see ourselves and the world, the situation of poetry is essentially the same.

But the audience had begun its exit with the invention of movable type over three hundred years before the Industrial Revolution. As Auden says in his trenchant introductions to the five-volume *Viking Poets of the English Language,* "Anglo-Saxon is the poetry of a tribe; Elizabethan poetry is the poetry of a nation." Tribal poetry is oral; as soon as writing is published, poetry is read, not heard, and reading is a skill that must be learned in leisure and is therefore a privilege of those who have leisure, namely the king, the clergy, the aristocracy, and, later on, wealthy merchants and bailiffs of manors. The concepts of universal education, even for Caucasian men only, didn't appear until the French Revolution. The province of poetry was the court, the rich and powerful, the aristocracy Yeats and Pound were nostalgic for; and court poetry, composed to be read, very quickly became intellectually ingenious to distinguish itself from the ballads continuing the oral tradition among the common folk. Auden says:

> We are so accustomed to a culture in which poetry is the highbrow medium, to be employed for communicating the most intense and subtle experiences, while the medium for everyday use is prose, that it is difficult for us to imagine a society [i.e., before 1300] in which the relative positions were the other way round, a time when verse was the popular medium for instruction and entertainment and prose, mostly Latin, the specialized medium for the intercourse of scholars.

By 1580, literacy was general among the nobility, the positions of prose and poetry had reversed, and the social utility of poetry was already in question. Sidney says in his *Apology:* "I have just cause to make a pitiful defense of poor Poetry, which from almost the highest estimation of learning, is fallen to be the laughingstock of children." His defense, borrowed from Horace (who found himself in a similar situation), is that the social value of poetry derives from its ability to teach and delight, "delight to move men to take that goodness in hand . . . and teach, to make them know that goodness whereunto they are moved." In other words, the social value of poetry lies in its efficacy as an instrument of knowledge and propaganda—without, for Sir Philip, the pejorative connotations of the latter term. Poetry, and poets, can be useful to society by identifying its moral ideas ("virtue") and causing citizens to believe in them.

It was a brilliant maneuver, and held as the predominant social— and human—justification for poetry until Wordsworth and beyond, and still recurs in places as seemingly diverse as monographs by English professors (such as Christopher Clausen's *The Place of Poetry*) and statements issued by the Soviet Writer's Union. Though reading made contact with poetry a solitary pleasure instead of a communal entertainment, and poetry was no longer needed to store and preserve knowledge, Sidney's poet theoretically serves one part of the social role of the Irish *file:* to dispense communal wisdom in an entertaining fashion.

Of course, it did not work out that way at all. The voice of the poet immediately became individual and personal, the dominant poetic mode lyric instead of narrative, poetic diction more refined and less like common speech, and poetic logic and structure more elaborate and less spontaneous. Elizabethan poetry was composed by a courtier or clergyman in a room by himself with his own thoughts, most often of his mistress or his God. The ballad tradition persisted among the lower classes, but, without a power base and therefore "moral" function, ballads became mere entertainment, usually bawdy entertainment, and soon evolved into broadsides and newspaper verse. Though Sidney's poet serves a very small audience—the court and nobles—it's a real and powerful one to whom he is at least theoretically important. Ben Jonson put the reigning idea with characteristic economy: "A Prince without Letters is a Pilot without eyes. All his Government is grasping."

In his *Apology,* Sidney performs a piece of sophistry worth noting because it shows how he must revise Plato's idea of poetry to keep poetry theoretically connected to the audience and useful to a civilized society. First, he affirms Plato himself "depended most of poetry" and is himself "of all philosophers . . . the most poetical." Then he argues that poets can't be liars because they do not labor "to tell you what is, or is not, but what should or should not be," adding that Plato meant to banish only the "abuse" of poetry—its causing wrong opinion— not the thing itself. Throughout, Sidney divorces Plato from his interpreters—a polemical strategy whose classical roots Sidney's contemporaries would have recognized—and ends this part of his argument with a key passage:

So as Plato, banishing the abuse, not the thing, not banishing it, but giving due honor unto it, shall be our patron, and not our adversary. For indeed I had much rather (sith truly I may do it,) show their mistaking of Plato, (under whose lion's skin they would make an asslike braying against poesy,) than go about to overthrow his authority, whom the wiser a man is, the more just cause he shall find to have in admiration; especially, *sith he attributeth unto poesy, more than myself do; namely, to be the very inspiring of a divine force, far above man's wit.* [my italics]

To speak to a civilized audience, and be socially functional, Sidney turns poetry into a civilized activity: rather than Plato's embodiment of a divine, unruly, dangerous force, it becomes for the sake of a moral and social good the expression of man's "wit" (which Hobbes defined a few years later as the "swift succession of one thought to another and steddy direction to some approved end").

Keeping Hobbes's definition in mind, the line from Sir Philip Sidney to Dr. Samuel Johnson can be seen as a straight one, despite the proliferation of individual styles during the two hundred years that separate them. Auden says:

> The real novelty in Romantic poetry is not its diction but its structure. If the Romantic poets, after rejecting Pope and Dryden, did not rediscover Donne and the Metaphysical poets, this was because the latter, no less than the former, organized their poems logically.

A radical change in diction like Wordsworth's actually forces a radical adjustment in structure, but Wordsworth and Coleridge did see clearly that "wit" was above all a structural principle that had to be overturned for its political no less than its poetic implications. For Sidney, the social value of "wit" ("the steddy direction to some approved end") is the foundation of its poetic value; by means of "wit," the shared moral values (the "approved end" of "virtue") are enacted by the poems. Without this social and moral foundation, poetry is frivolous and potentially harmful. For Samuel Johnson, *every* aesthetic value implies and requires such a base—hence his moral criticism of Shakespeare's "rough numbers," a poet's duty being reflected even in his prosody. To us, this may seem the reductio ad absurdum of the elevation of wit, but if poetic values are not based on moral values approved by the society, the poetry has no immediate authority, no social function, and no audience, and this was the overriding, legitimate concern for poets from Sidney to Johnson. When the Romantics replaced "wit" with the "imagination of the Poet," individual and unbounded, as the structural or, as Coleridge would say, "architectonic" faculty, theoretically they did so at this expense.

In practice, as soon as poetry had been composed in writing and preserved in books, as soon as wisdom and knowledge of the race did not need to be remembered with the aid and through the forms of stories and verse, poetry could and did become less and less important to the business of society. This situation, first lamented in England by Sidney, appears to us to have resulted in a great period of poetry. In the Elizabethan lyric alone, new prosodies were invented for songs and meditations, and many stanza forms developed from the sonnet in response to developments in music and logic—even though the greatest richness was the blank verse written for a thriving stage. If wit in Shakespeare's time was sometimes confused with ingenuity, by the eighteenth century its essential structural role in composition was firmly established, probably peaking in Pope's "Essay On Criticism," in which the word itself is used forty-six times. In 1819, when it appears in Hazlitt's essay "Wit and Humor," "wit" is a pejorative that denotes something artificial.

Hazlitt's essay begins: "Man is the only animal that laughs and weeps; for he is the only animal that is struck with the difference between what things are, and what they ought to be." This difference, in the eyes of the Romantic poets, widened at an accelerating pace during the latter part of the eighteenth century as England's economy shifted from an agrarian to an industrial base, and great technological advances improved life for the few and—as the poor could no longer live by farming and migrated to the cities—wreaked even more misery than usual on the many. In 1798, the year *Lyrical Ballads* first appeared, Thomas Malthus argued in his *Essay on the Principle* that poverty was the result of overpopulation and the best and simplest way to deal with the poor was to let them die off as quickly as possible, without the interference of organized charity. As the modernist revolution was a right-wing coup, the Romantics were of the Left; and, like the Bolshevik Revolution, the French Revolution raised great hopes among the Left for social justice and then shattered them. In the aftermath, the English Romantics, through various forms of exile, withdrew from society, but society had already withdrawn from them. Dryden and Pope could at least regard themselves as public poets whose audience was the elite of society; if Pope had only 575 subscriptions to his *Iliad,* he could boast with only some exaggeration that they included "almost all the distinguished names of Quality or Learning in the Nation." Whatever immediate, tangible social role the poet had in England after the Middle Ages he certainly no longer had by 1800, but what most clearly distinguishes the Romantic poet from his predecessors is his giving up the idea of one. Keats declared in a letter, "I never wrote one single line of Poetry with the least shadow of public thought." For Shelley, the poet is "a nightingale who sits in darkness and sings to cheer his own solitude with sweet sounds," a nightingale who doubles, perhaps on the dayshift, as "an unacknowl-edged legislator of the world." Appropriately enough, the "Defense of Poetry" in which this phrase appears was not only ignored in Shelley's lifetime; it wasn't even published until almost twenty years after his death. As a legislator of the world, he was certainly unacknowledged.

As Shelley's phrase indicates, the Romantic poets replaced the idea of the poet who promotes good by teaching virtue and moving his fellow citizens toward it with a considerably less modest and more abstract idea of his social role. This is how Wordsworth put it in the 1800 Preface to *Lyrical Ballads:*

> In spite of the difference of soil and climate, of language and man-ners, of laws and customs: in spite of things gone silently out of mind, and things violently destroyed; the Poet binds together by passion and knowledge the vast empire of human society, as it is spread over the whole earth, and over all time.

What Wordsworth did here is in its own way as ingenious and disfiguring as Sidney's transmutation of Plato. By imagining the audi-ence to be permanent and universal instead of immediate and particu-lar, Wordsworth awards the poet a larger, lasting, more important role in "the vast empire of human society,"—far beyond England in 1800—the actual nonreaders who would rather quaff Guinness in the local pub be damned. What's given up, besides the contact and correc-tive of a real audience, is the poet's role as citizen. By putting himself above the local and immediate, the Romantic poet becomes alien and possibly subversive. In this regard, Shelley's reading of Plato is more faithful than Sidney's. In his isolation, with a self-projected, imagined audience, the poet also acquires enormous potential for solipsism and self-aggrandizement.

The last part of Wordsworth's sentence is worth focusing on: "The Poet binds together by passion and knowledge the vast empire of human society, as it is spread over the whole earth, and over all time." Whereas Sidney is speaking literally and practically when he says the social function of poetry is "to teacheth and moveth to virtue," Words-worth's use of language here is terrifically figurative: the audience itself is imagined as all Humanity (capital *H*), and this Humanity is somehow metaphorically bound together by the poet's passion and knowledge. This seems pretty abstract now, and, though we may have some notion of what Wordsworth is talking about—since we work in the realm of his assumptions—it's an idea that's become impossible to swallow after the reports of Nazi concentration camp directors reading Goethe and listening to Beethoven as the day's allot-ment of Jews is being gassed. In our century, art does not necessarily "humanize," and even if it were a humanizing force, it has shown itself to be impotent against much more powerful forces of economics, technology, and history.

Wordsworth certainly believed that civilization was, in Pound's terms, a "botch," the main source of evil, brutality, and corruption of the human spirit. And he also believed poetry could do something about it:

> a multitude of causes, unknown to former times, are now acting with a combined force to blunt the discriminating powers of the mind, and, unfitting it for all voluntary exertion, to reduce it to a state of almost savage torpor. The most effective of these causes are the great national events which are daily taking place, and the increasing accumulation of men in cities, where the uniformity of their occupations produces a craving for extraordinary incident which the rapid communication of intelligence hourly gratifies . . . ; reflecting upon the magnitude of the general evil, I should be oppressed with no dishonourable melancholy, had I not a deep impression of certain inherent and indestructible qualities of the human mind, and likewise of certain powers in the great and permanent objects that act upon it, which are equally inherent and indestructible. . . .

These "great and permanent objects that act upon" the mind are, of course, the objects of Nature, and the "inherent and indestructible qualities of the human mind" are essentially two: memory and imagination. Most poetry since Wordsworth has dramatized possible interactions of the world with these qualities of the mind, and our current expectation in reading a poem is that in some way they will come into play. But for Wordsworth the interaction of memory and imagination with Nature has behind it a coherent moral force, a very definite idea of the poet's social function: namely, if people are reeducated according to Nature and the "inherent and indestructible qualities of the human mind," society will get itself back on the right path. The idea comes from Rousseau, whom Wordsworth read while living in France in the early 1790s, and it's this idea, not some disembodied aesthetic, that made Wordsworth think poems should be "a man speaking to men . . . in language really used by men."

In the same essay in which Wordsworth asserts that "the Poet binds together . . . the vast empire of human society," having imagined the grandest audience out of the thinnest air, he admits that, in fact, the poet's "own feelings are his stay and support." The whole drama of the poet's relationship to his audience becomes internalized in the theater of the poet's own mind, what Keats charitably called "the wordsworthian or egotistical sublime." Yet, in that theater, Wordsworth, no less than Sidney, wrote for an audience, and would not have conceded that his ideas contain the seeds of the *poète maudit,* the poet's final isolation from society, and the movement of art for art's sake that influenced the young Yeats. "What is the Character of the Poet?" is the question most frequently and urgently asked in Romantic poetics, because, in fact, what sort of person could possibly bind "together by passion and knowledge the vast empire of human society" against "the magnitude of general evil" and the destructive forces of civilization and still be his own "stay and support"? No wonder Shelley fell upon the thorns of life and bled.

As Auden says, for the Romantics, "To become a great poet was to become not only superior to other poets but superior to all other men." This pathetic self-delusion, one of our less happy inheritances from the Romantics, probably found its purest avatar in Pound. The elevation of art and the artist ("the unacknowledged legislators of the world") is only a compensation for his diminished social role, the other side of the coin to Rocky's "What do you want me to do? Stay at home all day and write *poems?*" In the absence of a living, breathing audience, in the presence of a grandiose, imagined one, the poet's self-aggrandizement is a natural trap. Romantic Ego and Romantic Agony are born of the same germ. The Great Man laboring mightily in solitude to produce Masterworks, the Genius with infinite energy and unstoppable will, as well as the self-destructive, drunk, deranged young poet, are mythic figures of our culture, to which too many poets have sacrificed themselves and their lives and everyone they loved. That poets are mythic figures may also explain the inevitably greater interest in their biographies after they are dead than in their poetry while they are alive. In 1765, Johnson said confidently that "all claim to poetical honours" must be decided by "the common sense of readers"; less than twenty years later, in 1784, Jeremy Bentham, who was known for his common sense, declared that in terms of social utility "pushpin is as good as poetry." When these two remarks are presented as the major and minor premise, Wordsworth's statement in 1800 that the poet's "own feelings are his stay and support" is the inevitable conclusion of the syllogism.

Walt Whitman read the Romantics carefully, no doubt including the preface to *Lyrical Ballads*. It's by now old news that this most insistently unliterary of poets put in many library hours of literary study, especially in the early 1850s, in preparation for his great, self-appointed task. The task was exactly what Wordsworth had named as the poet's function, only "the vast empire" Whitman hoped to bind together by his passion and knowledge was the vast empire of "these United States." Through *Leaves of Grass,* Whitman intended literally to "inaugurate a religion" in which the poet would be the new priest directing not only the cultural life but also, through his spiritual guidance, the political and social affairs of the young burgeoning nation. In the 1855 preface to *Leaves of Grass,* he wrote:

Of all nations the United States with veins full of poetical stuff most needs poets and will doubtless have the greatest and use them the greatest. Their Presidents shall not be their common referee so much as their poets shall.

And:

There will soon be no more priests. Their work is done. They may wait awhile . . . perhaps a generation or two . . . dropping off by degrees. A superior breed shall take their place . . . the gangs of kosmos and prophets en masse shall take their place. A new order shall arise and they shall be the priests of man, and every man shall be his own priest.

And:

The greatest poet hardly knows pettiness or triviality. If he breathes into any thing that was before thought small it dilates with the grandeur and life of the universe. He is a seer . . . he is individual . . . he is complete in himself . . . the others are as good as he, only he sees it and they do not.

Despite his superior eyesight, Whitman's poet is not superior to his fellow citizens. He "sees health for himself in being one of the mass." Though Whitman's great audience of initiates must also be imagined at first, he most certainly intends for it to become real and present. It is a nation, not an abstraction. He could and did go out and mingle in it, even if it wasn't aware of him. Though he knew from the start that the task would be difficult, he never intended that his "own feelings" would have to be "his stay and support." The last sentence of the 1855 preface is: "The proof of the poet is that his Country absorbs him as affectionately as he has absorbed it."

This was his ambition and his hope, and, despite such grandeur, the poet would retain his citizenship, like Sidney's moral instructor or the Greek craftsman-poet. In one bold stroke—there has never been one bolder in the history of literature—Whitman attempted to swoop up all past figures of the poet and carry them into the limitless future on the waves of his great rolling lines. Those figures would become just part of the multitude contained in the poem's enormous "I." It may have been his research into the origins of poetry that led Whitman to print the first edition of *Leaves of Grass* anonymously, with only an unidentified picture on the frontispiece of himself with an open collar, an outdoors man, virile and healthy, the ideal democrat, a "rough" who takes off his hat to no one and looks everybody square in the eye. This was the new poet, the midcentury American version of the shaman-priest, and the poem's continuous present represented a return to the mythic past, *in illo tempore,* a spiritualization of the daily world, an "ultimate vivification to facts, to science, and to common lives" without which "life itself" is "finally in vain."

The daily world of the 1850s was all expansion and possibility, very much like *Leaves of Grass* itself. The spirit of Manifest Destiny was in the air, and it suffused both the content and style of the popular orator's silver-tongued magniloquence. Boorstin says:

> Orations were a form of entertainment. In new towns . . . the spellbinding stump orator was a Nineteenth Century version of the bard, troubadour, or minnesinger. . . . On a historic occasion . . . sharing the orator's words was itself an act of community. Municipal authorities . . . would designate their official orator for each occasion. . . .

By absorbing the orator's spirit, *Leaves of Grass* might also absorb the orator's social role. After the Indians were pushed out, and sometimes before, towns further and further west sprang up out of nothing with amazing rapidity. The first building or tent to go up often housed a printing press that would announce the existence of a booming town and the golden opportunities to be found. The idea of the limitless future transformed the present in every aspect of American life, at least among white men. Mexico had been invaded for one reason only, and almost no one pretended otherwise: with all this land from Maine to California, and the wealth it represented, everyone wanted more. Whitman cheered the Mexican War. The town for which he was the booster, for which he mixed "visions and prophecies with current and negotiable realities," was a nation that he envisaged occupying the whole North American continent, plus Cuba, from the North Pole to the equator.

But Whitman's first political concern was not the expansion of the states but their union. The threat of "the Secession War," as he always called it, tinged the atmosphere; in the 1850s it was already a war of words, and represented the only significant threat to this potentially great nation of his. The "United States," in common usage, was a plural noun. Entirely unlike now, each state was independent and part of the federal union by virtue of consent as much as law; virtually no one, including Abraham Lincoln, questioned states' sovereignty and right to govern. In this context, the idea of Whitman's poem, and even what he believed it could accomplish in terms of actual political effects, seems almost plausible:

> I listened to the Phantom by Ontario's shore,
> I heard the voice arising demanding bards,

> By them all native and grand, by them alone can these States be
> fused into the compact organism of a Nation.
>
> ("By Blue Ontario's Shore")

Whitman certainly knew he had no audience. He wasn't just the author of his poem, he was its publisher and, in part, its printer. But exactly as a booster paper could create a town, a poem might create an audience, even a whole nation:

> a few first-class poets, philosophers and authors, have substantially settled and given status to the entire religion, education, law, sociology, etc. of the hitherto civilized world, by tingeing and often *creating* the atmosphere out of which they have arisen. . . . [my italics]

This is an idea he probably first discovered in Emerson, who told an audience at Harvard in 1833: "We have listened too long to the courtly muses of Europe . . . if the single man plant himself indomitably on his instincts, and there abide, the huge world will come round to him. . . . A nation of men will for the first time exist. . . ." Being a democrat, not a great but "feudal" poet like Shakespeare or Milton (such was Whitman's characterization of them), Whitman sought his audience by trying to derive "that average quality of the American bulk, the people, and getting back to it again." This meant that "the idea of beauty" would "need to be radically changed." The poet's subject would again be the tribe, "the best thoughts" of "mechanics" and "farmers" that "wait unspoken, impatient to be put in shape." "Every day," he wrote to Emerson in 1856, "I go among the people of Manhattan Island, Brooklyn, and other cities, and among the young men, to discover the spirit of them, and to refresh myself."

Whitman's taste for fraternizing with wagon drivers, steamboat captains, and soldiers may have preceded any use he might make of it, but there's no doubt that the great ruddy spirit, good cheer, friendliness, and what he called "amativeness" and "animal magnetism" were also part of his self-creation. Despite the purposefully scanty evidence Whitman left us, Paul Zweig's *Walt Whitman: The Making of the Poet* wonderfully tells the story of the willed transformation of Walter Whitman Jr., reporter and poetaster, into Walt Whitman, kosmos and prophet en masse, and of the poignant disparity between the grand vision and lonely life. *Leaves of Grass* was intended to create not only an audience and a nation but also its author. It was a Bible and an alchemical book. Whitman literally gave his life to it or, more accurately, to the idea it represented, and the whole enterprise, even with an intervening century of anything but reasons for optimism, still touches us. Whitman's absolute passion lives in the poem, in moments of beautifully rendered detail and of brilliant lightning movements between lines and stanzas, and still makes *Leaves of Grass*—despite its braggadocio, bad judgment, repetitiousness, and failed intention—an exhilarating, heartbreaking experience each time through.

> I depart as air . . . I shake my white locks at the runaway sun,
> I effuse my flesh in eddies and drift it in lacy jags.
>
> I bequeath myself to the dirt to grow from the grass I love,
> If you want me again look for me under your bootsoles.

As Whitman grew older, he more often characterized the force of his poem as a religious force. In the preface to the 1872 edition, shortly before the massive attack of paralysis that would make him an invalid, he wrote:

> As there can be, in my opinion, no sane and complete personality, nor any grand and elastic nationality, without the stock element of religion imbuing all the other elements, (like heat in chemistry, invisible itself, but the life of all visible life,) so there can be no poetry worthy the name without that element behind all.

Putting aside sanity and "nationality," and thinking only of what spirit is needed to fuel a lifetime of poetry, it's a statement for poets even now to dismiss at their hazard or, at least, at a hazard to their work.

Whitman's legacy is what John Updike calls "a totem-image . . . a kind of Excalibur that none but the pure of heart can seize and wield." Besides the religious passion that required a complete commitment to the great and grand (God or Democracy or, as Updike calls it, "Egotheism"), Whitman's poetry is made of and by no ordinary, everyday person—in Yeats's words, one who is "never the bundle of accidence and incoherence that sits down to breakfast; he has been reborn as an idea, something intended, complete." Although his poetry's texture and material was daily life, his focusing lens was the result of a self-transformation that couldn't be faked and would now be grandiose, anachronistic, misconceived, and willfully blind; in any case, we already know, thanks to Whitman, what waits at the end of this path. As a stylistic influence for poets writing in English, Whitman has been deadly. As a moral influence, the lessons of his miserable life, impenetrable personality, and sheer uniqueness loom powerfully. All the ersatz Whitmans that have come since—Vachel Lindsay, for instance—seem pathetic, and the many poets who have used and continued to use his rhetoric for the sake of producing what sounds like poetry have missed the point entirely:

it is not on "Leaves of Grass" distinctively as *literature,* or a specimen thereof, that I feel to dwell, or advance claims. No one will get at my verses who insists upon viewing them as a literary performance, or attempt at such performance, or as aiming merely toward art and aestheticism.

Without an absolute belief in Whitman's social program—which is certainly impossible now for anyone remotely sane—the style is an empty shell.

The most popular poet in England during Whitman's day was not Tennyson, even given the relatively large audience for a serious poet that he had, but John Keble, whose religious verses, *The Christian Year,* had sold 379,000 copies by 1873. It's Keble's audience, not Tennyson's (or Longfellow's)—or not only Tennyson's and Longfellow's—that Whitman was after, though his ambition obviously did not include the agreeable expression of conventional pieties, but of sentiments that Emily Dickinson, apparently never to read *Leaves of Grass* herself, reported that she heard were "shocking," in a manner that the young Henry James, reviewing *Drum-Taps,* said was "an offence against art."

This manner and style Whitman decided on in advance. For all his belief in the ineffable, the wordless, and the wisdom of the body, it's remarkable how conscious a designer he was. The few poems in the final edition of *Leaves of Grass* in rhyme and meter—including the anthology chestnut "Captain! My Captain!"—show how smart he was to adopt the long cadenced lines of the King James Bible as his prosody. There is no more extreme example of a preconceived idea of the audience and social function of a poem determining its whole character and, despite his famous pleasure in contradicting himself, this idea is consistent from the beginning (and before the beginning) to the end. In his earlier notebooks, he wrote these "Rules for Composition":

> A perfectly transparent, plate-glassy style, artless, with no ornaments, or attempt at ornaments. . . .
> Take no illustrations whatever from any ancients or classics. . . . Make no mention or allusion to them whatever except as they relate to the new present things. . . .
> Clearness, simplicity, no twistified or foggy sentences, at all—the most translucid clearness without variation.
> Common idioms and phrases—Yankeeisms and vulgarism—cant expressions when very pat only.

Such consistency over a lifetime is usually the result of will, and a willful resistance to change, and this, I think, brings out the shadow of Whitman's bright spirit in the same way his "grand and elastic nationality" looks less sweetly naive when one remembers the genocide of the

Indians he was willing to accept in payment for it. His relentless maintenance of his persona, even—I should say, especially—among his intimates and devotees was not accomplished without loss either to himself or to his poetry. In "A Backward Glance O'er Travell'd Roads," the afterword to the so-called Deathbed Edition of 1888, Whitman says in valediction: "the best comfort of the whole business (after a small band of the dearest friends and upholders . . . [)] is that . . . I have had my say entirely my own way. . . ." Small comfort that was, especially against the backdrop of his grand, great-spirited ambitions.

Whitman never reprinted the original 1855 preface but finally included in his *Collected Prose* what Justin Kaplan calls "a bobtailed and emasculated version"—another instance of Whitman's careful, useless attention to his image. Juxtaposing that original version against "A Backward Glance O'er Travell'd Roads" poignantly illustrates the vain hope of returning the poet to his central position in the tribe. At the beginning, Whitman set the criterion of his success, "that his country absorbs him as affectionately as he has absorbed it." At the end, he admits "That I have not gain'd the acceptance of my own time, but have fallen back on fond dreams of the future."

The future was always a crucial ingredient in Whitman's vision, as it is in all apocalyptic visions, but finally the themes he had reiterated thousands of times in his poetry, essays, letters, and conversations are stated with unusual quietness. In his "fond dreams of the future" he still, at least publicly, believed that there might "arise a race of poets, varied, yet one in soul—not only poets, and of the best, but newer, larger prophets—larger than Judea's, and more passionate—to melt and penetrate these woes, as shafts of light the darkness." But as far as *Leaves of Grass* was concerned, he had to concede his vision had been a chimera. He wrote in an anonymous review of himself that his poems "have fallen stillborn in this country. They have been met, and are met today, with the determined denial, disgust, and scorn of orthodox American authors, publishers, and editors, and in a pecuniary and worldly sense, have certainly wrecked the life of their author." Walt Whitman, the cheerful, white-bearded "good grey poet" Walter Whitman Jr. created to write *Leaves of Grass*, would never have published this under his own signature, but it gives us a heartbreakingly vivid picture of the person who had to live the good grey poet's life.

Asked for his opinion of Whitman's poetry, Wallace Stevens wrote, "It seems to me . . . that Whitman is disintegrating as the world, of which he made himself a part, disintegrates." On another occasion, he equated Whitman with a poetaster, Joachim Miller, and called him a "poseur." These remarks say more about Stevens than they do about Whitman, but none of the modernist poets—with the exception of Williams and Pound, who compared Whitman to a "pig-headed father"—had much interest in Whitman's poetry, his enterprise, or its failure. After World War I, the world seemed to be "disintegrating." "Poets in our civilization, as it exists at present, must be difficult," Eliot wrote, a sentence that Philip Larkin angrily said "gave the modernist poetry movement its charter." Just as Whitman's biblical cadences and "perfectly transparent, plate-glassy style" were designed to reach as many people as possible, Eliot's "difficult" style of juxtaposition, allusion, and disjointed syntax was meant to address, as he said, "the one perfectly intelligent reader who does not exist."

Ironically, of course, Eliot had many more readers in his lifetime than Whitman had in his, but if Whitman's idea of his audience predetermined his idea of his poetic style, Eliot's ideas were probably acquired concurrently. At the Harvard University that Eliot and Stevens attended, LaForgue's dandyism and the affectations of the *poète maudit* were de rigueur for the campus literati. It was the given that poetry was a "superior entertainment" for superior men. And the larger world for Eliot, as for the Symbolistes, was a "brutal mirage." This is the world that appears in *The Waste Land,* the poem that for Pound was "the culmination of our movement." Eliot's earlier poetic strategies and ideas about poetry are defensive—defensive of the poet's high cultural importance in the world that actually ignores him—and though he borrowed heavily from many different sources, the tenor of his ideas comes straight out of Romantic poetics, the Shelley he despised as well as the Coleridge he admired.

Obviously, the literary atmosphere has changed greatly since *The Sacred Wood* and *The Waste Land* and the halcyon days of Scofield Thayer's *The Dial,* but the fundamental situation of poetry has not. In the United States, the difference between the sales of five thousand copies of a volume of poems, which is almost unheard of, is the difference between minute fractions of 1 percent of the population. Every poet alive has felt the consequences of this fact in many forms, the most basic being that, unlike painters or novelists, a poet can never even hope to live from what he produces and therefore must continually do other things to buy time to write. TV and movies "teach" and "delight" the citizenry, not poetry. Whether or not Sidney would have recognized what they teach as "virtue," they most definitely do teach the values of the culture, the values of corporate capitalism.

Poets "teach," too, but in the classroom. "Academic poetry," after World War II, was initially a descriptive, not a pejorative, term. Modest as it may seem, classroom teaching—not his poetry—is currently the poet's main social utility. As for Dryden and Pope, the poet's social usefulness is the source of his livelihood, and the source of his livelihood has at least that much power to enforce aesthetic values. The genteel tradition that has forever confused the beautiful and the agreeable took root in American universities at their inception and has flourished there ever since in conservative political atmospheres. Further, as Larkin said, "the emergence of English literature as an academic subject" has led to a "consequent demand for a kind of poetry that needed elucidation." These two influences by themselves are enough to create the pressure for a poetic style that values ingenuity over profundity, nicety of expression over passion, restraint over candor, and complication—even opacity—over simplicity. Whatever else might be said about their poetry, this explains the academic approval of John Ashbery and James Merrill, and the styles of a number of younger poets who naturally, and probably unconsciously, gravitate toward the source of their livelihood.

But the university is an employer of teachers, not a patron of artists. The poet's dependence on the university is more complex and various and, as an economic source, the university is infinitesimal compared either to the relative wealth and power of the Church in Bellini's Venice or to the total economic resources available in the United States. A poet can survive on the fringes of the academy and outside of it if he has a marketable skill. Paradoxically, by virtue of the material worthlessness of his product, the poet may have a unique chance to become a free agent with a free imagination. He doesn't have to tack on happy endings or direct his message to urban dwellers between the ages of thirty-four and thirty-nine who make over $50,000 a year. Sensing how important this is in a putative democracy, this may be why foundations, endowments, and some college presidents do not want the poet starved into extinction, though the poets they choose to support are not likely to be the ones who challenge the ideological premises by which they themselves exist. A result of the poet's freedom is a dizzying proliferation of styles and almost no commonality of taste, which unhappily makes critical judgment seem arbitrary, reputations disproportionate, and awards meaningless. According to an ancient anecdote retold by Pliny, Polykleitos won an important sculpture contest in Athens because in the voting all the other sculptors picked him second, after themselves. By contrast, ten randomly chosen American poets picking their ten most esteemed contemporaries would probably result in a list of nearly a hundred names. Poets cluster around writing programs and magazines, all with circulations of fifteen thousand or less, usually much less, and, as a consequence, contemporary poetry is glutted by the "coterie writing" that Yeats warned against. The danger of writing for a small group is, of course, tunnel vision, mistaking the "accidental and temporary" for the essential and permanent. For Wordsworth, "pleasure" was "the grand elementary principle." And for Coleridge, the "origin and object" of poetry is "pleasurable excitement": "pleasure is the magic circle out of which the poet dare not tread." But without an audience at large, and with, at best, a specialized audience of academics and other poets who agree on almost nothing, how is a poet to judge what constitutes "pleasure," much less what is essential and permanent?

Poets themselves are often blamed for this situation, but it's only a reflection of the much-documented fragmentation of the culture as a whole. As Whitman demonstrated once and for all, the role of the poet in his culture is far beyond his individual desire and control. Even if by a miraculous conjunction of the stars, a real poet were to sell a million copies of his or her books, a TV show with only a million viewers is off the air the next day. And there are many television shows: in the average home, with cable, fifty-eight hours of them each week.

Simonides of Ceos, said to be the inventor of the mnemonic art, is also said to be the first poet to receive payment for his work. Enduring qualities of narrative and style—the memorable story, palpable detail, and powerful rhythm—made poetry the preserver of crucial information and cultural wisdom and thereby socially important and economically valuable. But from the beginning, memory had another aspect as well. As Gilbert Murray says, memory was " 'the waker of longing,' the enchantress who turns the common to the heavenly and fills men's eyes with tears because the things that are now past were so beautiful." Mnemosyne, the goddess of Memory, was the mother of the Muses, but she was also the daughter of Uranus and Gaea, Heaven and Earth, a Titan, one of the oldest order, born before the reign of the gods of Olympus. In this aspect, memory seems no less a part of poetry today than it was in ancient Greece, and the enduring qualities that made poetry memorable and "the waker of longing" are no less effective now. For Milton, these qualities were three: that poems should be "simple, sensuous, and passionate." In the same lecture in which he talks about the "magic circle of pleasure," Coleridge approves Milton's three qualities as a definition of poetry and adds: "Had these three words only been properly understood by, and present in the minds of, general readers . . . a library of false poetry would have been precluded or still-born."

It is a truism that at each moment of history the world has never existed in quite that way before. Sidney, Wordsworth, Whitman, and Pound, in their poems and essays, all felt their worlds to be a special case. But, even with this caveat, it seems that 1987 in the United States marks a unique historical moment. Besides the capacity for nuclear annihilation and the destruction of the natural world that continues almost invisibly through various forms of chemical pollution, we are now at the beginning of a time when language is neither the only nor always the most efficient means of communication and preservation of information, ideas, and feelings. "Speech alone has rendered man human," said Herder in the eighteenth century, and language certainly made the inheritance of tradition and the evolution and spreading of cultures possible. The invention of movable type expanded and accelerated information storage so that human memory began to exist, in a sense, outside the body. This process is now being accelerated again at the speed of light. No one knows what the long-term effects of this technology will be, any more than they knew that unchecked burning of fossil fuel would eventually destroy the ozone layer and make the earth a desert. It may even make us all into nicer people with our user-friendly machines. But, in any case, in this historical moment poetry seems both more anachronistic and more important as a custodian of time, a preserver of bodily memory in its rudimentary sense, the one million years of humanity and four billion years of life of the earth.

From this perspective, it's possible to see poetry as not just the product of individuals writing individual poems about individual experience. Heinrich Zimmer, in *The King and the Corpse,* says of the Indian storytellers: "Each poet adds something of the substance of his own imagination, and the seeds are nourished back to life." Against our culturally acquired way of looking at the world, it may be helpful to poets now to see their work also as a collective enterprise. The alternative was put succinctly by Wordsworth: "every author, as far as he is great and at the same time original, has had the task of creating the taste by which he is to be enjoyed." *Great, original, creating the taste:* these terms belong not only to our literary assumptions but also to a capitalist mythology of individual survival and dominance, as if we were not totally bound up with one another and all life on earth. It's the same mythology that makes the idea of writing poetry an absurdity to Rocky and to a culture that measures the quality of life in money and ego-rewards. It seems that there have been enough examples to show that these assumptions are self-defeating for a poet and that, given his lack of audience and social role, they breed humiliation, grandiosity, isolation, and bitterness. They have no necessary connection to poetry. They present the shortest view, of a set of Western countries, of a small percentage of the world's population, during a brief period of history. "It's what the tribe feels that is sacred." Our culture's elevation of individualism in all its forms does not by any means represent an absolute truth, psychological or moral.

Despite the possible uniqueness of our historical moment, biology still seems a stronger force than history. We are more like our ancestors, and like one another, than we are different. As Loren Eiseley put it in *The Immense Journey:*

> Unwittingly, man has assigned to his machines the selective evolution which in the animal changes the nature of its bodily structure through the ages. Man of today, the atomic manipulator, the aeronaut who flies faster than sound, has precisely the same brain and body as his ancestors 20,000 years ago who painted the last Ice Age mammoths on the walls of caves in France.

Wonderful poetry has been written out of the need to survive in isolation—Emily Dickinson's poetry, Hopkins's Terrible Sonnets, Stevens's late poetry written "not for an audience" but as "one of the sanctions of life"—but for all its intensity this poetry cannot communicate "the bloom of shared pleasure" that comes from collective emotions fundamental to human experience and therefore to art. "The bloom of shared pleasure" is Eudora Welty's phrase. She uses it to describe Jane Austen's novels, which Austen was not initially able to publish, but read, chapter by chapter, to her family. This is what an audience can do—it can make the writer feel the human community outside himself or herself that shares his or her love of what Stanley Kunitz calls "the sacred fire," a feeling that can change the character of the writing itself. There need be no dominance involved in this relationship, and it can provide an emotional support that between two people would be called love. As Gilbert Murray says, this spirit and this impulse—even when writing about the most internal, personal subjects—has existed since the beginning:

> Love, Strife, Death, and that which is beyond Death. Those are, it would seem, definitely the four themes about which our earliest bards sang, and, when singing was not enough to express all their stress of emotion, yearned and reached out their arms amid the dancers.

PART THREE *Manifest Apparitions*

The reflector of the inner eye
scatters the spectacle. . . .

The apparitions are manifest,
their bodies weigh less than light,
lasting as long as this phrase lasts.

—Elizabeth Bishop,
"Objects and Apparitions" (*For Joseph Cornell*)
Translated from the Spanish of Octavio Paz

REGINALD GIBBONS

Poetry and Self-Making

I

Anyone who has studied a book by Curtis Bradford called *Yeats at Work* knows that Yeats could begin with a very unlikely draft of what would eventually be a great poem. In his late work there's an untitled quatrain, a kind of fragment:

> The friends that have it I do wrong
> When ever I remake a song,
> Should know what issue is at stake:
> It is myself that I remake.

Does this little poem mean that *because* the poet revises his composition he inevitably changes his idea, his consciousness, of himself, also? Is this change, this reconstructing of the poet's identity, a kind of side effect of writing poems? Or could such reconstruction be the very purpose, even one of the supreme purposes, for Yeats, of writing and revising poems? Is this a narrower, writerly version of what Keats called Soul-making? A recognition of the way we continue to evolve through stages of life, as Erik Erikson theorized? Whatever the reality of life-changes for most people, I am convinced that Yeats expresses here a fundamental truth of the *writing* life—that a writer's being can be shaped by the way that he or she decisively uses language.

Ten years ago I instinctively set this quatrain beside a fragment by Osip Mandelstam that had been translated and sent to me in a letter by a poet friend, Kenneth Irby:

> How the feminine silver burns
> That's struggled against oxide and alloy,
> And quiet work silvers
> The iron plough and the poet's voice.

Mandelstam's silver is "feminine." I think he must have thought of this as meaning that, not acting on other things, silver is acted upon, by a tarnishing; but he saw also that it burns back against that dulling. In Mandelstam's poems, as he himself said of Dante's *Divine*

TriQuarterly 75 (Spring/Summer 1989): 98–118.

Comedy, one metaphor often launches the next. Here the substance—the noun, *silver*—changes to an action, a verb: "quiet work *silvers.* . . ." So the plough is pictured not as tearing through the earth (which would be "masculine") but as being polished to a bright shining (thus "feminine"). It is silvered by the softly abrasive, hissing sod through which it moves.

And then the last touch, which reveals what it was that sparked the metaphorical transformations, what difficult insistent notion it was that called for articulation: thus is the poet's voice like a thing polished, even silvered, as if changed from everyday iron to precious metal, by the softly abrasive work of writing, by the sod of language that goes by it and through which it moves, or is even dragged. Not farming, but the making of the poems is the poet's work, but like the realm of planting and harvesting to which the image of the plough sends us, the realm of poems is, by association, fruitful. Again, as in Yeats's quatrain, two related things are joined: (1) the poet's voice, which in the fullest sense is the poet's identity, and in another sense is metonymy for the made objects themselves, the poems that the poet harvests from his labor, and (2) the activity of writing.

Writing is a process in which we are engaged over time; how does our writing not only change all my available words into this particular poem, but also change me in the writing of the poem? I want to use these two little poems and some others to help reveal the relationship between what it is a poet, or more generally a writer, does, in writing and rewriting a piece of work, and who that poet or writer is and *is becoming.*

II

A poem's *worked* quality may show greater or lesser evidence of the poet's impulse to control language and form; the interesting thing is not whether this evidence is superficially greater *or* lesser—as between a poem written in a traditional verse form or one in free verse. The interesting thing is whether the poem gives evidence of having anything underneath it or inside it or behind it (all of these are metaphors) that would *require* artistic control in order to be articulated in the particularly intense way that (good) poems articulate feeling and thought. That is, a poem's *complexity* as an instance of language doesn't in itself reveal very much; a very poor poem can be full of tropes and highly organized rhythms and other complications or turbulences of language, and a very good poem can appear to be spontaneously uttered and almost simple.

But in many poems that we regard as good there is a sense, rather than of already *worked* language, of the *active* work of bringing feeling, thought, and language into an unusual intensity of meaningfulness and into an especially responsive representation of what we are coming to feel and think; both writer and reader are discovering what it is that the language in the poetic lines is coming to mean. That is, part of a memorable poem's power often lies in its conveying this work as if it were still going on, actively, in the poem as it comes into being once more in the reader's mind—or, often better, in the sound of its recitation in the present moment. This may be some of what Antonio Machado meant when he defined poetry as "the essential word in time." When we sense such an active working of the language in a poem, we may prize it more, it may be more precious to us, partly because it welcomes us as readers into that working, it gives us the chance to silver *our* voices as well. Let me give one example that I think is particularly pleasing and impressive, the opening sentence—the opening four lines—of C. K. Williams's poem, "My Mother's Lips":

Until I asked her to please stop doing it and was astonished to find that
    she not only could
but from the moment I asked her in fact would stop doing it, my
    mother, all through my childhood,
when I was saying something to her, something important, would
    move her lips as I was speaking
so that she seemed to be saying under her breath the very words I was
    saying as I was saying them.

The syntactical complexity of the sentence is like a riddle—it first makes apprehensible the complexity of the surprising moment Williams is portraying, and then, his mother's bizarre habit. The reverse order of these two things heightens our sense of what Williams's *present* understanding appears to be in the process of discovering. A larger version of this drama of becoming conscious of a new idea or feeling is played out most effectively in "Combat," which is also from Williams's book *Tar*. What the writing of the poem seems to represent, in part, is the hunt for a meaning that can only be discovered if the syntax can appropriately represent an evolving self-understanding.

This is not to say that all poets should place psychology at the center of their work or that they should imitate Williams's *style*—that's another question. What we may miss in a lot of poems, however, is the sense that what is going on in the poem is the poet's endeavor to understand, rather than merely to refer to or represent, his or her own psyche, or that of someone else; to identify what he or she understands; to discover and articulate what feeling it is that prepared for, or rises out of, that understanding; and finally, and perhaps most important to our excitement as readers, to create his or her identity out of that understanding. (Perhaps in lesser poems all this is missing because nothing of sufficient importance is informing that artistic illusion of the present struggle to articulate. The poem is striving to master and control nothing of sufficiently *un*controllable power to challenge either the writer or, subsequently, the reader.)

Now, if when I write I am struggling both to open myself to perception and feeling *and* to master my language, to free *and* to shape my thoughts and feelings in language, then I am writing *partly* in order to control or influence or determine in some way my own being, my *being-in-language,* by making visible and objective my own sense of language, by achieving a certain kind of victory—maybe it's just a little one—the evidence or result of which is a composed text.

From this it follows that, in writing, I am pursuing something not yet controlled or even controllable about my being and my being-in-language that I feel I must discover—if not fully, then at least as well as I'm able. But of course daily life careens this way and that because of events, persons, and forces that we *cannot* control. Out of this familiar unpredictability of life there come riddles of being and, more important to me as a writer, of being-in-language, that I want to unriddle. One of the oldest poetic genres is the riddle, and many great poems strive to *unriddle*—not *explain*—one mystery or many. (Explaining would only be a kind of neutralizing of the mystery, even a way of repressing it once more with bland assurances; but by unriddling I mean creating for the reader of a poem an active process of reading that answers or completes the active discoveries of writing.)

III

A sense of active discovering does not depend on syntax alone. Here is a riddle by Charles Causley, published in 1957 in his collection *Union Street:*

I AM THE GREAT SUN
(FROM A NORMAN CRUCIFIX OF 1632)

I am the great sun, but you do not see me,
    I am your husband, but you turn away.
I am the captive, but you do not free me,
    I am the captain you will not obey.

I am the truth, but you will not believe me,
    I am the city where you will not stay,
I am your wife, your child, but you will leave me,
    I am that God to whom you will not pray.

I am your counsel, but you do not hear me,
    I am the lover whom you will betray,
I am the victor, but you do not cheer me,
    I am the holy dove whom you will slay.

I am your life, but if you will not name me,
Seal up your soul with tears, and never blame me.

The poem leads us into a surprising recognition *in ourselves* of the figures of captive, child, lover, and holy dove, all of whom we would abandon or betray; and in our own historical context—that is, in Causley's as opposed to the context of 1632—we are also led into surprise when we find we have turned our distrust of power and domination against ourselves, for we ourselves are also the very captain, God, counsel, and victor from whom we shrink. The poem of 1632, if that's what it is, is very modern in showing me that I am divided against myself. Here the active poetic working of language is not in the complexity of the syntax, as in Williams, but in the formal parallelisms that organize the riddles so that they pile up on us faster than we can answer them. Because this is a poem, rather than another kind of organized language, both the sense of the words and also the formal organization of the poem create the poem's meaning, for it is the formal organization that reveals that the apparent uniqueness of each riddling line leads in all cases to one and the same answer. And in fact after we have assimilated the whole poem we see that the repeated beginning of each line, "I am," is at one and the same time the beginning of each riddle and the answer to it.

Despite its elegance and extraordinary formal symmetries, the poem is clearly meant not to provide a satisfying answer but rather to lead us through repetitions as if they were a ritual, and to lead our intuition through a satisfying variety of ways of putting the riddle. Poetry brings ritual into our presence because its highly deliberate organization of language, even in less traditionally shaped poems than this, returns us to the language of song, prayer, chant, and all other utterances in which repetition itself becomes a summoning and a fulfillment of feeling. Ritual is inherited, and may lose all connection with feeling or with the psychological reality that, in its oblique, riddling way, it so often represents or influences; yet it remains a scene in which the word and deed and word-as-deed are firmly ordered in time, and thus, like poetry, it can bring into us language that subtly alters our own language, and thus alters us. It can be used for good or ill. In Causley's poem, it seems to me, it is used for good.

Riddles, puns, paradoxes, and neologisms are most at home in poetry, of all the kinds of both oral and written texts, and nowhere are they more intensely concentrated than in the work of Paul Celan. Even in one of his tiniest poems we see another variety of the restless working of language I'm trying to point out—not only in the compound German word *vorgesichten,* for which there are many meanings, but also in how the poem is built on the way Celan, ordering the words strictly, draws a paradox out of a thing for throwing—the discus—which cannot throw itself:

WURFSCHEIBE, mit	DISCUS, with
Vorgesichten besternt,	Foreseeings starred,
wirf dich	throw yourself
aus dir hinaus.	out of yourself.

Figuring out what that word *vorgesichten* is doing is one riddle of the poem. *Vorgesichten* could mean "foretellings," "premonitions," perhaps a kind of clairvoyance: we know or see more than we can act upon. Is this the answer to the riddle: that each of us is the discus that has no one to throw it, no matter what hopes or predictions or expectations we may have of our lives? Does the poem suggest that we are inert things, and that it's impossible for us to make ourselves into more than inert things? In this little arena that Celan constructed for our thought, he seems to lead us toward a helpless inertia of self that is the opposite of Yeats's willed self-making. Yet at the same time, the intense concentration of language makes the reading of the poem an active process of discovery that gives at least the illusion of a movement in our thought. And if our thought can move, can't we move our lives, also? Which is the final riddle.

IV

It should be clear from the variety of these examples, so far, that no particular poetics will provide a mastery of language and poetic form; shall we pursue the question of writerly self-knowledge in this light? One way into this question is through some of the familiar maxims of writers.

Take the hoary advice "Write about what you know." It only trivializes a deep truth about all artistic expression, which is this: although any subject totally foreign to the writer isn't part of his or her daily struggle to be and therefore isn't likely to be a rich ground on which to play out the struggle to write, nonetheless no voyage into the known is worth making if there is not some unknown toward which we are sailing. In fact, you can't launch a boat, anyway, without a body of water on which to float it. If we are writers, our noticings and self-discoveries are the ground on which we work with language, and language is the ground on which we make our way not only toward discoveries of self but also toward perceptions of what is around us—what is *said to be* around us, and what is "really" there. (I don't mean that a writer must be one whose aural rather than visual perceptions are paramount. After all, Joseph Conrad wrote that the writer's task is to pay the highest possible homage to the *visible* world. But that homage is paid not in color and line but in words.)

It has seemed to many writers—I think of remarks by Robert Frost and E. M. Forster—that writing delivers us into discoveries of what, till we had formed some way to articulate it in language, had remained unformed, had been *unknown* to us, and that it must do this if it is to be at all interesting to anyone—even the writer! The articulation becomes the knowing; the knowing comes out of the process, and it refuels a further effort at articulation. A sense of ecstatic fruitfulness, of rich discoveries, of voyaging, comes to us in the exhilarating moments of being-in-our-work-in-progress. From this feeling comes a confidence not only in our powers of intuition but also of deliberateness and in our command of artistic form, and because of this achievement, when we return to the language of daily life, the language of all that time when we are not in the middle of our work, we are somewhat, somehow, changed.

There are a good number of writers, especially of fiction, who have described the creation of their first drafts as a kind of wild unleashing of whatever happens to come to them as they're writing—a free-associative sprawl from which, later, they will try to pick what is important, and then pursue its further articulation. Who knows, after all, what he knows? So there are any number of reasons why a maxim like "Write about what you know" is virtually worthless. Even on a superficial level, if I say to a fellow writer whose short story seems implausible in some ways, "Don't write about this, you don't know enough about it, it sounds like you're making it up," it should be that I mean to turn the writer back to the familiar not because it is manageable, but because on the ground of the familiar all the deep discoveries of the unmanageable and the unfamiliar are made. The sod is familiar to the plough, but the seedlings that arise from the sowing always seem miraculous. So instead of "Write about what you know," perhaps writers should say to each other, "Write about what you write about." Instead of telling my fellow writer "Don't write about this, you haven't got a handle on it," I should ask, "*Why* did you write about this? Why are you writing?"

V

Some of the literary conventions that rule us lead us to feel that a writer should try to dramatize, to enact, to present, rather than to editorialize, to explain, to abstract; and so we say, and hear it said, "Show this, don't tell it." There's no question that keeping ourselves away from insipid or uninformed opinions is a good idea. We have all come upon awful sentences or lines in our own work, as we are revising, that are nothing but some kind of shortcut around the kind of textured, vivid, lived quality that we want in our language. And we've tried to rewrite those passages in a more grounded, more realized or materialized way. But on the other hand there are *lots* of things in one's struggles both to live and to live-in-language that require a telling, not a showing. The conventional wisdom of this little maxim makes it all too easy for us not only to get out from under the responsibility of having something to say, but also of having to say *something*.

A telling is first of all dramatic; it creates an intimate moment of relatedness between two persons focused intensely on each other, the one who is telling and the one who is listening, as William Goyen often said. Therefore it is a brilliantly lit arena of knowledge and knowing—of others, of each other, of language. And in poetry as well as in fiction, there must be room for ideas and for ways of getting at experience and feeling that can only be found through the use of discursive language. So this maxim, "Show, don't tell," conceals and negates a deeper truth than the one it purports to reveal.

And if you look at a poet not spooked by these injunctions, the lesson to be learned is that while we may agree or disagree with a writer's beliefs or opinions, nonetheless the presence of belief, conviction, philosophical statement or opinion, stated discursively, has a vital place in poetry. A stark example from Philip Larkin's "This Be the Verse":

> They fuck you up, your mum and dad,
> They may not mean to, but they do—
> They fill you with the faults they had
> And add some extra, just for you.

When discursive language and belief are substantial, or themselves fresh, or when they help us to see with amazement the very conditions in the midst of which we are living, they consort very well with the most sensuous verbal textures and the most vividly presented sense perceptions.

I think that in passages of discursive directness, set against the textures of imagery, figurative language, and the highly deliberate poetic organization of sounds and syntax, the process of self-discovery makes its most impressive leaps. A strong example of this lies in Edward Thomas's "Owl":

> Downhill I came, hungry, and yet not starved;
> Cold, yet had heat within me that was proof
> Against the North wind; tired, yet so that rest
> Had seemed the sweetest thing under a roof.

Then at the inn I had food, fire, and rest,
Knowing how hungry, cold, and tired was I.
All of the night was quite barred out except
An owl's cry, a most melancholy cry

Shaken out long and clear upon the hill,
No merry note, nor cause of merriment,
But one telling me plain what I escaped
And others could not, that night, as in I went.

And salted was my food, and my repose,
Salted and sobered, too, by the bird's voice
Speaking for all who lay under the stars,
Soldiers and poor, unable to rejoice.

The final statement of the poem, because of the modest self-describing of the earlier lines, accomplishes an identification and leap outward from the poem that redefines the person whom we hear speaking it to us. His personal loneliness and isolation are matters to be described and presented in the first three stanzas, with all sorts of formal elegances of symmetry, syntactic deftness, and one rhyme, especially, that ties his state of feeling to the auditory image of the owl's voice ("I" / "cry"). But it's the last stanza that discovers what it is to which he can meaningfully link his own feeling, how it is that his own feeling can be made meaningful beyond his own experience. That going out of himself is what carries us outward, too—not the description leading up to it. So for comment or commentary to be proscribed from poetry or fiction only guarantees that the work must remain at best oblique to the actual circumstances of life. Behind striking images and showy language, in fact, a poet may hide a failure to seek any such engagement, or a lack of intellectual seriousness. Sometimes to conceal our opinions is only to present our work as something wiser than it is.

VI

"Find your voice." Hmm . . . As if it were there, waiting to be found? Or as if it might be only a gimmick, a technique? In such advice I hear neither true seriousness nor true play—both of which are essential to what we do as writers. After all, we cannot live a life that exists outside our own individual projects of living; our preoccupation with language is at the heart of the way each of us, as a writer, is continuing his or her project. So you don't "find" your voice, you create it, you continue to create it out of yourself and your work, and this continued creation is what changes it—or silvers it, as Mandelstam wrote. If mostly it's the same voice, because of the continuity of normal existence, yet each experience of composition, each poem and story and novel, carries us forward into the discovery of different inflections, modulations, and tones. What you *find,* if you're lucky, is a sense of the live pace of change in your own life and art, and therein, the reality of your feelings, the reality or truth of your intuition, the authority of your imagination, the words for what you now see you want to say—to paraphrase E. M. Forster.

VII

For Yeats, the motive for writing is in part to achieve a self-creation. Emily Dickinson offers us an account of a related, equally large motive, which I'll try to uncover by looking at an apparently theological poem in which she metaphorizes mortality as a condemnation by a court of law (#412):

> I read my sentence—steadily—
> Reviewed it with my eyes,
> To see that I made no mistake
> In its extremest clause—
> The Date, and manner, of the shame—
> And then the Pious Form
> That "God have mercy" on the Soul
> The Jury voted Him—
> I made my soul familiar—with her extremity—
> That at the last, it should not be a novel Agony—
> But she, and Death, acquainted—
> Meet tranquilly, as friends—
> Salute, and pass, without a Hint—
> And there, the Matter ends—

But of course the word "sentence" can also mean something quite different from a penalty of death imposed by God the judge—it can mean the sentence she is writing in a poem. Knowing the whole of her work, we can see a secondary reading. In the first stanza, she is asking if her expressive distortions of syntax are too difficult to be understood:

> I read my sentence—steadily—
> Reviewed it with my eyes,
> To see that I made no mistake
> In its extremest clause—

The next line expresses her sense that the whole enterprise of her work, in any case, confronts her repeatedly with such failure that the poems are a kind of crime (and surely we all recognize this feeling):

The Date, and manner, of the shame—

She implies, then, that there must yet be some merit—even if insuf-
ficient, then still deserving mercy—in her work:

And then the Pious Form
That "God have mercy" on the Soul
The Jury voted Him—

(The "Pious Form" in this second context would be the hymn-
meter of all her poems.)

Now, whereas in the first reading, the next four lines are the con-
demned prisoner's self-preparation for her execution, in this second
reading that I'm pursuing, these lines summarizing her existential proj-
ect also express her credo as a writer:

I made my soul familiar—with her extremity—
That at the last, it should not be a novel Agony—
But she, and Death, acquainted—
Meet tranquilly, as friends—

In these lines the apparent subject of the whole poem (that all mor-
tals are condemned to death) and the hidden subject (Dickinson's sense
of why she writes) are fused and no longer represent one level of
discourse that happens on close reading to reveal a less apparent one,
but rather a single yet complex *saying* that is highly and characteristi-
cally metaphorical. Knowing the "extremity" of her own soul—that is,
its imminent confrontation with death—and also the oddness, the diffi-
culty, the uniqueness, of her own temperament and the conditions of
her life, she has wanted to foresee *for herself,* in her multitude of poems
written with little hope of gaining readers, all the visions and versions
of extremity—from grief to happiness—that she can imagine, so that
the writing of the poems will extend her knowledge of feeling all the
way to her sense of her own death. She was obsessed by this subject just
as much as by her equally strong experience of isolated, ravishingly
wonderful moments of life. She is a poet of the dizzying freedom of
consciousness, a poet of the living of life and the living, as it were, of
death—as in "I heard a fly buzz when I died" and many other poems,
especially those in which consciousness of death offers her the opportu-
nity to be, as Cynthia Griffin Wolff calls it in her critical biography of
Dickinson, "proleptic"—that is, positing a condition that cannot be
(her having died already), and speaking from within it.

The unfettered aesthetic independence of her poems, and her re-
peated attempts in them to offer a symbolic reply to death, seem meant
to accomplish a work on her own consciousness, *upon herself.* If Yeats

wrote to take control of shaping his own temperament and person, Dickinson writes to extend (her) consciousness so that she might so thoroughly prepare herself for death that it would not be the terror that, against a small town of orthodox believers, she felt it must be:

> I made my soul familiar—with her extremity—
> That at the last, it should not be a novel Agony—
> But she, and Death, acquainted—
> Meet tranquilly, as friends—
> Salute, and pass, without a Hint—
> And there, the Matter ends—

The sense of this is, "I made my soul familiar with her extremity [so] that at the last, it should not be a novel Agony, but [rather that] she and Death, [already] acquainted, [should] meet tranquilly, as friends. . . ." Thus the terror of the first eight lines is tamed not by solace or illusion but by courage.

Another curiosity about this paradoxical poem is that until Thomas H. Johnson transcribed the poems as Dickinson in fact wrote them, the poem had been changed by early editors to four quatrains following the regularity of the hymn-meter. But as Dickinson wrote it out, she lengthened lines in what would have been the last two quatrains in order to make the poem come out to be fourteen lines long, and in fact she employed as a rhyme scheme a variation on the Italian sonnet form. Now, embarking on a sonnet is in the English tradition perhaps the most deliberate way for a poet to join a literary context of intense consciousness and self-consciousness, and of artistry carried to the level of the most highly-wrought (sonnets are not the form of spontaneity). Therefore, frequently the subject matter and the tropes of sonnets are characteristically paradoxical, compressed to the point of the cryptic, and so on. The very rarity of such a poetic form in Dickinson's work should alert us to her deliberateness in composing it; and in what better form could she have sought to express—as if for herself only—her own credo as a poet? The sonnet's characteristic volta, or turn, in feeling or thought, occurs right on schedule at line nine, the credo I quoted above—Dickinson's answer to the "sentence of death."

When Dickinson offers versions of more commonplace ideas about why poets write, they are also related to her acute consciousness of death. In poem #883 she constructs a modest consolation for herself, imagining the life of poetry after its author is dead:

> The Poets light but Lamps—
> Themselves—go out—
> The Wicks they stimulate—
> If vital Light—

Inhere as do the Suns—
Each Age a Lens
Disseminating their
Circumference—

But Dickinson does not seem to have meant that poetry is at all ethereal; in fact, she insisted on language as a living, uttered medium of the poet's work, for example in poem #1212:

A word is dead
When it is said,
Some say.
I say it just
Begins to live
That day.

And in poem #1651, probably dating from the last period of her life, when she returned somewhat to Christian faith after her early sustained rebellion against the incongruities and injustices that followed logically from belief in a supposedly just and omnipotent God, she began with the biblical creation of the Word made Flesh in order to suggest that all language that is "breathed distinctly," such as a poem, can defeat death in some way, and would only be *un*necessary if indeed God were to return:

A Word made Flesh is seldom
And tremblingly partook
Nor then perhaps reported
But have I not mistook
Each one of us has tasted
With ecstasies of stealth
The very food debated
To our specific strength—
A Word that breathes distinctly
Has not the power to die
Cohesive as the Spirit
It may expire if He—
"Made Flesh and dwelt among us"
Could condescension be
Like this consent of Language
This loved Philology.

Perhaps all the sensuous linguistic texture of poetry is evidence of its connection not only to thought but also to body; not only to feeling—that is, emotion—but also to feeling—that is, the perception of touch and of being touched; not only to psyche but also to eros. Poetry's peculiar intensity of linguistic effect, and also of meaning, gives it the power to work on us as readers, and to change us as writers, as if poetry were a material force confronting us. And Dickinson's phrase "A word that breathes distinctly"—embodying language itself to suggest this physical power of poetry—was echoed years later by Mandelstam, who said that the language of Boris Pasternak's poems made them such powerful breathing exercises that, if recited repeatedly, they could cure tuberculosis. This is an intensely material way of saying that Pasternak's poems are an *inspiration:* they work his lungs, they shape the way in which he breathes, and therefore in which, as a poet, he lives.

One last point suggested by this poem: Dickinson writes, "[T]his consent of Language / This loved Philology." This is to say, this gift as if from above us of a medium in which we can redeem ourselves, and this loved love of words. Our language comes to us from all who speak it around us. In our responses to it, in our choosing of whose language we wish most to hear and our resistance to language we dislike or distrust, we participate as writers in the social body in which we are formed and in which we struggle to form ourselves.

VIII

Dickinson is an extraordinary creator of metaphor, and one of the most striking aspects of her poetry is the compression and freshness of her figures of speech. I think our responsiveness to this, as opposed to the lack of responsiveness among her contemporaries, is very much a part of our cultural moment, and again implicates us in what we have inherited from the spate of post-Romantic, early-twentieth-century writers in various European languages who in one way or another claimed that the function of poetry was to defamiliarize the familiar, or refresh the sense perceptions, or, as Ezra Pound put it, to "make it new." One example: Walter Benjamin wrote of Brecht's epic theater that the art of it "consists in producing astonishment rather than empathy. To put it succinctly: instead of identifying with the characters, the audience should be educated to be astonished at the circumstances under which they function."

If I understand this correctly, it means that Brecht's plays, when successful, make it possible for the audience to feel astonishment at the circumstances of their own lives, which the plays force them to see stripped of mystifications and habitual attitudes. What Brecht seems to have been after was a way to create not only fresh perception and astonishment, but also conscience. It may be, although I can only speculate, that the process of active self-discovery and creation of one's being-in-language that I have been trying to point out in these poems has something to do, through some psychoneural connection we can only guess at, with the responsive and responsible part of consciousness we call conscience. This isn't to say that artistic activity can in any way infallibly re-create the artist as a more conscience-stricken person— there are many sad counterexamples among even great artists. But the activity of artistic making, especially when the medium is language, at least immerses the artist in that place where conscience is partly made, the realm of self-knowledge, self-acknowledgment, without which there can be little acknowledgment of others. In Dickinson's life, her paradoxical combination of reclusiveness and intensely solicitous concern for loved friends may be completely of a whole with the impression of a kind of metaphoric vertigo of speed and discovery that we find in her poems. What can make artistic life so confusing in our time, as it already did in hers, is that the language around us works against any freshness and cleanness of perception, against discovery, but steadily and relentlessly to strengthen the habits of thought and feeling on which commerce and power depend. Only in an illusory way does the commercial culture around us also prize the new, the novel. And it does so so superficially and insatiably that what we would try to refresh and "make new" with a word or an image can be immediately trumped by a crass advertisement, for purposes completely opposed to our own, even if those opposed purposes share with us certain rhetorical devices. For if indeed we find it exhilarating to be renewed, to be refreshed, to return to work and family and artistic creation with a sense of recharged resources, yet around us the advertising culture by which almost all communication is tinged works tirelessly to create a thirst for the new only so that our efforts to quench that thirst will never be satisfied, and we'll be thirsty again, and forever. Our "making it new," whatever that meant in Pound's day, is for us only an unintended echo of the driving mechanism of consumer culture, and we should give more thought to how to "make it last." Perhaps this is why, in poetry, there is now a vaunted trend to return to traditional poetic forms—as if to say, with this gesture, that the poet refuses to make the poem look like anything new at all. Such contradictions make it necessary for us to think about how we write and why we write in terms not only of artistic technique and craft but also in terms of how we as writers shape our own lives with our work.

IX

My last example is by César Vallejo, and in it I perceive all the things I've touched on—the deliberate self-making of Yeats; Mandelstam's sense of the poet's struggle with language as the ploughing that silvers us; Williams's emotional dramas of unfolding understanding; Celan's and Causley's riddling; formal patterns as ways of making meaning; discursive statement; and Dickinson's mortal anxiousness to find a way in her poems to address life and death. What I especially admire about Vallejo's poem is the way he unites his observations of the world outside himself with his self-questioning, to suggest that to remake his poems in response to this world is to remake himself as well.

Among the untitled posthumous poems called the *poemas humanos,* the "human poems," this one meets head-on all the artist's bafflement of conscience in the midst of those conditions of daily life that can call into question the value of making art and our motives for making it:

> Un hombre pasa con un pan al hombro.
> ¿Voy a escribir, después, sobre mi doble?
>
> Otro se sienta, ráscase, extrae un piojo de su axila, mátalo.
> ¿Con qué valor hablar del psicoanálisis?
>
> Otro ha entrado a mi pecho con un palo en la mano.
> ¿Hablar luego de Sócrates al médico?
>
> Un cojo pasa dando el brazo a un niño.
> ¿Voy, después, a leer a André Breton?
>
> Otro tiembla del frío, tose, escupe sangre.
> ¿Cabrá aludir jamás al Yo profundo?
>
> Otro busca en al fango huesos, cáscaras.
> ¿Cómo escribir, después, del infinito?
>
> Un albañil cae de un techo, muere y ya no almuerza.
> ¿Innovar, después, el tropo, la metáfora?
>
> Un comerciante roba un gramo en el peso a un cliente.
> ¿Hablar, después, de cuarta dimensión?
>
> Un banquero falsea su balance.
> ¿Con qué cara llorar en el teatro?
>
> Un paria duerme con el pie a la espalda.
> ¿Hablar, después, a nadie de Picasso?
>
> Alguien va en un entierro sollozando.
> ¿Cómo luego ingresar a la Academia?
>
> Alguien limpia un fusil en su cocina.
> ¿Con qué valor hablar del más allá?

Alguien pasa contando con sus dedos.
¿Cómo hablar del no-yo sin dar un grito?

A man goes by with a long loaf of bread on his human shoulder.
And after that I'm going to write about my double?

Another man sits down, scratches himself, nabs a louse in his armpit,
    then smashes it.
What's the good of talking about psychoanalysis?

Another has invaded my own body, with a stick in his hand.
So then, talk about Socrates later when I go to the doctor?

A cripple goes by with a boy, arm in arm.
And after that, I'm going to read André Breton?

Another man is shivering with the cold, he coughs, spits blood.
Will it ever be right to refer to the Inner Me?

Another is looking for meat scraps and orange rinds in the mud.
How can I write about the Infinite after that?

A mason falls from a rooftop, he dies, and does without lunch from
    now on.
And then I'm going to innovate tropes and metaphors?

A merchant cheats by one gram as he weighs out a customer's goods.
After that, talk about the fourth dimension?

A banker rigs his gold-balance.
Make a bawling scene at the theater?

An outcast sleeps with one foot behind his back.
And after that, not talk to anyone about Picasso?

Someone is on the way to a burial, crying.
How can one go join the Academy later?

Someone's cleaning his rifle in the kitchen.
What's the good of talking about the beyond?

Someone goes by counting on his fingers.
How can I talk about the not-I without screaming?

About Vallejo, what most appeals—because it gives a sometimes exaggerated, sometimes even threatening, edge to his poems—is that in nearly all he wrote he is working to make sense of the disparity between the straining yet exquisite concentration of artistic making and the intractable raw experience—his own or others'—that was the stuff of his poems. From the tilted lanes of his native village in the Andes to the streets of Paris he seems to have carried this disparity in mind, and one can sense in most of his poems how barely adequate a medium he found language itself, when he worked to express the anger and the awe that such divided consciousness caused him. In many of his poems, the complex torsions of syntax, the dissonant chords he sounds by employing starkly different sorts of diction, the difficult representational progress of many poems (that is, the progress of reference of the material images in his poems), all convey how hard it is not only to express powerful feeling and elusive insight, but also to discover them through the maddeningly complex medium of language. While the course of his work is toward less of this expressive torsion and distortion, till in the *poemas humanos* there is a greater simplicity of language, there is plenty of newness, freshness, and active struggle inscribed in his lines from earliest to last work.

It's not that Vallejo frequently wrote poems about poetry or about writing. But—to risk a definition—all poetry is language that is in some way also about language. Because this is so, all poetry, even the most intimate, is also in some way engaged with our social being, since language is the currency of our being with others. And because all poetry is in some way engaged with our social being, all writing is in some corresponding way a kind of self-making. One of Keats's most endearing qualities is the naked earnestness of his youthful ambition to make a place for himself in the wider world, and his ambition to do so *as a writer*. In the same letter of 27 October 1818 to his friend Richard Woodhouse in which he wrote of "the poetical Character" that "it is not itself—it has no self—it is every thing and nothing," he also wrote, "I am ambitious of doing the world some good: if I should be spared that may be the work of maturer years—in the interval I will assay to reach to as high a summit in Poetry as the nerve bestowed on me will suffer." These statements suggest that Keats's idea of a poet connects an openness of being and becoming, with a preparation for some useful, even if postponed, involvement in the lives of others. And in the famous letter of 1819 to his brother George and his wife Georgiana, written only a few months before his greatest, and last, poems, Keats said,

Call the world if you Please "the vale of Soul-making [. . .] I say 'Soul making' Soul as distinguished from an Intelligence—There may be intelligences or sparks of the divinity in millions—but they are not Souls till they acquire identities[.]

Keats's metaphor for the process by which an intelligence becomes a soul is that of *reading*—an engagement with language:

> I will call the *world* a School instituted for the purpose of teaching little children to read—I will call the *human heart* the *horn Book* used in that school—and I will call the *Child able to read, the Soul* made from that school and its hornbook. [. . .] Not merely is the Heart a Hornbook, It is the Mind's Bible[.]

And because his own engagement with what he was reading, especially Shakespeare, so clearly fed his own artistic powers in this period of his life, his experience of language must have been as rich and intense as any poet's has ever been.

In May of that year he wrote the odes to the nightingale and to the Grecian urn and other poems. In August he wrote in a letter to a friend, "I am convinced more and more every day that (excepting the human friend Philosopher) a fine writer is the most genuine Being in the World." And to another friend, "I am convinced more and more day by day that fine writing is next to fine doing the top thing in the world." His excitement is evident. About what, exactly? Given his sense of his own painful limitations both as an artist and as a person, his passionate commitment to writing, and the almost total lack of appreciation for his work from readers of his time, isn't it hard not to see in these statements Keats's intuition that the intensely focused artistic powers that he could feel ripening in himself, and which he poured into his greatest poems in these few months, had given him the hope that against his failing physical health he was working furiously to create a self that could survive even indifference and illness? Keats's struggle to create himself fully before he died is a story in which the poems appear as the evidence of the extraordinary changes through which his soul-making carried him.

The conclusion I come to for myself, after pondering these poems and matters poetical, is that why I write, and why I want to write, is because I find myself preoccupied with being attentive *with the instrument of language* to the life inside and around me. Maybe that's because I want to change that life. But maybe we write not first out of conscience, but first because the way it has turned out for us is that we're haunted by the sound of the language in our heads, in our own mouths, in the mouths of others, and obsessively we listen to it, ponder it, rework it; we're following a thread of linguistic clues to understanding what this life is good for. And so writing becomes our way of discovering and shaping our own understanding, and maybe thereby our own lives, and a way to share the self-empowering we gain from this preoccupation and artistic work with others. Out of my experience of that process, which strengthens me, I believe, in my artistic will the more I have of it, comes some sense of progress toward what it is I would like my work to become, and who I might have to be in order to write that work. As Yeats—with whose opinions I'd argue, but whose great poems, and whose engagement with others and with the artistic and social life around him, I admire— wrote to explain why he revised his poems so much,

> The friends that have it I do wrong
> When ever I remake a song,
> Should know what issue is at stake:
> It is myself that I remake.

HEATHER MCHUGH

Moving Means, Meaning Moves
Notes on Lyric Destination

This essay first took form as a lecture given in Bergen, Norway (a place where, as no tourist agency likes to tell you, it rains 305 days a year; in some senses, every destination is unexpected). I was there for one academic quarter, without the benefit of any knowledge of Norwegian, and it reminded me of the general truth that poets bear a naive or estranged relation to language. For example, it kept striking me as concretely evocative that the word for *speak* was *snakker:* "Snakker du engelsk?" smacked of "Do you eat the English?" (not the fast food of choice, in America). And every time I saw that perfectly innocent Norwegian phrase meaning "Very good," I was subject to a sudden sense of titillating oxymoron: the Norwegian reads *bare bra* and cannot help packing, in an American eye, considerable wallop. This is the curse of a poetic or naive relation to language: you don't know where it's going but you're very susceptible to traveling whatever road it takes you down.

At every corner store in Bergen was a large sign saying, "SPILL HER"; in fact this turned out to mean something rather less mythic, and more mundane, than my persistent mental image of great vessels of Norwegian womanhood, brimming over and ready to be tipped. For Americans, the phrase is "fill 'er up." Americans love their cars. It sometimes seems they'd rather give up their spouses than give up their wheels. In a nation of highways, three thousand miles across, where you can drive ten hours a day and in five days still not hit its other coast, it's no wonder that the cultural consciousness is filled with so many versions of the driving romance: the chase scene, the getaway car, Route 66, Jack Kerouac.

But the romance of hitting the road has two sides to it. On the one hand, it's the romance of reassurance: service stations when you need them; a Motel 6 right down the next off-ramp; McDonald's every sixty miles, with dependently identical features—unfailingly fast cash registers, smiles canned at McDonald's University, and fresh wishes, a thousand times an hour, half-a-million times a year, that you should have a nice day. But there's also the other American automotive romance, the romance of freedom *from* the predictable, the romance of the highway adventure, the wild encounter, the unfamiliar sight, romance of unknown destination. In a sense, these two desires also govern a reader's passage through a poem, and the poem fails us if it doesn't deliver us some of both—the pulmonary pleasures of recurrence and the breathtaking spikes of surprise.

A poet is materially engaged in estranging language, all the time— her own language must become strange to her. The motion of a poem (in Norwegian "motion" is *fart*) is, in some essential way, an estranging motion. A poem means to move you, but in unexpected directions. I fall into spatial metaphors, perhaps because I think a poem is a *passage* in a more literal sense than a prose piece is. By this I mean that a lineated lyric draws a reader's attention, by design, more to immediate spatial and structural relations—to the course the reader travels from departure to arrival point, the pattern of curves en route. In prose the margin's arbitrarily placed; you're not supposed to notice it. Not so in poems. In poems, the convention of continuance is always being queried by poetic structure: a lineated poem is constantly ending. A sentence can have many line breaks in it, and each line break significantly reconceives not only the status of the sentence, but the status of the narrative the sentence stands for. Line breaks willfully remind us of the wordlessness that surrounds and shapes the verbal passage; one could even say (if one wished to sabotage a fashionable critical locution) that in poetry the margin isn't marginalized.

Indeed, the margin's of the essence—it's an absence that makes its presence felt at every turn. As every student knows, the root of the word *verse* lies in the Latin for "turning." As every student also knows, the Greek root of *poetry* (*poesis*) means "making"; but a lineated poem is a making full of breakings. A poem is, in other words, not only *in words:* it is a structure of internal resistances, and it's no accident that paradoxes arise at the very premises of its act. This is, I think, the most fundamental sense of Whitman's saying, "Do I contradict myself? Very well, I contradict myself," and Keats's insistence on negative capability. A constant unsettling in the grounds of the poetic, an obsessive literalness about approaching the edge, forcing each line of thought to walk the plank, again and again, to a provisional end where it must hang, for a moment, at the edge of wordlessness—these features of the lyric definitively undermine the constitutional groundwork of narration. We are creatures of habit; given a blank we can't help trying to fill it in along lines of customary seeing or saying. But the best poetic lines undermine those habits, break the pre- off the -dictable, unsettle the suburbs of your routine sentiments, and rattle the tracks of your trains of thought.

What *moving* means, in poems, is very physical, however often poems are mistaken for sentimental instruments. To *feel* a poem is to run your senses over the directions, speeds, angles, and densities of its poetic objects, in relation to its poetic subject. The two poems to which I commend your attention here are, like all lyrics, equipped with points of departure, points of arrival, and trajectories between. Both narrators arrive, by car, at destinations that turn out to contain more than meets, at first, the passing eye—more than *could* have met the eye in passing—, and more than a presupposing eye would ever have recorded. Indeed, though the speakers of both poems identify themselves as travelers first and foremost, the crucial turns, and the greater identification, turn out in both poems to happen when the car comes to a halt. The vehicle of metaphorical impulse can outgun the delicate tenor. To that extent, these are poems about what a poet, as long as he's caught up only in the motorworks of his craft, might miss entirely.

Let me start with "The Right of Way," a William Carlos Williams poem from the book *Spring and All,* written in the mid-1920s, when the early models of the Ford motorcarriage were changing the American landscape and psyche. It seems somehow no accident that William Carlos Williams, the name itself as an act of language, ends where it began (the surname seems a simple plural of the Christian name), and that there intervene, between these almost identical ends, a plural article (*los*) and a singular vehicle (*car*). Such nominal peculiarities are not lost on poets. In English, the "right-of-way" the poem starts with is both a legal concept or abstraction, and also a perfectly solid material thing: a roadbed. It is characteristic of Williams that he puts his pedal to the *mental,* as surely as to the metal, when he accelerates: his way of engaging matter and mind at once, in each shift of gesture, is (poetically) his trademark.

THE RIGHT OF WAY

In passing with my mind
on nothing in the world

but the right of way
I enjoy on the road by

virtue of the law—
I saw

An elderly man who
smiled and looked away

to the north past a house—
a woman in blue

who was laughing and
leaning forward to look up

into the man's half
averted face

and a boy of eight who was
looking at the middle of

the man's belly
at a watchchain—

The supreme importance
of this nameless spectacle

sped me by them
without a word—

Why bother where I went?
for I went spinning on the

four wheels of my car
along the wet road until

I saw a girl with one leg
over the rail of a balcony

The speaker of Williams's poem starts "in passing." The sense of this phrase, with nothing before it to condition it, is casual; there's nothing on his mind but the moving—the right of way that is a right of passage. The passage is, for us, his passengers, a literary one, a poem, and ultimately it can be read as being about how a lyric disposition grasps the world. The poem's speaker speeds by in his vehicle, and as he does, he sees the world in fragments, in frames—still-frame glimpses that result from his own motion. The glimpsed people achieve a kind of stillness, becoming almost mythically representative: he sees an old man, a woman, and then (between them, as if produced by their convergence) a boy. The boy is gazing at a timepiece; all this can be seen in a grand and emblematic poetic light—for in glimpses the occasional can look eternal, and the momentary be taken for the momentous.

This is an effect like what optical studies call retinal retention—only here the retentive organ is a psychodynamic one—the persistence in the recording organ of what was in fact a merely transitory image or gesture. The world can seem a sum of such frozen images only from

the perspective of the passerby, the detached eye, the eye of the out-
sider. In that regard, the old man may seem fixed on a farther—or
cooler—than human horizon ("to the north past a house"), and the
laughing woman, whose gaze is fixed less far-off (to, and into, the
man's face), can be seen as a figure caught up in the middle distances of
human relation; while the boy's gaze is fixed at the nearest distance—
the navel, the belly, and the time-chain. It would not be hard to read
large gestures into these glimpsed poses—gestures toward death, sex-
ual love, and time. In many ways the positions, and the pre-positions,
of this poem powerfully suggest the cool approaches of art criticism:
life seen as art, in angles of relation, available as symbol, something to
be fixed, rather than followed, by the roving (if appreciative) eye.

Five stanzas from the end of the poem, Williams makes so grand a
rhetoric of claims about these glimpses ("The supreme importance /
of this nameless spectacle"), it would seem to be sarcastic, were it not for
the modesty of its own self-rebuke ("without a word"). It's not with-
out portent, the irony of this turn. (There are three great turns of
attention or changes of gear in the poem, marked by capitalizations—
at the first, the tenth, and the twelfth stanzas.) Attaching as it does to
glimpses of unknown people caught in the happenstances of street life,
people doing nothing (on the face of it) that one would ordinarily call
significant, the hyperbolic flavor of the "supreme importance" stanza
prepares, in us, several understandings: that there is for Williams im-
portance in the human figure in its *accidents* of incarnation, flashes of
gesture seized out of motions; that these accidents and moments
glimpsed as spectacle are significant in terms we'd usually reserve for
the immortal ("supreme importance"); and that, as the speaker says,
this importance *sped him by them*—that is, the speed with which he
passes is *itself* a coefficient of significance, high speed making it pos-
sible, even necessary, to excerpt their gestures so, and to cast them in
the light of the universal.

The paradox here of course is that one expects a poet to be *aiming for*
the supreme importance, and when he's found it, to stop there, to
make that his poetic destination. But that's not the case with Williams.
Because were he to stop, these people would then have to be seen as
moving, rather than fixed in the postures of the perennial: their ges-
tures would lose their fragmentariness and connect into meanings, and
all too frequently the meaning of movements in daily life is trivial.
The man who seemed to be looking off into the distance could turn
out to be thinking about his hemorrhoids; the woman peering in at the
man could be looking not for love or wisdom, but at the bit of spinach
on his chin; the boy could be turning his head with the ultimate
intention of looking, not at the mysteries of time, but at the pinball
arcade across the street. This too is life, after all, a lot of unromantic
particulars. The sense of the mythic or momentous circumstance is

bestowed by the vantage of the traveler in motion, a vantage that confers on human partialities an aspect of the eternal, and that seizes moments out of time into a kind of romantic imperishability.

Indeed, throughout this poem, one has the feeling that just behind the local, or just under it, something larger is always turning: wheels within wheels from the very beginning of the poem, where what's "in the world" and what's not in it are the declared province of the poetic attention. At the juncture where the triangulation of man, woman, and child comes, pointedly, down to the belly button—comes, that is, down to where *we* all come from—at that point any sense of destination shifts, and the speaker asks (perhaps facetiously, of readers intent on finding out his poetic destination), "Why bother where I went?" He immediately goes on, nevertheless, to flirt with a where, and turn to a how: "For I went spinning on the. . . ." Here the line break becomes telling. The question "Why bother where I went?" might lead us to expect more in the grandiloquent mode—why bother what my local destination was, because in the wake of the supreme importance, one remembers one's planetary wheels—one goes spinning, for example, on *the earth*. But this flash of impression doesn't survive the line break. What he does deliver is surprisingly concrete (or rather, rubber and concrete): "for I went spinning on the / four wheels of my car / along the wet road. . . ." We must readjust our assumptions, and realize he's returning to the level of the local—and positing vehicle and road as sufficient to any question about "where I went," though that wet road is a sign of slippery grounds. No image seizes *him* out of the fleeting and peremptory presence of his *own* motion on earth *until*—until he hits that "until."

"I went . . . on . . . until" can be read as the mark of the next significant turn in the poem's passage. It's an augury, a foretelling hint: it suggests we're about to be introduced to the event or sight that stopped him. And what *is* the sight before which he stops? The sight of the incarnation that was missing in the triangulation of man, woman, and boy: he stops at the sight of a girl.

At once our readerly appetite to know a narrative destination seeks out a likely story. (A poem's lineation is always working with and against the narrative urge in readers toward the story's one-and-only end, toward an exhaustive answer—that is, lines work with and against the sentence.) Perhaps the first girl who comes to mind, the mind conditioned by the three figures preceding, is the little girl counterpart to the boy—an idle figure, one in a trail of happenstance figures, and one the speaker will bypass like the others, as he goes on. But such an explanation leaves unregistered the clearly distinguishing effects of Williams's efforts to frame her in poetic suspense: his keeping the whole engine of poetic progress rolling toward that word "until," with its power to arrest; his posing her at the end of the poem, rather than in the course of it (where she too could have been left in the dust of his passage); his bringing the poem completely and abruptly to a halt the moment her figure has been introduced. All these moves conspire to distinguish her from the other figures, and make us consider her in a different light.

In the service of our will to identify her as destination, the second figure that proposes itself to a reader's mind, or rises to the mind's eye as being by nature eye-catching or arresting, may well be the girl as erotic figure—a girl with her leg hooked over a balcony. It could *be* a hooker he's stopping for; he could be stopping in a moment of semiotic fidelity, stopping because he's in the red light district. (In Norway the word for aim or goal or end is *slutt,* though it's pronounced like *slit.*) But the *line break* almost simultaneously draws our attention to another possibility. For this may alternatively be a girl who *has* only one leg. (Williams's career as a doctor often sent him on house calls, and many of the poems are actually sympathetic yet unflinchingly honest portraits of patients in various conditions.) In this case, that is, if we read the girl to be one-legged, the last line's prepositional phrase ("over the rail of a balcony") attaches not to the noun *leg,* but rather to the verb *saw:* over the rail of a balcony is where he saw her positioned, relative to him.

Aesthetically speaking, this pair of angles on the figure of the girl is structurally satisfying, and makes a virtuoso gesture toward symmetry, since one is the girl whose professional skills he might have reason to use, and the other is the girl who might have reason to use *his* professional skills. It would have been a rich enough *coup de force,* compositionally speaking, to have conflated these two versions of the female figure at the end of a poem—the one a *femme fatale* and the other a *fille mortelle*—and it is surely a stroke of genius to incorporate, in this second and crippled girl, so literal a version of discorporation—of the human fragmentariness that has, up until now in the poem, seemed to be the governing metaphor. It bears remarking, however, that the fragmentariness of the other human beings was qualitatively different from *her* fragmentariness: the girl with one leg will remain one-legged no matter how long he studies her; her partiality is permanent, unlike that of the man with the half-face, whose partiality is conditioned by time and the moving vantage of the observer; in his case, the missing half of his face, though not visible, nevertheless exists: it's a question of appearance, not essence. If we think of these matters in terms of art criticism, rather than philosophy, then a comment Gertrude Stein made about Picasso seems apropos. She said that when we see a figure, part of which is always necessarily hidden (by its orientation, or a shadow, or—she adds, in a moment of Steinean peculiarity—by a hat), most of us fill in, in our minds, the missing part, to keep the idea of the body whole; but, Stein said, when Picasso saw a single eye, for him there was no other eye. (This is a nice reversal of the cliché about Picasso, that he saw all sides at once.) Williams knows that the reader's mind will naturally fill in gaps; it is the mind's socialized *disposition* to connect. But the girl who has lost her leg cannot be made whole in a glance or a thought or a lifetime, and if she takes on a mythic status in the eye of the poem's traveler, it would have to be the status of the human figure enduring by enduring, the figure who sustains the damages of living, and lives on.

But the poem provides no single, exclusive narrative relief or answer to a reader's avid curiosity to know the secret of the relationship between the driver and the girl before whom he comes to a stop. Really it's a question about the poem's destination. The poem stops before we know what the driver intends with her, what the poet *means* by her. Yet there is, in the absence of a single narrative answer, nevertheless a wealth of lyric answer. I mean, there are answers even beyond the counterpoise of hooker and halt.

For there is a fourth girl one might see in this, the poem's last moments, a girl the driver couldn't have foreseen, but the seeing of whom might well compel his attendance. Indeed attendance—in the Frenchest sense, the sense of waiting or staying—is much to the point here, since this fourth girl's fate is linked to his choice to go or stop, to questions of motion and vision, perspective and time. She could, that is, be a girl about to jump or fall from a high balcony, a girl about to plunge, in the seizure of whatever melancholia or misjudgment, to her death in the street below.

All the other human figures in the poem were engaged in the passing indirections of happenstance, engaged in living, that is; to bypass them consigned them to postures that *greatened* our sense of their significance: the old man then could become a figure for all old men in that moment of looking beyond the ranges of the domestic, and the woman looking up "into the man's half" could become, in that moment, the universe of women in a moment of relation with their "other halves," and the boy could seem to be youth itself, regarding the mechanisms of time. The girl who is the missing fourth in the symmetries of this scene shifts quickly into the temptress whose mythic status (the oldest profession) comes with her pose, and suggests urgencies in the speaker's future; or into the one-legged girl, whose peculiarity, even, can be understood as a universalizing gesture, since her partiality makes all the preceding partialities so much more literal; she too, thus, can be "kept" in mind—hers is the sign of survival: an urgency in the past.

But the fourth incarnation, the figure of the girl as potential suicide or fatal faller, is an urgency in the present. She can't be kept in mind; she has to be stopped. If the driver (or poet) *does* stop, then he has to attend to her gesture's intent, its direction, its consequence. Its meaning is *in* its motion. Can the driver—or can the poet—or can the reader—afford to zoom past individual human gestures, framing them

in lyric moments, detaching them from the gravity of local conse-
quences? Not this time, however large his motives as an artist may
have seemed. The kind of imperishability his passing conferred on the
others seems suddenly insignificant before this figure's proposition of
urgent and actual perishability. If the driver stops for this fourth fig-
ure, he commits himself to a relation in time, not timelessness.

The driver and the suicide are intimately related, in their way: both
think they are heading for nothing. (That's what the speaker said at the
outset his mind was on, "nothing in the world.") The nothing in the
world *she* has in mind is the flat fact of the street; her ground for
stopping forever is his ground for forever moving. The driver of the
poem must, as Rilke says, change his life. And this poem addresses the
poet as witness of life, and the reader as witness of poems. The mind
that was on nothing in the world has come suddenly face-to-face with
a more compelling nothing *in* the world: the nothing-in-the-world
that is death. There's a critique of aestheticization at work in this
fourth figure's claim on his (and our) attentions. For the aestheticizing
momentum that redeemed the other figures can only doom this girl.
An old man looking "north past a house" can suggest a figurative
relation to death; the destination of the girl who would plunge from
the balcony cannot be aestheticized that way: her death proposes to be
no far or pale or polar latitude, no Hebrides of a heaven. This girl
means to smash—more or less immediately—into the concrete. At the
borderlines of such actuality, there's no time or place for the vehicular
recourse of metaphor.

In a sense, the figure of impending death is the accident the speaker
"had coming," on that wet road: she's the intersection of the local and
the universal, the moment she moves to die. Unlike the accidentalities
and happenstances of most moves in daily life, the last motion is
anything but trivial. Hers *is* no longer a daily life; it is rather, all at
once and for the only time, a living daylight—certainly a living day-
light is what might be scared out of a passerby discerning her intention
to jump. And that is the moment the poem means to ask us to con-
sider: the moment when we, the passengers of poems, can no longer
dash along, insulated, untouched. Had the poem driven on, the girl
would have been just another figure like the others—a glimpse that
remains installed in its pose, girl on a balcony, the girl in works of art,
impending, suspended. But if in real life—life that isn't lost in
emblems—she is bent on suicide, then if he passes by she'll not remain
in the world as a girl of any kind. So Williams the caretaker must, I
think, ask us what he asks the driver of the car of the poem—to take
note of this fourth possibility, the most urgent girl, beyond the
quicker figures we neatly identified by habit of bypass, arrest of lust,
or gist of lost limb. To think that this girl is about to die must change
the premises of thinking: for her status in that thought has to be

changed, from representation to presence. It's one thing to be carefree; it's another not to care. Williams stops the poem, as he would the car itself, at the sight of the girl whose particularity most calls out for intervention, the girl whose time could end in the flash of his passing, the one who takes living so seriously she's about to take her life. The poem ends abruptly at the encounter with such ferocious *presence*—at the point where act must overwhelm aesthetic.

"To name is to destroy," says Mallarmé; "to suggest is to create." Elizabeth Bishop's poem, "Filling Station," is spoken by a fastidious character quite intent on disparagement by name-calling. Like the speaker of "The Right of Way," she recounts an arrival by automobile at some destination that turns out to be more compelling than it first appeared. In the Williams poem, that destination was the figure of a woman who, at first glance, seemed erotic, but whose impending meaning was necrotic. Until that moment, Williams proceeded by the study of *objects;* but the girl about to fall is less an object than an impending *act,* an enlistment of subjectivity; and the shift from object study to an act of self-involvement is the true trajectory of the poem. Compare that driver's journey to this one's:

FILLING STATION

Oh, but it is dirty!
—this little filling station,
oil-soaked, oil-permeated
to a disturbing, over-all
black translucency.
Be careful with that match!

Father wears a dirty,
oil-soaked monkey suit
that cuts him under the arms,
and several quick and saucy
and greasy sons assist him
(it's a family filling station),
all quite thoroughly dirty.

Do they live in the station?
It has a cement porch
behind the pumps, and on it
a set of crushed and grease-
impregnated wickerwork;
on the wicker sofa
a dirty dog, quite comfy.

Some comic books provide
the only note of color—
of certain color. They lie
upon a big dim doily
draping a taboret
(part of the set), beside
a big hirsute begonia.

Why the extraneous plant?
Why the taboret?
Why, oh why, the doily?
(Embroidered in daisy stitch
with marguerites, I think,
and heavy with gray crochet.)

Somebody embroidered the doily.
Somebody waters the plant,
or oils it, maybe. Somebody
arranges the rows of cans
so that they softly say:
ESSO-SO-SO-SO
to high-strung automobiles.
Somebody loves us all.

Elizabeth Bishop's speaker stands aloof, characterizing the objects and circumstances of the filling station at which she's forced—reluctantly—to wait; but finally time itself, the time she spends looking deeper into the life of this object-world, discloses her sympathetic relation to it.

Look how the language of the poem proceeds—there's a gradual but sure shift from consternation and fastidiousness, evident in the first stanza's recoil (the general oiliness of things seems to her not only distasteful but even threatening: "Be careful with that match!"); this fastidiousness develops through the second stanza's dehumanizing account of the family of men who run this filling station; but it begins to relent, in the third stanza's curiosity about what lurks behind these people's occupational *use* to her. The figures of the filling station attendants begin to take on depth, just as her field of vision deepens to comprehend, behind the grease-monkey facade of the service station, a porch, a couch, and a family dog. By stanza four we have perfectly unexpected domestic details—comic books, lacework, a matched set of furniture, and an ornamental plant. That she cannot relinquish her native fastidiousness is evident in the repeated (though decreasingly frequent) references to oil: they become the comic recapitulation of a minor poetic theme—she uses the word "dirty" four times, and "oil-" or "grease-permeated" another four times, just in the first three stanzas—so we come to see it as part of *her* character, as much as the scene's; we expect it (as we expect features of human character) to continue. But, instead, our prim motorist begins to change, getting drawn into the humanity of the situation—and, where a shadow of her old fastidiousness arises, this change affords it some fairly hilarious (if irrepressible) variations, as in the characterization of the doily as "dim," the crochet as "gray," and the plants as oiled. What started as name-calling, as hasty and derogatory epithets (*dirty, disturbing, saucy, greasy*—indeed so many *esses* in the first two stanzas one might well hear hissing in them), later begins to weave a more generous art of variation, relieve itself with tinges of comedy, as she begins to see evidence of the domestic life she knows and values. In other words, name-calling turns to poetry.

Remember that this is not, as all poems are not, to be understood as spoken by the poet, only. In this case the character or persona who speaks at the poem's outset may very well be distasteful to Bishop herself. But as this character, Bishop's motorist, continues to observe, looking more deeply into the scene, as she gives up the denunciations of naming for the sympathies of suggesting—that is, gives up the motorist's habit of cursory looking at objects, in favor of the abider's more patient inquiring into acts of life—in the time it takes for objects to turn into subjects—she becomes a far more sympathetic character, can make a little poetry of her variations on the "dirty" words, and can intimate a caretakerly presence not only behind the surfaces of service stations, but behind the workings of the world at large.

It must be observed that her alienation from the very start seems gender-related—it is the alienation of a fastidious femininity before domains that remain even today potently, perfunctorily male. (The cheesecake calendar in the auto mechanic's back office seems some-times to serve as a sign of *that* realm's own brand of exclusivity.) What enlists the sympathy of Bishop's evidently female motorist reveals her own expertises: she notices not just furniture but *wickerwork,* not just cloth but *doily,* not just footstool, but *taboret;* she knows what kind of plant it is, and appreciates the details of the embroidery (she knows a daisy stitch when she sees one). The richness of her namings of these details (contrasting as it does with the verbal poverty of the mere blunt repetitive moralizing to which she was relegated at the realm of the gas-pump) points to a richness of sympathies in her, and begins to suggest a missing figure, a like-minded one, who has embroidered the evidences and who takes care of the men.

This introduction, into the brute mechanical scene, of the pos-sibility of caretaking changes her relationship *even,* finally, to the outer male domain. For it is not without sympathy and humor that she observes the begonia is "hirsute," and that it may be oiled regularly rather than watered. By now the sympathies brought out in her by the tracery of the feminine in the landscape, the whisper of a missing mother or wife behind this family filling station, can apply themselves not only in the far ground but also in the foreground: even the oilcans now seem to have been arranged by a caretakerly impulse, and the mechanisms of car care seem now able sympathetically to animate the men's world. (Notice how automobiles themselves become humanized for her at last—she calls them "high-strung," affording them all the delicacy of a social euphemism.) Looked at cinematically, the trajectory of her regard, of her insight, has zoomed in past the gas-pump surfaces of things, deep into the family background, and is now, in the final lines, drawing back again to see the whole—a vision this time informed by new sympathy: she's drawing back not to recoil, as at the outset, but because she's able to see more capaciously now—even to the extent of considering the world at large to be in the care of some invisible and loving presence.

"Somebody loves us all" is a declaration so overarching it can't fail to suggest a divinity—and divinity of the kind that makes all her previous distinction-makings seem trivial. For hers can now be no automatic god, no mechanic of the universe, merely of *use* as we motor our way through life; no mere deus ex machina, the dictable god. Nor can it be, by the way, any longer a god figured only as father or son. After she has taken time to see things in the light of that female caretaker whose traces she has detected, it's no accident that the "somebody" at the poem's end is scrupulously *not* named or gendered, but rises above the world of partialities. The fastidious motorist has, like Williams's motorist, been seized out of her usual lines of thought, out of the numbing horizontality of the world seen in passing, and into the axis of the vertical; her flight of magnanimity at the end suggests some line of celestial transport.

This speaker has come a long way. A poem is a vehicle. As you can see, it was not a casual impulse that led me to pick two poems in which the automobile brings the character to a moment of moral understanding. In America, the life of motion has been, preeminently, the life of the highway, and our moral understandings take place where we live. Often we live in passing (where Williams's poem begins). But in both of these poems, the aesthete's taste for glimpses of a nice clean complete artfully arranged life of objects comes unexpectedly face-to-face with life's messier demands—the demand that he or she get involved, participate (as readers also must) in the moving moment, and in time be committed to acts of living sympathy.

The true poetic moment is the moment the uncontainable shines through, or bursts out, spills over beyond the objective limits of the poem. That is the essential nature of the lyric, to suggest (over against all formulas) the form (as subject) of a moving meaning. To really enter a poem is not to escape; it is to have your mental map revised.

Little does the reader dream that the "Right of Way" might lead to the possibility of suicidal downfall, nor that the "Filling Station" might end up in transports of love—but that's what makes life and poems interesting—precisely that we don't know where we're going. Their richness is the richness of possibility. Even now, we can't say, at the end of "Filling Station," whether the "somebody" who loves us all is god or man or woman, but the poem has moved us beyond whatever automatic prejudice the speaker may have had about whether god is figured *only* male. Immediately after "The Right of Way" in the original volume *Spring and All,* Williams wrote, "in the condition of imaginative suspense only will the writing have reality." The senses of suspense at the end of "The Right of Way" are literal, metaphorical, and more: suspense in this poem is not meant, as many novelistic suspenses are, to be gotten rid of. We'll never be able to say we *know,* with any probity, whether the girl at the end of the poem is prostitute or cripple or soon-to-be literally fallen. But the poem has moved *us,* that much is sure, beyond whatever prejudice might have made us identify her in only one way. She is "suggestive" in a much broader sense than we would have obtained if we thought the driver were stopping merely to use her, just as the driver in "Filling Station" (and we) would have missed the richer understanding of love if she had persisted in seeing the men merely as *useful* to her, merely as serviceable. Poetry is not of use, in that small sense. It is a vehicle to move us from the smaller *to* the larger senses of destination: to move us out of our casual readerships, out of passing disregard, out of passivity itself, our habit of auto-immunity, and into that most mortal vulnerability: the capacity to respond.

ELLEN BRYANT VOIGT

Image

. . . an intellectual and emotional complex in an instant of time.

—Pound

There are two usual ways to praise the image. The first derives essentially from what can be called imitative or representational theories of art, what M. H. Abrams characterized so succinctly as "art-as-mirror," art whose primary function is to record and embody the shared reality we think of as the world. (He actually called these theories "mimetic," but I would like to reserve that term.) From this largely classical aesthetic position, the image is particularly valued as "a picture made out of words," and "the sensuous element in poetry":

> An image is the reproduction in the mind of a sensation produced by a physical perception. . . . When Archibald MacLeish says, in "Ars Poetica," that a poem should be "Dumb / As old medallions to the thumb," he not only means that the language of poetry should make important use of imagery, he also exemplifies what he means by expressing it in terms of imagery. . . . When, however, he says "A poem should not mean / But be," his meaning is the same but his language is not, for this statement is abstract rather than concrete and imagery-bearing, dealing as it does with an idea or concept rather than a perception or sensation. . . . (*Princeton Encyclopedia of Poetry and Poetics* 363)

The list of opposites is important: concrete rather than abstract; sensation rather than idea; perception rather than concept. Which is to say, allied with the body rather than the mind, even as examples of the type range from the literal use of concrete nouns (what I will call narrative detail) on the one hand, to the use of simile and metaphor on the other. That range is apparent in this passage, for instance, which begins in narrative exposition and ends in figure:

> About halfway between West Egg and New York the motor road hastily joins the railroad and runs beside it for a quarter of a mile, so

New England Review 13, 3–4 (Spring/Summer 1991): 254–68.

as to shrink away from a certain desolate area of land. This is a valley of ashes—a fantastic farm where ashes grow like wheat into ridges and hills and grotesque gardens; where ashes take the forms of houses and chimneys and rising smoke and, finally, with a transcendent effort, of ash-gray men who move dimly and already crumbling through the powdery air. (Fitzgerald 23)

Detail suggests empirical evidence; it makes the text plausible. A figure, by comparing an object or experience to something familiar, adds clarity; it makes the text accessible. When one assigns the primary allegiance of poetry to the world beyond poet and poem, the value of the image is its representational power—its ability to create in the mind a color, say, which is an "ostensible copy or replica of the objective color itself" (*Princeton* 363). Thus, while most textbook definitions of the image acknowledge all five senses, the primary—that is, most efficacious—sense is sight, and the sister art to poetry is painting.

The second usual way to praise the image presumes a different function, or purpose, for the poem. Here, M. H. Abrams's figure, in opposition to the mirror, is the lamp, and his term for the opposing set of assumptions, brought into play by the Romantic movement, is "expressive theories" of art. Abrams quotes Bishop Lowth, one of the Longinians:

The language of reason is cool, temperate, rather humble than elevated, well arranged and perspicuous. . . . The language of the passions is totally different: the conceptions burst out into a turbid stream, expressive in a manner of the internal conflict. . . . In a word, reason speaks literally, the passions poetically. The mind, with whatever passion it be agitated, remains fixed upon the object that excited it; and while it is earnest to display it, is not satisfied with a plain and exact description, but adopts one agreeable to its own sensations, splendid or gloomy, jocund or unpleasant. For the passionate are naturally inclined to amplifications; they wonderfully magnify and exaggerate whatever dwells upon the mind and labour to express it in animated, bold and magnificent terms. (Abrams 77)

Abrams follows this with general summary:

Figurative language, thus, is the spontaneous and instinctive product of feeling, which modifies the objects of perception. . . . (77)

Earlier, he quotes John Stuart Mill:

In so far as a literary product simply imitates objects, it is not poetry at all. As a result, reference of poetry to the external universe disappears . . . except to the extent that sensible objects may serve as a stimulus or occasion for . . . poetry. "[T]he poetry is not in the object itself," but "in the state of mind" in which it is contemplated. When a poet describes a lion he "is describing the lion professedly, but the state of excitement of the spectator really," and the poetry must be true not to the object, but to "the human emotion." (24)

So the image is no less valuable to expressive theories of art. It is still more or less a tool for imitation, but what is imitated shifts, and the list of suspicious elements—abstraction, idea, conception—is refurbished and restored along with "feeling": the poet's vision supplants the objective or empirical world, and the classical virtues of clarity and precision take second place to passion and sweep. Fitzgerald's extended imagery is seen to serve a new function—it gives us access to the writer's "symbolic vision" by "wonderfully magnify[ing] and exaggerat[ing]" the landscape he is describing:

Occasionally a line of gray cars crawls along an invisible track, gives out a ghastly creak, and comes to rest, and immediately the ash-gray men swarm up with leaden spades and stir up an impenetrable cloud, which screens their obscure operations from your sight. (23)

The importance of image, from this vantage, derives less from what we see through the lens and more from what we deduce from the smudges on it—in this case, the corruption and rootlessness of Tom and Daisy Buchanan. The passage washes over us like music.

In those lucid introductory chapters to his thorough study of the development of Romanticism, Abrams's interest is historical; mine is pragmatic. What interests me is how, two centuries after that great shift in underlying presumptions about art, the image is still so differently championed and defined by essentially opposing camps, although with the distance narrowed on that mind-body spectrum.

As others have pointed out, it was not a very large step from Romantic theorists' view that "the objects signified by a poem . . . [were] no more than a projected equivalent . . . for the poet's inner state of mind" to "the practice of symbolists from Baudelaire through T. S. Eliot" (Abrams 24–25). Here is Eliot's update, from his essay on Hamlet:

The only way of expressing emotion in the form of art is by finding an "objective correlative"; in other words, a set of objects, a situation, a chain of events which shall be the formula of that *particular* emotion; such that when the external facts, which must terminate in sensory experience, are given, the emotion is immediately evoked. If you examine any of Shakespeare's most successful tragedies, you will find this exact equivalence . . . the state of mind of Lady MacBeth walking in her sleep has been communicated to you by a skilful accumulation of imagined sensory impressions. . . . (100)

As is often the case with poets who undertake essays and lectures on poetics, Eliot was both justifying and camouflaging his own poetic practice: specifically, he seems busy erasing any tracks back to the mind/psyche/internal conflict of the poet as originating source and primary allegiance for his work. But his formula has held with remarkable tenacity: as intervening years and poems have taught us, though the "passionate are naturally inclined to amplifications," the expressive impulse needs embodiment in "external facts," in those images that mediate between poet and reader. Consider, for instance, this "expressive poem" of statement:

POPPIES

Little poppies,
Do you do no harm?

I cannot touch you,
And it exhausts me to watch you. . . .

There are fumes that I cannot touch.
Where are your opiates, your capsules?

If your liquors could seep to me, in this glass capsule,
Dulling and stilling. . . .

The tone is clear enough—erotic, tender, a bit impatient. But what is missing is motivation: we don't know why the speaker is seduced by, or seducing, the flowers, and we are shut out from the experience. This dilemma will not be helped much by restoring the purely descriptive, or representational, figures, those images that provide a "reproduction in the mind of a sensation produced by a physical perception" (*Princeton* 363):

POPPIES IN JULY

Little poppies, little flames,
Do you do no harm?

You flicker. I cannot touch you,
I put my hands among the flames. Nothing burns.

And it exhausts me to watch you
Flickering like that, wrinkly and clear red.

There are fumes that I cannot touch.
Where are your opiates, your capsules?

If your liquors could seep to me, in this glass capsule,
Dulling and stilling. . . .

The poppies are beginning to take shape, but to what extent are
they an "ostensible copy or replica"? "Flickering" should tip us off: it
invites us to stare at poppies in a way most of us probably have not,
would not—to stare long enough for the flowers to waver. What is
beginning to emerge is not objective, recognizable blossoms but the
agitated mind looking at them. The title is another clue: the titular
object is a totem. Here is the actual poem, with all its imagery and
figure restored:

POPPIES IN JULY

Little poppies, little hell flames,
Do you do no harm?

You flicker. I cannot touch you.
I put my hands among the flames. Nothing burns.

And it exhausts me to watch you
Flickering like that, wrinkly and clear red, like the skin of a mouth.

A mouth just bloodied.
Little bloody skirts!

There are fumes that I cannot touch.
Where are your opiates, your nauseous capsules?

If I could bleed, or sleep!—
If my mouth could marry a hurt like that!

Or your liquors seep to me, in this glass capsule,
Dulling and stilling.

But colourless. Colourless.

Sylvia Plath, whose poem this is, no doubt read Eliot's essay;
perhaps read it again or recalled it that last year of her life when she

wrote home jubilantly that she'd found a way to do it—to write poems directly from her own exhilarated, defeated, swirling emotional state. In poem after poem, it is the image that mediates between poet and page, between page and reader, to articulate the interior landscape and weather that is her subject. That penultimate verb—"marry"—for instance, doesn't enter the poem by accident; in July she was burning Ted Hughes's letters and papers while he was in London, probably for a tryst. In September, as the death poems began to take shape at an astonishing rate, she had, as she told friends, "thrown Ted out." The autobiographical circumstance infuses everything, muddying the lens—hell flames? The skin of a mouth? A mouth just bloodied? Bloody skirts? The size, color, and texture of the poppies shift and veer. Her subject, of course, is not poppies, nor does she expend much effort to render an exact description of them as things of the world; rather, it is the very discrepancy between these poppies and "real" or familiar poppies that makes the imagery an efficient means by which to embody, enact, dramatize the speaker's mind under threat, much as Lady MacBeth's incessant handwashing does.

The idiosyncrasy of the figures does not necessarily make them decorative or indulgent: they are the weight-bearing walls of the lyric structure. If the poem succeeds, it is because what might otherwise be abstract or inaccessible or private or alien—the speaker's desperation—floats between us and the "relict" in our minds (of real poppies) like a cluster of eye-motes. If the poem works, it is because the poem—and others in *Ariel* and eventually the flood of biographia—establishes the persona: that is, it works dramatically. And if it fails, it fails dramatically: the persona remains too idiosyncratic or unarticulated for the reader to understand her experience.

Given the neo-Romantic nature of confessionalism, to have recognized the need for mind to be embodied, for the text to make its case through the objects of the world, would seem to mark a victory for the other camp—poem-as-painting over poem-as-music. But the classicists have had to compromise as well. Thom Gunn, reviewing Christopher Isherwood in *Threepenny Review,* praised his "power of objective perception" this way:

> Too much has been made of his phrase "I am a camera," as Isherwood himself knew, but nevertheless—given the fact that humans are creatures of almost uncontrollable bias—a camera is not a bad thing to emulate. Even the practice of analogy is not completely un-camera-like: cameras often record that one thing resembles another, a church is like a knife, for instance, or foam on a brown stream like stout. The attempt to represent with clarity is always worth making, however impossible it is to achieve in absolute terms. (We may

call the attempt "fairness.") There is no danger of the writer's ever turning into a real camera, but the imitation of the camera may be good training. And its faithfulness of attention to physical imagery is valuable because through it we may learn about the appearance of the world outside of us, or in other words about things we didn't know before. Doing so helps us to escape from the singleness of our minds, which, if lived in exclusively, become prisons. (6)

The primacy of the world has been reasserted, and precision over magnification, but with a wistfulness: the imitative project is now a moral issue, "the attempt to represent with clarity" recognized as "impossible . . . to achieve in absolute terms," given the "almost un-controllable bias" of humans. This is the late-twentieth-century up-date, post-Heisenberg. The primary virtues and functions of the im-age remain the same: recording the dependable concrete nouns of our common reality, uncovering the congruence among them. But one expects the fog of the individual sensibility settling inexorably on the lens. I've concocted a three-stage exercise to demonstrate how that might happen in the drafting of a poem:

ON TOP OF A GREENHOUSE

The wind in one's britches,
the splinters of glass and dried putty,
the chrysanthemums through streaked windows,
flashing with sunlight,
a few white clouds, a line of elms,
and a crowd of people below.

This entry starts where Gunn urges us to start, and tries hard indeed to emulate a camera—a task that poses no real danger here since this isn't a real poem. More probable in composition is the movie camera:

CHILD ON TOP OF A GREENHOUSE

The wind billowing out the seat of my britches,
my feet crackling splinters of glass and dried putty,
the chrysanthemums facing up
through streaked glass, flashing with sunlight,
a few white clouds moving eastward,
a line of elms plunging and tossing,
and everyone pointing up and shouting.

Clearly, the text has taken on energy and color with the addition of movement, those present participles that agitate the long sentence fragment. But something else has been added too—a human figure. The pull of what Gunn calls with a certain ironic pleasure "uncontrollable bias" has been away from imitation, toward dramatization. And as the poem yielded to that pull, we might suppose, "the conceptions burst out into a turbid stream, expressive in a manner of the internal conflict," since here is what Theodore Roethke actually wrote:

CHILD ON TOP OF A GREENHOUSE

The wind billowing out the seat of my britches,
my feet crackling splinters of glass and dried putty,
the half-grown chrysanthemums staring up like accusers,
up through the streaked glass, flashing with sunlight,
A few white clouds all rushing eastward,
a line of elms plunging and tossing like horses,
and everyone, everyone pointing up and shouting!

What is rendered is not just a scene but what it felt like to be that boy. "Half-grown chrysanthemums staring up like accusers" is both representational, in that it seems a vivid and precise rendering of actual flowers growing in the greenhouse, *and* expressive, because a child doing something forbidden and risky would have seen them that way. "A line of elms plunging and tossing like horses" is a plausible "relict of a known sensation," as I. A. Richards defines image (*Handbook* 232), but it also articulates the rush of exhilaration experienced by the child, the freedom from and even power over the others, whose attention he has wholly secured while remaining firmly out of reach.

Of course, the first two "versions" of the poem are not drafts any more than were my "versions" of Plath; we don't know if Roethke set out with some equivalent of Gunn's injunction in mind and was pulled away from visual representation toward music and feeling, or began with an autobiographical, charged memory and worked toward its correlative in images that could make it available to the reader. Probably neither—probably, composition was the far less linear process described by Susanne Langer in *Philosophy in a New Key:*

A subject which has emotional meaning for the artist may thereby rivet his attention and cause him to see its form with a discerning, active eye, and to keep that form present in his excited imagination until its highest reaches of significance are evident to him. (203–4)

This is what she calls "presentational apperception," and it at least addresses, in ways that conventional notions of the image do not, the extent to which Roethke's realistic images of the greenhouse feel totemic—like Plath's grotesque poppies, like Kunitz's "root images."

In this poem, the contrasting similes ("like accusers," "like horses") and the crucial adjective "half-grown" seem not accidentally coincidental to both vegetation and child, equally attributable to the empirical world and to the internal conflict. They function as lyric signals in a way that parallels those moments of repetition in the texture of the sound:

> staring up like accusers,
> UP through the streaked glass

and

> everyone, EVERYONE pointing up and shouting!

Clearly, just as the symbolists tried to make abstraction corporeal, representational imagists (concrete *rather than* abstract, sensation *rather than* idea, perception *rather than* concept) must recognize Gunn's overlay of "bias" in what they record—not merely the objects of the world but those objects seen, touched, heard, smelled, tasted: rendered with a halo of human response. For the contemporary poet of classical OR Romantic affinity, then, the most useful function of the image would seem to be less "imitation" than "dramatization."

Both Gunn and Eliot suggest poem making as a kind of continuum, with the completed poem, and the reader in a box seat, somewhere dead center—Gunn being dragged there from the far left or representational position, from the world, from the unbiased camera eye, from the dependable senses, by the magnetic pull of the insistent subjective expressive sensibility on the right, Eliot's own point of departure. But for both, the image is the crucial mimetic device, essential for its power to enact not only what the writer-as-scientist has uncovered in the empirical world, or what the writer-as-ecstatic has isolated and articulated from the whirl of the individual psyche, but the moment when both are fused.

In other words, our usual ways of praising, defining, and understanding the image are trapped in a historical dichotomy we have since outgrown. Susanne Langer says:

A mind that works primarily with meanings must have organs that supply it primarily with forms. . . . [T]he world of sense is the real world construed by the abstractions which the sense-organs immediately furnish.

The abstractions made by the ear and the eye—the forms of direct perception . . . are genuine symbolic materials, media of understanding, by whose office we apprehend a world of things, and of events that are the histories of things. To furnish such conceptions is their prime mission. . . .

Visual forms . . . are just as capable of *articulation,* i.e., of complex combination, as words. But the laws that govern this sort of articulation are altogether different from the laws of syntax that govern language. The most radical difference is that *visual forms are not discursive.* They do not present their constituents successively, but simultaneously, so the relations determining a visual structure are grasped in one act of vision. Their complexity, consequently, is not limited, as the complexity of discourse is limited, by what the mind can retain from the beginning of an apperceptive act to the end of it. (73–75)

The power of an image, in a literary work, derives largely from its own essential paradox—a "picture in words" is a nondiscursive articulation rendered through the discursive systems of language, the body "thinking" through its senses, the mind embodied—which reflects the paradox of human consciousness: the fact that mind *is* body, whether sense organs or cerebrum. Thus the most effective images in poetry may be those in which the two opposing poles, the two ends of that mind-body spectrum, are collapsed in on themselves—those images that duplicate what Langer calls "presentational logic," delivering simultaneously the concrete and the abstract, the objective and the subjective, the representational and the expressive, the empirical and the assumed.

If the image, then, can reproduce not only what the poet sees but at the same time *how* the poet sees, one need not choose one over the other, the mirror over the lamp. That opposition, I believe, resulted from the constrictions of the term "imitation," which came to be lodged in the poetics of both camps through the customary mistranslation of the Greek work *mimesis,* which had

a different and somewhat broader range of meaning than the English word. Ultimately derived from *mimos,* which in the historical period denoted the "mime" or an actor therein, *mimesis* seems to have meant originally the mimicking of a person or creature through dance, facial expression, and/or speech and song. But the object so "imitated" might be a god, a mythical hero, or a fabulous creature, e.g., the Minotaur; in other words, mimesis could refer to an idea. . . . (*Princeton* 501)

Mimesis was the shared function Aristotle affirmed in all modes of poetry—even as he distinguished among them:

Epic Poetry and Tragedy, Comedy also and Dithyrambic poetry, and the music of the flute and of the lyre in most of their forms, are all in their general conception modes of mimesis. They differ, however, from one another in three respects—the medium, the objects, the manner or mode of mimesis, being in each case distinct. (*Poetics* 20)

To translate *mimesis* as "imitation" is to place it in opposition to "expressiveness," but Aristotle included expressive, or musical, poetry under its rubric. Eliot's formulation better secures the original notion—the mind perceiving or responding must be embodied, or dramatized, as Lady MacBeth's mind has been, through "a skilful accumulation of imagined sensory impressions"—but that too maintains the separation or difference between the concrete and the abstract. Mimesis was intended as not a "counterfeiting of sensible reality but a presentation of universals"—that is, "the permanent, characteristic modes of human thought, feeling and action" (*Princeton* 379).

For Aristotle, although the manner or mode of mimesis varied—with Tragedy the most efficacious, as Plato recognized in the *Republic*—in all the forms of poetry "the pleasure which the poet should afford is that which comes from pity and fear through mimesis . . ." (32). The allied modes, of course—"Epic Poetry, Tragedy, Comedy, Dithyrambic poetry, music of the flute and of the lyre"—have since hardened into distinct genres, with the first three split off now from verse and assigned to plays and to the novel, our contemporary epic. Thus all contemporary poets may be said to be, in light of his categories, writing lyric poems. Nevertheless, his classifications, and his notion of shared mimetic purpose, are still helpful in examining contemporary lyrics—poems that increasingly borrow strategies and values from narrative, drama, and essay or discourse.

What Aristotle meant by "pleasure . . . from pity and fear" was *catharsis:* the audience front-row center, the characters or actions sufficiently representational to be recognizable, or accessible, sufficiently expressive to be enlightening and moving. My thesis here is that the image, capable simultaneously of the "representational" and the "expressive," is the chief agent for mimesis in a poem written for the page—an equally effective tool no matter where the poet is located on the Gunn/Eliot spectrum, no matter now much the individual lyric poem may yearn for its allied modes. And it would seem, too, that the yearning occurs less between two points of a straight line than around the rim of a wheel, or circle. The issue seems as much pragmatic as theoretical, with Gunn advocating the virtues of narrative, of a self-contained world maintained by linear plotline, direct exposition, recognizable concrete detail, and what could pass as "objective perception"; and for its opposite, Eliot's slightly decadent, architecturally formal, paradox-ridden, individuated lyric. For contemporary poetry, which travels from one formal allegiance to the other at will, the more crucial choice, the real division, may be the vertical coordinates: discourse, on the one hand, encountered most purely in the essay, and on the other the highly presentational and mimetic forms of drama. After all, as Langer says, "the logical structures underlying all semantic functions . . . suggest a general principle of division. . . . [D]iscursive and presentational patterns show a formal difference" (83).

MEDUSA

I had come to the house, in a cave of trees,
Facing a sheer sky.
Everything moved,—a bell hung ready to strike,
Sun and reflection wheeled by.

When the bare eyes were before me
And the hissing hair,
Held up at a window, seen through a door.
The stiff bald eyes, the serpents on the forehead
Formed in the air.

This is a dead scene forever now.
Nothing will ever stir.
The end will never brighten it more than this,
Nor the rain blur.

The water will always fall, and will not fall,
And the tipped bell make no sound.
The grass will always be growing for hay
Deep on the ground.

And I shall stand here like a shadow
Under the great balanced day,
My eyes on the yellow dust, that was lifting in the wind,
And does not drift away.

The structure of Louise Bogan's poem is a familiar one—the "when/then" arrangement of so many sonnets, cast here into past/future, then and forever. The poem opens with a narrative gesture: two statements, one a past perfect narrative summary, one past expository:

I had come to the house, in a cave of trees,
Facing a sheer sky.
Everything moved,—

The stanza concludes with what the textbooks call two images and what I prefer to call one descriptive detail and one figure:

> —a bell hung ready to strike,
> Sun and reflection wheeled by.

And the meter and rhyme are, not accidentally I gather, those of the traditional ballad.

The next stanza prepares us syntactically, and with somewhat strained description, for some event or action—

> When the bare eyes were before me
> And the hissing hair,
> Held up at a window, seen through a door.

But the linear narrative movement is stopped by the period, which converts the three lines to a sentence fragment, just short of a real predicate—short, too, of the satisfying completion of the alternating rhyme scheme. Mid-stanza the little story seems to start again, with a further look at those concrete nouns, eyes and hair:

> The stiff bald eyes, the serpents on the forehead
> Formed in the air.

At last the rhyme scheme has been completed (hair/air) and the stuttered sentence is completed—or is it? Could "formed" in fact be only a past participle? If so, the entire stanza lacks an actual predicate, lacks the verb that is so essential to story, since story is so thoroughly caught in time. Or, if this *is* a predicate, what a curiously inactive and abstract one it is. The narrative is left hanging; cast entirely into subordination by the syntax, and the literal, physical detail suddenly seems, well, figurative—eyes aren't usually "bald" and hair doesn't hiss. As it happens, the image formed here is entirely referential—"conceptions burst[ing] out"—to the Medusa head of myth: to idea.

That's all we get for "then": the climactic event is curiously blacked out. We open the third stanza with what our encyclopedia called abstraction, three declarative independent clauses in a row, the first, with its severely passive construction, providing the only present moment in the poem, as a pivot—

> this is a dead scene forever now

—and the next two in the future tense that will dominate the poem's second half:

> Nothing will ever stir.
> The end will never brighten it more than this. . . .

At exactly the place where a good narrative would deliver its compli-
cating action, where the cameras should roll, where literal, concrete,
sensuous, representational images seem most appropriate and needed
to convince us, Bogan eschews them. But somewhere in the recesses
of our reptilian brains, we've noticed that the meter of the lines is that
of the opening stanza: initial irregular tetrameter, followed by a fully
end-stopped trimeter, then a third line of rough iambic pentameter,
and a final, shorter end-stopped line that delivers the rhyme:

> Nor the rain blur.

It is as if she were starting over—and in a way she is, going back as she
does to the dramatic setting. But what we get is not story, not a
sequence of events or actions, but two stanzas of dramatic imagery:
first, returning to the same scene in the continuous future, in succes-
sive declarative sentences with the most active predicates the poem has
used thus far:

> The water will always fall, and will not fall,
> And the tipped bell make no sound.
> The grass will always be growing for hay
> Deep on the ground.

And then turning the focus back to the speaker, the "I" who opened
the poem, Medusa's victim, in one sensuous sentence:

> And I shall stand here like a shadow
> Under the great balanced day,
> My eyes on the yellow dust, that was lifting in the wind,
> And does not drift away.

If Bogan starts the poem with Gunn's restrained camera, she
moves subsequently into Eliot's objective correlative. The recurrence
of the bell marks the shift. While "the bell hung ready to strike" is a
"relict of a known sensation," a familiar bell, an empirical bell, the
"tipped bell that makes no sound" is not—it does not exist in the
natural world. Concrete, sensual, specific, recognizable, the images
of water, bell, grass, shadow, and dust can also be called "idea-
bearing"—dependent as they are on the Medusa myth even to make
sense: suggestive as they are of other sorts of paralysis of the will, a
recurrent subject of Bogan's: congenial as they are to the general
dilemma of the lyric poet.

Though taxonomy may be of limited use, I think of these images
in the last two stanzas as dramatic images, distinguishable from the
detail ("house," "cave of trees"), description ("a bell hung ready to

strike") and figure ("hissing hair") of the first two stanzas. By dramatic, I do not mean to suggest they are used to further or enhance dramatic structure: the poem seems, in fact, to avoid assiduously both dramatic action and dramatic pacing in an extreme instance of the lyric's affinity for a fixed or frozen moment. Rather, such images may be thought dramatic because of their mimetic and presentational effectiveness.

In the Bogan poem, it might be argued that this effectiveness derives from an expressive impulse given over to what is, after all, a mask or assumed persona (Medusa's victim), a "represented" voice or sensibility, an actor who "mimes" or "mimicks" the experience in order to produce "catharsis" in the reader-audience. What may be of greater persuasiveness, then, is a poem less firmly lodged in the lyric hemisphere of that circle of forms, one that lacks a first person pronoun—and one that also shares with much contemporary American verse a greater interest in the discursive, a more liberal use of statement, and a more narrative structure. My example is from Philip Larkin—whose prose writings, at least, would appear to place him in the Gunn/Isherwood realistic camp of "objective perception."

THE EXPLOSION

On the day of the explosion
Shadows pointed towards the pithead:
In the sun the slagheap slept.

Down the lane came men in pitboots
Coughing oath-edged talk and pipe-smoke,
Shouldering off the freshened silence.

One chased after rabbits; lost them;
Came back with a nest of lark's eggs;
Showed them; lodged them in the grasses.

So they passed in beards and moleskins,
Fathers, brothers, nicknames, laughter,
Through the tall gates standing open.

At noon, there came a tremor; cows
Stopped chewing for a second; sun,
Scarfed as in a heat-haze, dimmed.

The dead go on before us, they
Are sitting in God's house in comfort,
We shall see them face to face—

Plain as lettering in the chapels
It was said, and for a second
Wives saw men of the explosion

Larger than in life they managed—
Gold as on a coin, or walking
Somehow from the sun towards them,

One showing the eggs unbroken.

The poem is structured around narrative—the story is told in the first five and the seventh stanzas in a fairly straightforward way. Stanza one sets the scene, stanza two introduces the main characters, stanza three offers partial and characterizing action, stanza four summarizes, stanza five provides the crucial event foretold by the title, a false or temporary climax, and stanza seven gives the concluding action-event. Missing a first person lyric speaker, the poem nevertheless skillfully establishes a point of view with its diction—pithead, pitboots, slagheap, moleskin, God's house—and develops tone through the relationship between the declarative, occasionally inverted syntax and the Anglo-Saxon music of those spondees and others throughout these stanzas: oath-edged, pipe-smoke, lark's eggs, nicknames, heat-haze.

But what I want to stress is what happens in the second half of the poem—gratuitous to the narrative, essential to the poetry. The formal arrangement of the poem thus far has been syntactically idiomatic: each of the first five stanzas is end-stopped with a period—each forms a complete, rhythmically and grammatically independent sentence. But stanzas three and five differ from the others in the sheer number of active predicates and in the disjunction between line length and phrase length. Stanza three is the most narratively active moment of the poem—

chased after rabbits
lost them
came back with a nest of lark's eggs
showed them
lodged them in the grasses

and the parallel predicates are anchored even more firmly by rhythmic and exact repetition:

lost them;
showed them;
lodged them.

Thus the throwaway narrative moment is given structural importance. It continues to resonate subliminally when we reach stanza five, with its three predicates, where the central narrative event is triple-stitched, rendered first discursively:

> At noon, there came a tremor;

then, severely enjambed, with a narrative detail:

> cows
> Stopped chewing for a second;

and finally, in awkward, nonidiomatic syntax, with a descriptive, or representational, figure:

> sun,
> scarfed as in a heat-haze, dimmed.

Three lines, three delayed caesurae, three final isolated stresses.
    That rhythmic pattern continues into the next stanza—

> *The dead go on before us, they . . .*

—to maintain the slower pace and keep the poem steady as the voice changes radically. It is the voice from the pulpit, again in a triple unit—three clauses as openly declarative as the previous lines were formally, then syntactically, strained, and the figure so far from fresh or colorful as to read as cliché:

> *The dead go on before us, they*
> *Are sitting in God's house in comfort,*
> *We shall see them face to face—*

This feels like an aside, lengthening as it does the natural pause of the held moment of the explosion, but remarkably, despite the shift in tone, it proves not an interruption but an announcement of what is to follow, as if the narrator of *Our Town* had come to the edge of the stage and told us what to watch for. Pure exposition—

> Plain as lettering in the chapels
> It was said, and for a second
> Wives saw men of the explosion
>
> Larger than in life they managed—

is followed by the same triple-stitching used for the trauma itself—here, first figure ("Gold as on a coin . . ."), then narrative detail ("walking / Somehow from the sun towards them . . ."), and finally dramatic image ("One showing the eggs unbroken").

That structural, syntactical symmetry of course gives the last three lines of the poem weight equal to the three that contain catastrophe—and that is partly why they are so convincing. In addition, as with Bogan's bell we greet those eggs with a shock of recognition. They appeared early, in the most caesura-ridden stanza of the poem, the most active, the most "narrative":

> One chased after rabbits; lost them;
> Came back with a nest of lark's eggs;
> Showed them; lodged them in the grasses.

Appeared, that is, as a passing detail; but now they reappear, with the same generalizable singular pronoun ("one"), with the same uncomplicated gesture ("showed them"/"showing them"), in the same matter-of-fact understated tone, its tenderness this time radiating out from the gesture of one of the men and encircling them all, as if the pronoun had changed referent. This image provides the poem's only attempt to validate the idea at the center of the poem: that the men may in fact be in heaven, "sitting in God's house in comfort." The poem's strategy is to let us see what the wives saw, or thought they saw. The descriptive figure "Gold as on a coin," by comparing the vision to something already known, already familiar, makes it vivid and clear, which is to say makes it accessible. The descriptive detail "walking / Somehow from the sun towards them" yields empirical evidence, which is to say makes it plausible. But it is with the last line that we experience pity and terror, Aristotle's catharsis: it is there that we feel what the wives felt, their wish not only to reverse time to the earlier moment in the day, restoring the lost to the earth, to their casual pleasures of chasing rabbits and finding a lark's nest, but to mend the exploded bodies—

> *The dead go on before us, they*
> *Are sitting in God's house in comfort,*
> *We shall see them face to face . . .*

> One showing the eggs unbroken—

and we feel it not through exposition, or description, or narration, but through the mimetic power of the final dramatic image.

WORKS CITED

Abrams, M. H. *The Mirror and the Lamp*. Oxford 1953.

Aristotle. *Poetics*. In *Criticism: The Major Statements*. Ed. Charles Kaplan. St. Martin's 1986.

Bogan, Louise. *The Blue Estuaries: Poems 1923–1968*. Ecco 1977.

Eliot, T. S. *The Sacred Wood: Essays on Poetry and Criticism*. Methuen 1920.

Fitzgerald, F. Scott. *The Great Gatsby*. Scribner's 1925.

Gunn, Thom. "Christopher Isherwood: Getting Things Right." *Threepenny Review*, Summer 1990: 5–9.

Larkin, Philip. *The Collected Poems*. Farrar, Straus, Giroux 1989.

Langer, Susanne. *Philosophy in a New Key*. Scribner's 1953.

Plath, Sylvia. *The Collected Poems*. Harper and Row 1981.

Plato. *Republic*. Trans. Alan Bloom. Basic Books 1968.

Princeton Encyclopedia of Poetry and Poetics, The. Ed. Alex Preminger. Princeton 1974.

Roethke, Theodore. *The Collected Poems of Theodore Roethke*. University of Washington 1982.

Richards, I. A. Quoted in Holman, C. Hugh, *A Handbook to Literature*. Bobbs-Merrill 1972.

STEPHEN DOBYNS

Writing the Reader's Life

A piece of writing is a body of information governed by a purpose and that purpose determines how the information is ordered. Actually two purposes govern any piece of writing: the purpose of the particular category of writing (menus, traffic tickets, poems) and the purpose of the particular example of writing. The purpose of the particular category of writing is determined by its function, which, in art, may be no more than to give pleasure, which further means that it must be communicated to an audience. That function also governs the individual example of writing.

Function directs purpose. A specific poem, for instance, may try to make the reader see the world in a new way. It may try to engage the reader's emotion. It may try to amuse or frighten or teach or do all the above. These are aspects of a specific poem's purpose. At the same time, a certain tension exists between the form as it is defined at any moment within the culture and the individual example of the form. A reader is always reading a poem through his or her opinions about poetry as well as through every poem he or she has ever read, and the writer is writing the poem through his or her opinions and through every poem ever read. We call a work original when it surprises these opinions and expands our preconceptions of the limits of the form.

Purpose is predominantly communicated through structure. It is through structure that a piece of writing releases its information to the reader. Most simply, structure is strategy imposed upon time. The fact that the piece of writing has a purpose makes it necessary that it have a structure, which means, in turn, that it must have a beginning, middle, and end. But the writer can have no real sense of the beginning, middle, and end until he has a sense of the work's purpose. Even the most original and avant-garde work can be seen to have a beginning, middle, and end, although perhaps only when the piece is long over and has been subjected to strict analysis. Otherwise, the piece of writing can be no more than a fragment.

Structure is two things at once. It is the order in which the information is released and it is also information itself. This double function of structure becomes most important in the arts where the structure of a poem or story or novel can carry as much information as the actual

One Meadway (Spring 1991)

content. We can further define structure as the formal elements of language, texture, pacing, and tone imposed upon the informal elements of action, emotion, setting, and idea. In this definition, form becomes an element of structure so that structure is both the order and the manner in which the information is released. This information is composed of those elements that the writer feels are important and that are intended to affect the reader, and clearly they are chosen from a much larger body of information. Consequently, we can further define structure as the selection and organization of significant moments of time. The decision of what is significant is one of the functions of talent, which Chekhov once defined as the ability to distinguish between the essential and inessential.[1]

Aristotle described structure as the most important of the principles governing a work of art.[2] No matter how brilliant the writer's idea or how strong the emotion, if the structure is weak, everything else fails. Structure then is not only what allows the work to be complete in itself but also what enables the work to be communicated and become a source of pleasure.

A work of art has certain requirements that make it a work of art and not something else, such as a restaurant menu or instructions on how to operate a car. A work of art must engage the intellect. It must engage the emotions. It must engage the imagination. It must function as metaphor. It must contain within it some definition of beauty. Why it must be these things is perhaps another matter, but it must be these things to the writer and it must be these things to the reader. Consequently, the structure too must engage the intellect and emotions and imagination. It too must be beautiful and function as metaphor. The structure of Pope's "Rape of the Lock" is, among other things, a metaphor of Pope's perception of the world: a world that is orderly and rational. The structure of Apollinaire's "Zone" is a metaphor of Apollinaire's perception of the world: a world that is disorderly and surprising.

Structure cannot be accidental. Even if structure is determined by chance methods, the use of chance constitutes a chosen method. Additionally, structure not only conveys information but it is also a thing in itself, beautiful, metaphoric, and so on, although divorced from its content it is nothing. Information without structure is cacophony. Structure without information is a theoretical abstraction. One can speak of certain traditional forms, such as the sonnet form, but that form is only a small part of the structure of a particular sonnet. But the fact that structure itself may be informative and beautiful allows us to have many novels or stories or poems on similar subjects. We have an unlimited number of ways to present a limited amount of information.

It would seem that the world itself has no structure other than what is given to it by the passage of time, while entropy, gravity, the alternation of light and dark, and the cycles of reproduction become elements of its form. Human beings require structures, looking for them either in the master plan of some deity, or imposing them to protect life and to protect and increase property. Consequently, the creation and imposition of structure is done both to protect against and in defiance of the apparent anarchy of what exists. The imposition of structure makes human beings feel they have some sort of control over the anarchy. A government is an imposed structure, as are the Ten Commandments and the Bill of Rights. One of the functions of these structures is to give us the apparent ability to divide actions and events into right and wrong, good and bad.

Structure in a piece of writing allows us to divide actions not into good and bad—that may come afterward—but into probable and improbable. A main requirement of a piece of writing is probability. A story must be probable. Even if it is fantastic or surreal or a fairy tale, it must be probable within its governing situation. The world itself need not be probable. That is one of the things we find most frightening about it. In the world, the hero may be struck by lightning as he is getting ready for battle. In a story, that lightning, if it is to exist, must be explained. One of the functions of the gods in *The Iliad* is to make lightning bolts probable.

We read a work presuming that nothing is accidental, all is purposeful, whether consciously or unconsciously, and so we move through a story or poem by asking questions of it—why this, what's that? By coming up with answers we separate the possible from the probable and follow the trail of probable. We try to do that in the world as well, but the world is not governed by any such rules of probability, or rather there are far more things affecting events than we can possibly see, and the result is a sense of randomness. One of the ways that fiction and poetry work is by making the reader anticipate what is going to happen next and, further, by making the reader want to know what is going to happen. Always balanced against our anticipation is possible frustration, the fear that the whole thing is going to fall apart. But the reader is only going to anticipate and want to know what is going to happen if he trusts that the events stretching ahead are in some way probable within the whole, that they are not gratuitous or arbitrary or merely possible. This suggests something about art: that we require of it certain conditions that we don't find in life, that is, that it be probable. The ending of a story may be tragic or comic or surreal or trivial, it may surprise and shock but it must also be probable and, ideally, inevitable. That is one of the paradoxes of writing, that the conclusion of a given piece must appear both inevitable and surprising. This inevitability is something we find particularly satisfying. It suggests the world has an intrinsic structure that it in fact may not have. Virtue is rewarded; the guilty are punished; love prevails.

A poem or piece of fiction exercises the imagination like little else. Not only do we imagine the scene we are reading but we also imagine what might happen next and then measure what is happening against what we imagined was going to happen. Also, if the work has engaged us, we have a series of desires and fears about what may lie ahead: desires and fears that may actually become painful. Furthermore, as we read, we are measuring what we are reading against all we have ever read. Whenever we read a poem we are also, at some level, holding that poem against every other poem we have ever read. We don't necessarily judge the new poem against the others, although we may, but we are using our previous reading to help us anticipate what might happen next in the poem presently at hand. Whatever we read is always filtered through what we have ever read; in the same way it is filtered through where we are in history, filtered through our culture and psychology, our various ideologies, our precarious card house of opinions. Ideally, the writer knows this and makes use of it. Structure is not only a matter of knowing what word to put down next, but also knowing how the reader will respond to that word, knowing how you want the reader to respond and why.

Any work is tied to the writer's life even if it isn't specifically autobiographical. Structure always reflects the writer's view of the world and is tied to the writer's psychology. Whenever we write, we describe ourselves. The writer is not presenting us with reality. That has been a critical fallacy that has moved in and out of popularity since Plato: that art attempts to imitate reality. Rather the writer gives us a metaphor for the writer's own emotional/psychological/intellectual/physical relationship with what he or she imagines reality to be, a metaphor that we value in part because either it is similar to our own relationship with reality (or what we imagine reality to be) or simply because it wakens us to our relationship with reality.

Reality itself is a hidden thing. The word forms a paradox because it stands for a great mystery. A child is born into this mystery. Then two things happen: he gathers information about it and he grows used to it. Both are necessary. But because the child grows used to the mystery, he feels that his information about it must be correct. This is not necessarily true. The function of his information (apart from its possible validity) is to make him feel comfortable in the world around him: that medium in which his time is spent. In fact, the world continues to be as much a mystery as it was at the beginning, but now as an adult he has formed opinions and grown used to it, meaning he has worked to diminish its oddness, its menace, and its surprise.

Neurosis, according to Freud, allows us to believe the lies we make about the world in order to reduce its threat and be able to function within it. Neurosis shields us from the fact of our mortality. We constantly speculate about reality, but we are unable to see it accurately because of (1) our conditioning (social, cultural, class, and family background); (2) our psychology; (3) our limited perspective in space and time; (4) the questionable trustworthiness of our senses (is the blue that I see the same blue that you see); (5) the degree of our intelligence and imagination; (6) our emotional engagement; (7) our dependence on language, which is reductionist and inexact, and so on. But despite our ignorance, we do know a few things and that little knowledge is backed up with endless opinions.

Perhaps we would not care so much if we didn't know that reality can hurt us. In fact, it will someday kill us. And so we gather information about it. This is one of the reasons we read fiction and poetry. It gives us information about our lives. We read in part to see ourselves. We read to see what our future will be. We read to see that our most private joys and fears are in fact shared within the human community. And we read to have our opinions about the world challenged or even strengthened. Our question is what is it to be a human being, what is it to be me. At some level the subject of any story or poem is always the reader, and the writer who ignores this does so at his peril. No matter how caught up we are in the story of *Lord Jim*, the novel is finally a metaphor of how human beings behave in this world. We read it to learn about ourselves.

We read to learn about our lives and be distracted from our fate. And the more the writer engages our attention and makes us want to read, the more we are distracted. Clearly, some writing offers more distraction than information, but we value the information more than the distraction, and if we sufficiently value the information, then we call the writing literature. Dostoevsky's *Crime and Punishment* and Raymond Chandler's *The Big Sleep* are both mysteries, but we value Dostoevsky more because (1) he gives us more information about the world, (2) his novel is not limited by its conception, which, in the Chandler, is simply the problem of who killed whom, and (3) he creates a metaphor that tells us something about our own lives.

All fiction and poetry begin in metaphor. We sometimes forget this in fiction because the narrative, during the act of reading, tends to overshadow the metaphor, but the work still began as metaphor and if it remains important to us, it remains important as metaphor. Joyce's *Ulysses* began as a metaphor that stood for the author's relationship with some aspect of reality, a subjective reality. The same is true of Conrad's *Lord Jim* or Yeats's "The Second Coming" or Chekhov's "The Duel" and so on.

The act of inspiration is, I think, the sudden apprehension or grasping of metaphor. When we understand a metaphor, that understanding comes all in a flash. At one moment the mind is blank—it is merely questioning—and in the next there is knowledge. Look at these metaphors or aphorisms from W. S. Merwin's *Asian Figures:*

Thief
plans even his naps

Quiet as
a crane watching
a hole over water

Tree grows the way they want it to
that's the one they cut first

Don't curse your wife
at bedtime[3]

The move from ignorance to knowledge in these examples seems spontaneous. Actually what we do is imagine a past and future and this provides a context in which to understand the single moment presented by the metaphorical aspect of the aphorism. A metaphor has an image (or an analog) and an object. For instance, quiet is the object and the crane poised over a hole in the water is the image. Inspiration is the act of hitting upon something that will function as the image for a particular object. The act of writing most usually begins with this discovery. Even if what is discovered is no more than a sound or picture or word, our attentiveness to it, as writers, is caused by the fact that we see it potentially functioning as metaphor.

We write in part to discover why we are writing. The work begins in the intuition and, by writing and learning about what we have written, we carry that intuition toward consciousness.

A major idea of the Romantics was that the writer surrenders himself to the process of writing. The work must emerge from the whole of the writer's personality (possibly even from outside him), not just from his ego. The writer cannot force the work into existence. The writer must submit himself to the metaphor in order to discover its meaning, not seek to dominate it. These ideas continue among us. But where they split into several different theories is in the amount of conscious control that the writer asserts in the revision process.

On one side, it is felt that the writer should take no control, that to tamper with the intuition is to diminish it. "First word, best word," Allen Ginsberg has said. On the other side is the belief that the intuition is only so much raw material that the revision process shapes, much as a sculptor shapes his stone. Baudelaire mocked those writers who "make a parade of negligence, aiming at a masterpiece with their eyes shut, full of confidence in disorder, and expecting letters thrown up at the ceiling to fall down again as a poem on the floor."[4] He also wrote, "Everything that is beautiful and noble is the product of reason and calculation."[5] Poetry has swung back and forth between these two positions since before Homer.

Personally, I feel that structure isn't intuited so much as chosen. That original inspiration gives us metaphor and may prioritize a series of images, but it doesn't show how to arrange the words. It simply gives information. The work can only be structured when the writer has a degree of understanding about his or her meaning and purpose, and that may require a lot of writing and revision. The writing itself is a process of discovery, the discovery of the meaning of the metaphor. But eventually the writer decides what he or she is about and at that time the work evolves into its final form.

In praising Edgar Allen Poe's control of the short story, Baudelaire wrote,

> If the first sentence is not written with the preparation of the final impression in view, the work is a failure from the start. In the whole composition, not a single word must be allowed to slip in that is not loaded with intention, that does not tend, directly or indirectly, to complete the premeditated design.[6]

What Baudelaire was praising was structure. He was saying that each poem, story, or novel has an optimum number of words, an optimum number of pieces of information, that their order must be determined by the writer's intention, and to go over or under even by one word weakens the whole. In fact, he argued that anything that does not contribute to the whole, detracts from the whole. "There are no minutiae in matters of art," he said.[7]

It is often a weakness of beginning writers to see structure in terms of chronology: first this happened, then this. But the selection and organization of significant moments of time in no way requires one to be chronological. The first sentence has to be written, as Baudelaire points out, with the final impression in view. "Everything for the final impact!" he quoted Poe as saying.[8] Chekhov encouraged writers to take the story they had written, throw away the first half and start in the middle. He was urging writers to start with action, not background. But Chekhov's dictum had another purpose than just starting with something important. His purpose was to start with something that would actively engage the interest of the reader.

Interest is partly created by making the reader ask questions, by creating tension. Chekhov argued that if a pistol is introduced at the beginning of a story, it must be fired by the end of the story. The introduction of that pistol creates tension in the form of suspense. Reading is done partly with our memories: we know that pistols get fired and people get killed. Inevitably, the presence of the pistol affects our expectations.

Structure is nothing without creating in the reader a desire to know what is going to happen. Once that desire is created, then the reader's attention is driven forward by means of pacing, which is effected by creating patterns of tension and rest, by making the reader anticipate, then sometimes frustrating and sometimes rewarding that anticipation. The energy in a work—meaning whatever keeps us reading—comes in part from (1) the balance between what we know and what we don't know and (2) how well the writer has made us want to know. A failure in much writing, especially poetry, is that the writer has not created sufficient tension, has not done enough to make us want to know. If the writer takes the reader's interest for granted, then he or she will fail.

So far I have been lumping fiction and poetry together but here we come to a division. Fiction requires narrative: events moving from one moment in time to one or more other moments in time. It may even be a prerequisite of fiction that it have narrative. We go to fiction for the story and the writer creates the tension to make us read by creating suspense, by making us want to know what is going to happen. Once the suspense is created, the writer controls our attention by varying the mix of primary and secondary information. Primary information is "Bob shot Alice." Secondary information is "It was a sunny morning in the second week of June." Secondary information is completely necessary. It gives the setting, controls our sense of space and time, develops the characters, and may present ideas, but it also stands in the way of what we want to know most: is Bob going to get away with shooting Alice? This is a difficult balance. If there is too much secondary information, then we don't care what Bob did. If there is too little, then the situation is not plausible and we don't believe in Bob and Alice. Obviously other things also effect tension in fiction but primarily it works by the writer making us want to know and then creating suspense by delaying our access to primary information.

In much poetry what is important is the lyric moment, a sort of crescendo when the emotional world of the writer joins with the emotional world of the reader. The primary function of narrative in poetry is to set up these moments. We are more interested in these moments than we are in the story. Also, in a poem, there is not this same mix of primary and secondary information. And clearly, a poem need not have any narrative at all, or perhaps only the smallest degree of narrative, since an element of narrative exists whenever one has two moments of time. This limits the role of suspense in poetry. Of course, some suspense may occur within the narrative and suspense may also be created by other means. When Philip Larkin titles his poem "The Explosion," he is creating suspense. But in poetry, what the writer most often uses to create tension is surprise. In fiction, because of its use of narrative, the main element of tension is suspense and the secondary element is surprise. In poetry, however, suspense tends to be secondary to surprise.

Both suspense and surprise affect our anticipation, and again I want to stress that one reads on four levels of time. One reads in the present, word by word. One reads in the future, anticipating what will happen next. One reads in the past, remembering at any moment what has already happened. And one reads in the more distant past, through one's knowledge and the books one has already read. But it is our anticipation and curiosity that keep us reading. Without that, we stop. The writer seeks to control the degree of our anticipation and curiosity through suspense and surprise. Both deal with the future. Suspense is a state of mental uncertainty. It means wanting some specific thing to happen or not happen. Surprise is the sudden occurrence of an unanticipated event that creates tension partly by shaking our faith in our anticipation and producing uncertainty. All good metaphor incorporates surprise. Here are three more of Merwin's *Asian Figures*.

> Sudden
> like a spear from a window

> His hundred days of sermons
> all gone in one fart

> Full of danger
> as an egg pyramid[9]

Our understanding in each case is sudden and unexpected. A good poem constantly uses surprise. Even originality is a form of surprise. A poem works by setting up various patterns that heighten the reader's anticipation. Rhyme and meter are the most obvious examples but there are also repeated words, half-rhymes, alliteration, and other more complicated patterns. Once a pattern has been established, then any variation creates surprise, while any unexpected rhyme or half-rhyme or any aural echo can also become a surprise. And clearly, line breaks can create surprise as well. Look at Philip Larkin's poem "The Explosion."

> On the day of the explosion
> Shadows pointed towards the pithead:
> In the sun the slagheap slept.

> Down the lane came men in pitboots
> Coughing oath-edged talk and pipe smoke,
> Shouldering off the freshened silence.

One chased after rabbits; lost them;
Came back with a nest of lark's eggs;
Showed them; lodged them in the grasses.

So they passed in beards and moleskins,
Fathers, brothers, nicknames, laughter,
Through the tall gates standing open.

At noon, there came a tremor; cows
Stopped chewing for a second; sun
Scarfed as in a heat-haze, dimmed.

The dead go on before us, they
Are sitting in God's house in comfort,
We shall see them face to face—

Plain as lettering in the chapels
It was said, and for a second
Wives saw men of the explosion

Larger than in life they managed—
Gold as on a coin, or walking
Somehow from the sun towards them,

One showing the eggs unbroken.[10]

Although there is suspense in the fact that we suspect an explosion is going to occur, Larkin greatly diminishes the actual explosion, reducing it to a tremor that makes the cows stop chewing for a second. What we have instead is the great surprise of the eggs: eggs that are transformed from a piece of secondary information to the primary metaphor of the poem, a metaphor that tells us something about the immortality of the soul.

Larkin surrounds this surprise with other surprises. For instance, the poem is written in trochaic tetrameter, and the use of the same meter as Longfellow's "Hiawatha" is itself a surprise. Through the first four stanzas the meter is regular and each line is end-stopped. In the fifth stanza, the stanza of the explosion, Larkin completely overthrows the meter and enjambs the lines, making a small metaphor for the explosion itself. The next stanza, from the prayer book, also comes as a surprise and again the meter is thrown over and the first line is enjambed. The first line of the seventh stanza reasserts the meter. The next line breaks it and the third line reasserts it. The first two lines of the last full stanza reassert the meter and then Larkin breaks it again in the last two lines, a metrical surprise to go with the surprise of the eggs, while the presence of the one line by itself also forms a surprise.

There are additional surprises. For instance, Larkin uses a series of spondees or double stressed words in the first half of the poem: pithead, slagheap, pitboots, oath-edged, pipe-smoke, larks' eggs, moleskins, nicknames, tall gates, heat-haze. They are not placed in any particular pattern yet after a bit we come to expect them, while their irregular appearance creates a surprise. He also uses alliteration to make small aural surprises, as in his use of the ss and ps in the first two stanzas. Although there is no regular rhyme, there is a lot of irregular rhyme, such as coughing/shouldering, lost them/showed them/lodged them, brothers/laughter/tremor, standing/chewing. Each of these rhymes creates a small surprise. Some of this is simple texturing but much of it directs our attention or underscores particularly important parts of the poem.

In terms of the arrangement of information, the first stanza establishes the context and the second stanza begins the action. We are given two different times: the time of the explosion and the time in church. In the first, there is a sort of stationary camera. Then the camera disappears in the prayer and reappears at the end. There are two kinds of language: that of the poem and that of the prayer. There are two realities: the events around the explosion and the vision of the women in the chapels. The shifts in time, language, and levels of reality all create surprises, that is, they are unexpected. We have not anticipated them. These surprises leave us uncertain as to what lies ahead and set us up for the main surprise, which is the reappearance of the eggs.

These surprises build tension. Tension is also affected by line breaks. An enjambed line creates tension and an end-stopped line relaxes tension. Sentence length and syntax affect tension. Rhythm affects tension. Tone and pacing affect tension. Tension can also be increased and relaxed by moving back and forth between obscurity and clarity. The poet uses tension to drive the reader through the poem, to make him want to read and anticipate what is going to happen. Consequently, tension becomes a key element of structure, since if the poet has not made the reader want to read, the rest doesn't matter. Tension is the fuel that propels the reader through the landscape that the writer has created.

Fiction does it a little differently. First of all, far greater importance is given to narrative, character, and conflict. Frank O'Connor once wrote:

There are three necessary elements to a story—exposition, development, and drama. Exposition we may illustrate as "John Fortescue was a solicitor in the little town of X"; development as "One day Mrs. Fortescue told him she was about to leave him for another man"; and drama as "You will do nothing of the kind," he said.[11]

In this definition suspense becomes part of drama: what will happen next? Exposition, development, and drama form part of plot, which Aristotle called "the first principle, and, as it were, the soul of a tragedy."[12] Plot is the ordering of information, the arrangement of incidents within the narrative to create a pattern of causality. *A Handbook to Literature* defines it as a "planned series of interrelated actions progressing, because of the interplay of one force upon another, through a series of opposing forces to a climax and a denouement."[13] In fiction plot forms a major part of structure. It is not so necessary to poetry, since plot requires narrative and poetry need not have narrative. Also, as already indicated, narrative in poetry often works to set up certain lyric moments, not necessarily to move us toward a climax and denouement. But, because the writer is always working against the reader's anticipation, the future has to be made uncertain and the poet creates this uncertainty through surprise. Suspense is the foremost method of creating tension in fiction; surprise is the foremost method of creating tension in poetry.

Consider this tiny piece of fiction by Lon Otto called "A Very Short Story."

> A man is at a party with his former lover and her new husband. She is in one part of the room with her husband, talking with some old friends. He is a little way off, telling a story. And then he starts making a peculiar kittenish, rhythmical crying sound, then continues with his story.
>
> She and her husband do not look at each other. It is the sound she makes while making love. He does not pay any attention to them. The story is not about her; it is just that the woman in his story makes the same sound in bed as she makes. There is a certain tension in the room.[14]

William Trevor defines a short story as "the art of the glimpse"[15] and that is what Otto has given us: a glimpse. Of course he is making a joke with his title, but he is also setting up certain expectations. The first sentence creates suspense by giving us a triangle. That suspense depends a great deal on our own life experience. We know that triangles are potentially dangerous. The second and third sentences give us the scene and the beginning of the action. The fourth sentence gives us a very detailed and strange action, the "peculiar kittenish, rhythmical crying sound." It is moderately surprising but what we mostly feel is curiosity.

Otto heightens this curiosity with the first sentence of the second paragraph: the fact that the husband and wife refuse to look at each other. The sentence delays us and we are also uncertain whether it is secondary or primary information. The next sentence identifies the peculiar sound. Then Otto seems to pull away from the triangle. The former lover apparently isn't aware of what he is doing, although he may be aware and this ambiguity itself creates tension. In the last sentence, Otto glides out of his story with his remark about tension, a tension that is obviously felt by the newly married couple: the husband aware that his wife had been involved with the storyteller, the wife's awareness of this awareness and perhaps, too, the wife is struck by how completely she has gone out of her former lover's head, that she has become invisible to him, and perhaps the husband is also struck that his wife is someone who has become invisible to her ex-lover, that this woman he loves, his new wife, is ultimately very forgettable. Furthermore, there exists the possibility that the ex-lover has created this situation on purpose—to suggest that he has forgotten when he has not forgotten—and that perhaps he does this out of revenge.

One could expand the Otto story, flesh out the characters, give more action, but that wouldn't change the "glimpse" that is at the heart of the story. Otto leaves out nothing that is necessary to that glimpse and he creates the tension right at the beginning that propels us toward it.

Structure, then, has two parts. It is the formal elements of language, texture, pacing, and tone imposed upon the informal elements of action, emotion, setting, and idea. And it is the creation of tension to make the reader want to know what is going to happen: the making and controlling of anticipation. Both parts are governed by purpose, which means that the writer must discover his or her intention, must discover the meaning of the work. Only after that discovery can the work be properly structured, can the selection and organization of the significant moments of time take place. The writer must know what piece of information to put first and why, what to put second and why, so that the whole work is governed by intention.

It is this perfection of structure that allows the work to transcend its author, allows the work to be complete by itself. If the structure is imperfect, then the work remains tied to the writer and dependent on his or her psychology for completion and interpretation. But the work belongs to the reader. Its hidden subject is the life of the reader. It is through structure that the writer moves the work from his or her life to the reader's life, that the metaphor is moved from the quirky specificity of the writer's life to the greater universality of the reader's life. We write, finally, to be free of things, not to express ourselves; to become articulate, not to mumble to ourselves; to drive our feelings and vague ideas into consciousness and clarity. Structure is our pri-

mary means of achieving articulateness and consequently of communi-
cating our discoveries.

NOTES

1. Anton Chekhov, *Anton Chekhov's Life and Thought: Selected Letters and Commentary,* ed. Simon Karlinsky (Berkeley: University of California Press, 1975), 104.

2. Aristotle, *Poetics,* in *Criticism: The Major Texts,* ed. Walter Jackson Bate (New York: Harcourt Brace and Co., 1955), 23.

3. W. S. Merwin, *Asian Figures* (New York: Atheneum, 1973), 38, 11, 4, 65.

4. Charles Baudelaire, "Further Notes on Edgar Poe," in *Selected Writings on Art and Artists,* trans. P. E. Charvet (Cambridge: Cambridge University Press, 1972), 206.

5. Baudelaire, "The Painter of Modern Life," in Charvet, 425.

6. Baudelaire, "Further Notes on Edgar Poe," 200.

7. Ibid., 206.

8. Ibid., 202.

9. Merwin, 37, 41.

10. Philip Larkin, *Collected Poems* (New York: Farrar, Straus and Giroux, 1989), 175.

11. Frank O'Connor, *The Lonely Voice* (Cleveland: World Publishing Company, 1963), 26.

12. Aristotle, 23.

13. William Flint Thrall and Addison Hibbard, *The Handbook of Literature* (New York: Doubleday, 1936), 356.

14. Lon Otto, *A Nest of Hooks* (Iowa City: University of Iowa Press, 1978), 77.

15. William Trevor, "The Art of Fiction *CVIII,*" in The *Paris Review* 31 (Spring 1989): 135.

TONY HOAGLAND

On Disproportion

For the purposes of generalizing, the world of poems might be divided into two large camps: the conservative, well-wrought, shapely poem, and the deformed, admirably lopsided, zany, and subversive one. Of course, poems don't truly belong entirely to either category—they are neither Democrats nor Republicans; they don't have jerseys stenciled with *A* or *D* for Apollonian or Dionysian. Any good poem tames the savage or savages the tame to some degree; the best-mannered poem holds certain opposing energies in containment and bulges with the effort; likewise, the poems we admire for their sprawling shagginess obviously have integrity and unity in ways that make it possible for us to apprehend them as completed wholes.

Proportion and disproportion turn out to be slippery terms. Yet in this essay in favor of "disproportion," I want to admire some poets' conscious indulgence in stylistic effects, and to advocate indulgence of the unconscious impulses that occur in our writing, even when such indulgences distort the "packaging" of the poem.

Let me begin with the premise that form and value are always associated. Moral prescriptions perennially are affiliated with choices about whether to be formal or not. We can see such tendencies in Horace's essay "The Art of Poetry":

> If a painter chose to set a human head on the neck and shoulders of a horse, to gather limbs from every animal and clothe them with feathers from every kind of bird, and make what at the top was a beautiful woman have ugly ending in a black fish's tail—when you were admitted to view his picture, would you refrain from laughing, my good friends? . . . such a book . . . will be like a sick man's dream, in which no two parts correspond to any one whole. . . . [Imaginative liberty does not extend to the point that] savage should mate with tame, serpents couple with birds, or lambs with tigers.

When Horace makes his statement of dos and don'ts, his mustn'ts, he appears to have a somewhat realistic, mimetic poem in mind. His persuasive technique is social; he threatens us with ridicule. And then

Parnassus: Poetry in Review 19, 2 (Winter 1994): 110–27.

there is an odd, inadvertently mythological quality to his negative examples—mermaids, griffins, flying snakes—which will come to seem significant. But Horace himself likes art that harmonizes and subordinates parts to a whole; that keeps things, or places them, in perspective. Horace was an exceptionally sane poet. If we want to see his artistic ideals embodied, we might look at his own poem, "Rectius Vives," alive with rectitude:

> The proper course in life, Licinius,
> is neither to always dare the deep, nor,
> timidly chary of storms, to hug
> the dangerous shore.
>
> Who values most the middle way
> avoids discreetly both the squalor
> of the slum and a palace liable
> to excite envy.
>
> The gale shakes most the lofty pine,
> tall towers fall with the louder
> crash, and the highest peaks most often
> are struck by lightning.
>
> Hopeful in evil times and cautious
> in good, ready for weal or woe,
> be prepared. Jupiter imposes
> the ugly winter,
>
> but then withdraws it. Bad luck
> is not forever: Apollo varies
> his archery sometimes by harping
> to waken the Muse.
>
> In difficult straits show spirit
> and fortitude, but on the other hand
> always shorten the sail when you
> run before the wind.

It is remarkable, reading this essay-poem, to observe how constant our expectations about what a poem can be have stayed over 2,000 years. Legions of poets today share Horace's idea of what a poem is. In means as well as theme, "Rectius Vives" is classically proportioned. As it is a poem about keeping one's wits amid changing circumstances, its concrete materials are constantly shepherded by their regularly reiterated thesis: "the middle way is best, be prepared." In good essay form, the poem builds its case, sandwichlike, with alternate layers of assertion and illustration. The poem achieves its "depth," its third dimension, by directing the reader's eye back and forth between the levels of the universal and the particular. The imagery, drawn principally from weather and navigation, is consistent in nature and degree, type and scale. The figures digress but briefly and always relevantly. The poem never "adheres" to its details, or lingers over them, but proceeds at a steady pace. Formal yet fluent, rhetorical yet conversational, the style itself is a model of temperance. The poem projects an admirable vitality and freshness, despite its age and its civility; surely civilization was fresher then.

Here is a more contemporary example of the "well-proportioned poem," William Carlos Williams's "Pastoral":

> The little sparrows
> hop ingenuously
> about the pavement
> quarrelling
> with sharp voices
> over those things
> that interest them.
> But we who are wiser
> shut ourselves in
> on either hand
> and no one knows
> whether we think good
> or evil.
>   Meanwhile,
> the old man who goes about
> gathering dog lime
> walks in the gutter
> without looking up
> and his tread
> is more majestic than
> that of the Episcopal minister
> approaching the pulpit
> of a Sunday.
>   These things
> astonish me beyond words.

The conventions of this poem seem all Williams. In its descriptive method and its celebration (and canonization) of the unpoetic ordinaries of dog lime and sparrow, the style has an appealing plainness and directness that seem open and American, exemplary of its message. For all its apparent spontaneity and candor, though, Williams's poem, like Horace's, is didactic in its intention and argumentative in its structure; and despite its spirit of democratic subversiveness, its poetic proportions could be called architectural and conservative. A formal, not a mimetic, concern for proportion accords each character in the poem a roughly equal number of lines—two pairs of subjects are descriptively compared to illustrate the thesis that birds are superior to people and dog lime gatherers more noble than Episcopal ministers. The poem is carefully balanced; linguistically, the number of lines and words assigned each "frame" of the poem accords with the conceptual hierarchy endorsed by the poem: seven lines for sparrows, six for humans; dog lime gatherers, six; ministers, three.

The sections of the poem are basically equal in conceptual and linguistic weight; the poem maintains a consistent distance from its scenery and topic. It is symmetrical and lucid. Though the suburban landscape, juxtaposed with the poem's title, declares that Williams is revising the traditional pastoral, the title nonetheless declares his consciousness of its literary and formal heritage. Its paternity, like its formal balance, is clear.

Oscar Wilde, an unlikely source for defining proportion in art, usually argues that all art is exaggeration. But in "The Decay of Lying" he remarks:

Enjoy nature! I am glad to say I have entirely lost that faculty. . . . What art really reveals to us is nature's lack of design, her curious crudities, her extraordinary monotony, her absolutely unfinished condition. . . . If nature had been comfortable, man never would have invented architecture, and I prefer houses to the open air. In a house we feel all the proper proportions. Everything is subordinated to us. . . . Egotism itself, which is so necessary to a proper sense of human dignity, is entirely the result of indoor life.

Wilde's praise of housing, which is also his praise of art, implies that making is a matter of editing and arranging. Though he concedes that such order may be illusory, Wilde doesn't care; he is probably the kind of individual who, in another era, would have said that reality is for people who can't handle drugs, or for people who don't realize that art is infinitely preferable. He is more frank than most artists about the ego drive that lurks beneath making, and the need to make the ego feel safe. The goal, as he presents it, is a sense of mastery. The method is subordination: subordination, for example, of illustration to concept. In an artwork governed by such values, we might well expect the use of figurative language to be rationed and extraneous detail to be excluded. Psychologically speaking, Wilde depicts repression as a useful agent in creative shaping.

This may sound like a harsh summation of the proportion agenda, but all—or at least, most of us—have internalized it anyway. We reveal the presence of such biases when we say a poem should be "economical" and "efficient," applying commercial terminology to art; we go to *work*shop, not to playshop, where we decide whether a poem *earns* our attention or not. A real poem gets its *work* done without dallying or distraction. But of course, control exacts a cost too: It is often achieved at the expense of discovery and spontaneity.

What is art that does not subordinate parts to the whole, or to the self, or offer perspective? We might logically call it *insubordinate,* and it is a variety of insubordinations that I wish to praise.

Disproportion as Extravagance: Stevens

Wallace Stevens may have been the first poet in whose work I recognized elements of style as deliberately excessive. Stevens is sometimes called baroque, a term originally used to describe irregularly shaped pearls. Its application to art originally was negative in connotation, but applied to literature *baroque* is defined as "the breaking up and intermingling of classical forms" to achieve "elaborate, grandiose, energetic and sometimes highly dramatic effects."

There are many kinds of excess in Stevens to admire, or, depending on your temperament, to dislike. As an inexperienced reader when I came to him, deaf to most nuances of language, I needed a style as potent and clownish as his to alert me to the existence of such a thing as style and its possibilities. The oddity, for example, of the second stanza of the poem "Loneliness in Jersey City" intrigued me:

> The deer and the dachshund are one.
> Well, the gods grow out of the weather,
> The people grow out of the weather;
> The gods grow out of the people.
> Encore, encore, les dieux . . .
>
> The distance between the dark steeple
> And cobble ten thousand and three
> Is more than a seven-foot earthworm
> Could measure by midnight in June. . . .

What, I had to ask myself, was a nonsense verse, a stanza that seemed to belong more to the oeuvre of Dr. Seuss in his Circus McGurkus period, doing in a poem by the renowned Wallace Stevens, a poet noted for his formidable difficulty and dignity? Why was metaphysical assertion—"the gods grow out of the people"—framed in the Howdy Doody rhythms of nursery rhyme? Such childlike liberties pointed me to other tonal exaggerations in Stevens's work, and to interpret them as playfulness rather than loftiness. Thus while Stevens, in poems like "Sunday Morning" or "The Idea of Order at Key West," was represented as being grand, it was the grandiose Stevens that I loved; the mock-heroic rather than the heroic, the polka rather than the waltz, the tuba and the pennywhistle rather than the violin sonata.

From Stevens, that noble rider, I learned something about the role of self-indulgence and spontaneity in writing; that pleasure was permissible as an end in itself, that insubordination was desirable; that a poem could be elastic in form instead of architectural, more like a Slinky than a Grecian urn. Consider the shameless sonic extravagance of the beginning of "Bantams in Pine Woods":

> Chieftain Iffucan of Ascan in caftan
> Of tan with henna hackles, halt!
>
> Damned universal cock, as if the sun
> Was blackamoor to bear your blazing tail.
>
> Fat! Fat! Fat! Fat! I am the personal.
> Your world is you. I am my world.

I am my world, says Stevens, in these erratically linked, eruptive couplets. Is this the cry of a major poet or a giant, sophisticated infant? If maturity is defined as the ability to defer immediate gratification in favor of long-range goals, as surely patient Horace would contend, Stevens is an often immature poet.

But the truth is not so simple. Stevens leads us to appreciate that excess and pleasure are, if not synonymous, at least related. Freud calls pleasure as motivator the "pleasure principle," and saw it accurately as the adversary of hierarchical, organized, "adult" civilization. Adulthood, he said, requires not only restraint, but the internalizing of social structures, priorities, taboos, deferments. And of course, much of our best poetry is exactly about such growing up, about the recognition of and compromise with external realities. The architectural poetry of perspective is precisely about the organization of desires in the context of possibility and limitation.

Yet Stevens never quite took this lesson to heart. Instead, the independence of song from factual possibility, the self-sufficiency of art, and the joys of self-creation compose easily half of Stevens's theme. His willingness to gallop off, his love of stylistic prodigality, allowing language to balloon into clause upon clause, is partly related to his nature as a lyric poet, innately more loyal, involved, immersed in the passionate moment than in the long perspective. He celebrates experience, or he creates it, but he is not really interested in organizing it into hierarchic modules. Often, Stevens's poems are poorly organized; or rather, they are ordered by their self-generating music and whimsical associations rather than by beginnings, middles, and ends, by story or argument. There are no true narratives in Stevens, and few "facts"; all things are rather images, linguistic slide shows that bloom and vanish on the billowing clouds of his lyric.

It is this pleasure-oriented style rather than any concept or event that is the *originating* impulse for many of his poems. "The Bird With the Coppery Keen Claws," to take just one example, is nothing more than a fantasy about a supreme parakeet. Or consider the alchemical exaggerations of "Sea Surface Full of Clouds," all pomp and style, with its oceanic, masturbatory, rhythmic descriptions of the same scene over and over again, with microtonal variations:

> The slopping of the sea grew still one night
> And in the morning summer hued the deck
> And made one think of rosy chocolate
> And gilt umbrellas . . .

> The slopping of the sea grew still one night
> At breakfast jelly yellow streaked the deck
> And made one think of chop-house chocolate
> And sham umbrellas . . .

> The slopping of the sea grew still one night
> And a pale silver patterned on the deck
> And made one think of porcelain chocolate
> And pied umbrellas . . .

And so on. Stevens's pleasure here is brazenly associated with excess instead of wisdom, with fantasy instead of fact, with opulence instead of utility. His spoofing of the reality principle is in part spiritual, of course, asserting the supremacy of the imagination over reality. But Stevens dynamically and intentionally subverts the powerful superego of poetic tradition, which designates the poet as the merchant of meaning, custodian of morality, truth, etc.

Despite the examples I have provided so far, the pleasure principle in Stevens is the source not just of comic, mock-elegant effects, but of a sometimes far-reaching heartiness. It seems important to emphasize the human value of flamboyance in a time when the plain style predominates, when what elegance there is tends to exhibit the virtues of the austere style, when ornamentation is viewed suspiciously as "mere style." How many poets would be nervy enough to end a poem as Stevens concludes "The Man on the Dump": "Where was it one first heard of the truth? The the." Or as he ends "On the Road Home":

It was when I said,
"There is no such thing as the truth,"
That the grapes seemed suddenly fatter.
The fox ran out of his hole.

You . . . you said,
"There are many truths,
But they are not parts of a truth."
Then the tree, at night, began to change,

Smoking through green and smoking blue.
We were two figures in a wood.
We said we stood alone.

It was when I said,
"Words are not forms of a single word.
In the sum of the parts there are only the parts.
The world must be measured by eye;"

It was when you said,
"The idols have seen lots of poverty
Snakes and gold and lice,
But not the truth;"

It was at that time, that the silence was largest
And longest, the night was roundest,
The fragrance of the autumn warmest,
Closest and strongest.

"On the Road Home," I admit, is different from the other Stevens
poems on exhibit here, in that it has an implied, nearly believable
landscape, two people, even dialogue. It asks after perspective, rather
than filling a universe with the speaker's consciousness. We can recog-
nize, in the regularly paced, measured, qualifying stanzas of the poem,
units of an *argument*. The world described is not dominated by mind,
or pleasure, or language, though in it language catalyzes certain trans-
mutations. It is a world without fixed points of truth, not flooded
with human consciousness but inhabited by, among other things,
speech. It is a poem about reality with a small r rather than the big R of
Stevens's other work.

But even the relative groundedness of the poem and Stevens's un-
characteristic acknowledgment of limitations does not explain the dar-
ing closure, with its heap of reverent, rhythmic superlatives. Here,
Stevens's extravagance of affirmative language seems exciting in a

way that is more than linguistic or self-regarding because his praise for the surrounding inhabited world is a genuine response that resists being reductively apprehended.

Hyberbole as Style

Stevens is often labeled as a poet of style, of manners, in a dismissive tone that implies the poet of experience is ultimately more valuable. These days the unadorned poetry of autobiography crowds the pages of literary magazines, proclaiming the virtue of the raw, the mimetic, and the experiential. In the face of those poems of sensational trauma and loss, those iron lungs and cluster cancers, the wheezing and sucking of the life support systems, the needles and tubes running in and out of the poem, dripping juices, how can style compete? What kinds of advantages does extravagance offer? What particular depths and dimensions is it capable of imparting to a poem?

We've seen one example in "On the Road Home." Now I want to turn to several examples of hyperbole. Hyperbole is a peculiar instance of disproportion in which perspective is warped, a language event in which the naming of a thing inappropriately exceeds the size of the thing named, thereby causing a lopsidedness that threatens to capsize the poem. Consider the hyperbole with which Stevens begins "Two Figures in a Dense Violet Light":

> I had as lief be embraced by the porter at the hotel
> As to get no more from the moonlight
> Than your moist hand.
>
> Be the voice of night and Florida in my ear.
> Use dusky words and dusky images.
> Darken your speech.
>
> Speak, even, as if I did not hear you speaking,
> But spoke for you perfectly in my thoughts,
> Conceiving words,
>
> As the night conceives the sea-sounds in silence,
> And out of the droning sibilants makes
> A serenade.
>
> Say, puerile, that the buzzards crouch on the ridge pole
> And sleep with one eye watching the stars fall
> Below Key West.

Say that the palms are clear in a total blue,
Are clear and are obscure; that it is night;
That the moon shines.

Reading this overture, we entertain again the fleeting chance that we will encounter an actual relationship between two characters in a Stevens poem. This turns out not to be the case. Ultimately, the "Other" here is a sort of stand-in for the muse. Notice, though, the complex kinds of distance made possible by multiple types of inflation in the first stanza:

I had as lief be embraced by the porter at the hotel
As to get no more from the moonlight
Than your moist hand.

In the elaborately delayed syntax, the archaic diction ("as lief"), the crabby overstatement of the speaker's petty preference, and the fantastic alternative to reality proposed (embracing the porter at the hotel), we get what amounts to character description. The speaker is simultaneously capable of self-mockery and the insulting observation about the moistness of his companion's palm. The courtly, archaic, gibing use of the adverb "as lief" likewise frees us from the obligation to identify with the situation. The exaggerated poeticalness underscores the petty spirit of the complaint, and does so at an early point in the sentence. This style could be said to be uneconomical—the marriage of a lot of fancy words to a little bit of situation—but the result of this inflation is that we feel protected. We are provoked to recognize that here the gap between words and things is large, and that we are living in the roomy language-half of the equation. The safety of that license frees us to admire and enjoy the poet's ability to inflect reality in ways that an exclusively plain style never could.

From the linguistic vaudeville of this highly stylized beginning, the poem takes an unlikely direction, eventually arriving at a tone of grave sincerity. For though the hyperbole of the opening is mockery, it nonetheless establishes a high rhetoric, which enables the poet to segue into a boozy eloquence and then into a serious invocation. Logically, perhaps, such a transition should not be possible. But Stevens demonstrates an important truth: that our tolerance for inconsistency, our ability to change direction in an artwork, is greater than we commonly suppose.

A passage from Denis Johnson's early poem, "It's Thursday; Your Exam Was Tuesday," shows how a seemingly prolix style can add unique dimensions to a narrative. Johnson plays with the extravagant distance between language and actuality to create a complexly accented perspective:

And then—ascending
over the rooves, the budded tips
of trees, in the twilight, very whole
and official,
its black

markings like a face
that has loomed in every city
I have ever known—it arrives,
that gigantic yellow warrant
for my arrest,
one sixth the size
of the world. I'm speaking
of the moon.

The most literal-minded of readers might charge that the poet wastes
twelve lines to say nothing more than that "the moon came up."
Johnson's unhurried description does in fact suggest the physical slow-
ness of the moon's rising. The superlatively unlikely and warped meta-
phor, however, "that gigantic yellow warrant / for my arrest / one
sixth the size / of the world," is both comic and stylistically effective in
communicating the speaker's paranoia. Moreover, its absurdity, plus
the skillful, self-conscious use of slow motion line breaks and delayed
information, communicates the speaker's ironical awareness of his
own mental imbalance. Style and a highly controlled poetical excess
again make possible psychological nuances that would be impossible
for the plain style. The prolonged, imaginative, mock-gothic suspense
of the arrest warrant imagery heightens our involvement and pleasure
in the poem, and the bump of the literal, when it finally arrives—the
flatly spoken "I'm speaking of the moon"—both recalls us from our
involvement with the speaker's fantastic subjectivity and condemns us
to a less exotic confrontation with the circumstances of his reality. Like
him, we discard our excessive emotional and poetic baggage and see
what is before us. Johnson integrates high style and dirty substance;
stylistic pleasure enhances the genuine seriousness and despair of the
poem as a whole. Comedy and pathos coexist.

The Ecstatic

Multiple types and degrees of disorder, of disproportion or insubordi-
nation, are encoded in poems. One important case is that of ecstatic
poetry, defined by sudden lateral movements and disorganized surges
of language and psyche that might be edited out of a Horatian poetry.
Though Stevens's inflections are majestic, hedonistic, and spontane-
ous in their way, they are so self-contained that they resemble power

steering. Dionysian frenzy is beyond them. Stevens is not truly interested in losing control; rather, his songs tend to prove his omnipotence. Because he isn't really penetrated by anything external, he can only give birth to himself over and over again. Stevens, oddly enough, is sensuous but bodiless.

But the god of ecstacy is Dionysius, the irrational, blissed-out deity who at birth was torn apart and reborn; this rending is itself analogous to the rending apart of the rational and linear by intoxication. The poetry of rapture embraces categorical confusion; it desires to lose control and enter the vertical moment, to lose balance and escape from time and the self.

Susan Mitchell's *Rapture,* surely one of the most exciting collections published in 1992, is full of titled perspectives and beautifully written, unconventionally proportioned passages. One thing that unifies the collection is a fascination with loss of control, both perceptual and linguistic. In *Rapture,* the sustained tension is between Mitchell's desire to be consumed by experience and the guarded indifference required by life in the material world. In a style alternately plain and plush, alternately swooning with verbal sensuality and withdrawing into arch skepticism, Mitchell makes rapture believable and contemporary.

Though one theme of the collection is the poverty of words to register emotional complexity, the poems delve deep into language in a quest for the ultimate articulation, pushing the speech envelope towards incoherence or glossolalia. I offer this passage from a longer poem, "Cities," as an example of writing that is allowed to dilate elastically, far beyond the bounds that most of us would allow in our more missionary, perspective-ridden poems:

> I want something else in my mouth
> Bread and butter, coffee and cream, blink and stutter
> *In the city where I was born*
> but not so fast—
>
> I want something other
> the *cough* in *coffee* and the *cawf* in *cough*
> the *dog* in *doggerel* and the *dawg* in *dog,* not *god*
> but *gawd.* Forget *gaudy,* forget *gaudeamus igitur.* I want
> the *gutter* in *gutteral* and syllables like crates loaded
> onto barges rusted, planks swollen, gangrenous, bitter
> as iodine and its ignominies, the conglomerates stuffed
> into my mouth before my tongue
> was pulled out by the roots, I want my crooked teeth, language
> before orthodontia, the sounds unbarred, the buck
> and buckle and overlap. . . .

In rock music, feedback occurs when a guitarist moves his instrument too close to its amplifier—an ugly screeching, burning sound is the result. Of course the sound is often produced deliberately; in Mitchell's poem, we see what happens when speech becomes its own object, pushing against the perimeter between music and noise, between language and the pure voluptuousness of sound that would mean escape from consciousness and the self. Pushing, in a very basic sense, on the limits of form.

To some degree such moments occur in everybody's writing, when the language is energized, dilates, balloons, proliferates, and begins to write us. That experience is one of the rewards of writing. Yet I am quite certain that such Dionysian moments are commonly trimmed back, controlled, wrought into shape, perhaps eliminated entirely to conform to standards of economy and proportion. We discard such insubordinate language because it doesn't match the rest of the furniture in the house, because we aren't supposed to allow an elephant in the living room: It makes ownership unclear.

From one of Tess Gallagher's poems, I find another example of lateral acceleration. The instability of Gallagher's poems causes some people to like them and others to dismiss them. I admire them because their disorder maps, with remarkable precision—though the cost may be "neatness"—the rich fission and fusion of psyche itself as it occurs at the moment when the poet is seized by the muse (the medievals called it the *furor poetica*) and carried away. For me these runs of metaphor/thought/perception, when they work, are thrilling; the rational pace of standard discourse is thrown aside in a canter of irregularly unfolding, often fantastic figures for knowing and sensing. Here is an extended passage from "Legend With Sea Breeze," a refusal-to-mourn poem, that shows the ignition and blast-off of such a moment:

> Oh my black horse, what's
>
> the hurry? Stop awhile. I want to carve
> his initials into this living tree.
> I'm not quite empty enough to believe he's gone,
> and that's why the smell of the sea
> refreshes these silent boughs, and why
> some breath of him is added if I mar the ritual,
> if I put utter blackness to use
> so a tremor reaches him as hoofbeats, as
> my climbing up onto his velvet shoulders
> with only love, thunderous sea-starved love,
> so in the little town where they lived
> they won't exaggerate when they say
> in their stone-colored voices

that a horse and a woman flew down
from the mountain, and their eyes looked out
the same, like the petals of black pansies
schoolchildren press into the hollow
at the base of their throats as a sign
of their secret, wordless invincibility.
Whatever you do, don't let them ring any bells.
I'm tired of schooling, of legends, of
those ancient sacrificial bodics dragged to death
by chariots. I just want to ride my black horse,
to see where he goes.

The whirling extension and complication of the figure into a nar-
rative-legend is not tidy or architectural; it is sidereal, digressive,
frenzied. There are accompanying confusions: Whose "velvet shoul-
ders," for instance, is the speaker standing on? To what use is "utter
blackness" put? This poem qualifies as insubordinate because the
writer has followed the bursting of imagination into psyche and
language into bravado: "I just want to ride my black horse, / to see
where he goes."

Let us pause, and ask here, is it any coincidence that this deforming,
disproportionate burst ends with the image of a woman joined to a
horse, the very sort of image that our civic, civilizing poet Horace
warned us about? And is it a coincidence also that Freud, in his essay
about the pleasure principle and the reality principle, on the page
beside a cartoon of the brain—a lumpy little thing—anatomizes the
relative position of the ego and the id this way:

> the ego in relation to the id is like a man on horseback, who has to
> hold in check the superior strength of the horse; the analogy might
> be carried further. Often a rider, if he is not to be parted from his
> horse, is obliged to guide it where ever *it* wants to go. . . .

The unruly "galloping" in these excerpts from Mitchell and Galla-
gher can be seen not only as an ecstatic "giving in" to linguistic and
imaginative inspiration, but also as a rebellion against the predictable
development of more generic poems. As Mitchell says, "*In the city
where I was born* / but not so fast." Gallagher's poem also explicitly
wishes to "mar the ritual" forms of poetic mourning she is engaged in.
"Legend With Sea Breeze" explodes a poem of mourning into a liberat-
ing celebration of self. Such subversive balkings and flurries may be
psychologically expressive, but they also represent strategies of deliber-
ate "ugliness," a disordering of what is called, significantly, "the well-
executed poem." Psychoanalytically, again, let us once more recall
Horace's images—these poems are griffins, a woman's body joined to

a fish's tail, snakes coupled with birds, the tame and the savage laughably or horribly joined.

Excesses, this essay argues, are good. In capable hands, they demonstrate freedom, give pleasure, celebrate artifice, react against convention, and illustrate the healthy, complex earthiness of the maker. But how much digression, wildness, lack of control, tumult of style and content can a poem contain? Until rapture ruptures? The easy answer and the only true one is that it will take as much as it takes. The final standard is whatever works.

·A friend who once edited a poetry magazine used to return manuscripts with a note saying, "a little more savoir faire, please." I now understand, I think, what he meant by this arch and arrogant advice. Reading many poems, I too often want to say, "a little more excess, style, violence, savoir faire, please." It was Rilke, our great model for the ecstatic poet, who asked in the Ninth Duino Elegy, "Are we not here, perhaps, simply for saying, *House, Bridge, Gate, Jug, Olive Tree, Window,* possibly *Pillar, Tower?*" His question suggests a life's work in the plain style: that an artist would be well-exercised if kept on a diet of nouns only.

But Rilke the poet, in the poem itself, hardly slows down at his own suggestion; he pirouettes, leaps, spins, commands, begs, refuses—and goes on to add, "but for such saying, remember, as never the things themselves hoped so intensely to be!"

For it is the job of the poet to give pleasure, to amaze and exhort as well as testify to the real. Song is heroic. It has its place even at a funeral. How else will we remember that anything is possible?

GREGORY ORR

Four Temperaments
and the Forms of Poetry

Now there are diversities of gifts but the same Spirit.
— 1 Corinthians 12:4

I'd like to propose that poets are born with a certain innate form-giving temperament that allows them to forge language into the convincing unities we call poems. This form-giving gift is more important than any other a poet might possess. Different poets are born with different temperaments, and the nature of their temperaments determines essential qualities of the poems they write.

To my way of thinking, there are four distinct temperaments. If a poet is born with one temperament, then he or she grows as a poet by developing that temperament, but *also* by nurturing the others. The greatest poem is one in which all four temperaments are present in the strongest degree, though no one in English but Shakespeare could be said to exhibit all four in equal vigor. The main point is, great poems show the presence of all four, though in varying proportions.

A Glance at Characteristics and Dynamics

The four temperaments are: story, structure, music, and imagination.

1. Story: dramatic unity—beginning, middle, and end. Conflict, dramatic focus, resolution.

2. Structure: the satisfaction of measurable patterns. It is akin to higher math, geometry, theoretical physics—the beauty and balance of equations. It manifests itself in sonnets, villanelles, sestinas (closed structures) and, to a lesser extent, in metrical lines, rhymed couplets, and repeated stanza patterns (open structures).

3. Music: rhythm and sounds. It includes syntax, the syllabic qualities of English that determine rhythm (pitch, duration, stress,

From *Richer Entanglements: Essays and Notes on Poetry and Poems,* 3–14 (Ann Arbor: University of Michigan Press, 1993). Copyright 1993 by Greg Orr. First published in *The American Poetry Review* 17, 5 (Sept./Oct. 1988): 33–36.

loudness/softness), and the entire panoply of sound effects (alliteration, assonance, consonance, internal rhyme, etc.). (I realize that music is an old metaphor for the texture of rhythm and sounds in a poem, and perhaps not a very adequate one, but I'm going to use it anyway.)

4. Imagination: the flow of image to image or thought to thought. It moves as a stream of association, either concretely (the flow of image) or abstractly (the flow of thought).

It is essential to recognize that the four temperaments form another pattern. Story and structure are *intensive* in their impulse; music and imagination are *extensive*. Story and structure concern limits and correspond to our desire for and recognition of the role of law. Music and imagination concern our longing for liberty, the unconditional and limitless.

Limiting impulse: Limitlessness:
Story   Music
Structure   Imagination

Although each of the temperaments is capable, in and of itself, of creating the unity we call a poem, for a poem to have the stability and dynamic tension that comes of a marriage of contraries it must fuse a limiting impulse with an impulse that resists limitation. Thus Dylan Thomas's most successful poems are those in which his primary musical temperament is constrained by the limiting qualities of structure (the villanelle "Do Not Go Gentle into That Good Night") or of story (the minor but effective story progressions of "Poem in October" or "Over Sir John's Hill"). Likewise, Richard Wilbur's structural temperament has need of those qualities that resist limitation, as when the run-on syntax, alliteration, and elaborately varied vowels of "A Baroque Wall-Fountain in the Villa Sciarra" enact a watery music that flows around and over the structure.

If the minimum formula for a poem's success is a kind of Chinese menu—one from Column A (the limits of story and structure), one from Column B (the limitlessness of music and imagination)—then it should be added that combining two impulses from the same column can be fatal. Hart Crane's reputation, despite his great gifts, is precarious in large part because he so frequently relied on a fusion of music and imagination to make his poems. One can say the same of Dylan Thomas, or Swinburne for that matter. Such a marriage makes it almost impossible to create closure, to constellate a wholeness. If the dangers of a music/imagination combination are quite obvious, the converse—a fusion of story and structure—also presents characteristic problems. The prime example of this is the later Wordsworth. His great early work was sustained by a tension between the poles of imagination and story. When he lost faith in his basic story of the benign interfusing of man and nature ("Elegiac Stanzas on a Painting of Peele Castle in Storm" dramatizes this loss), Wordsworth felt burdened and alarmed by the chaotic flow of imagination ("Me this unchartered freedom tires" he laments in "Ode to Duty"). His response was to repudiate imagination and turn to structure. Seeking "brief solace" in the rigidity of their structural constraints, he created hundreds of hollow sonnets through which his basic story echoes faintly, unconvincingly.

Story

Aristotle is full of insights into the nature of story: the primary importance of action and event; the need to create dramatic focus around a single action. "So too the plot of the play, being the representation of an action, must present it as a unified whole; and its various incidents must be so arranged that if any one of them is differently placed or taken away the effect of wholeness will be seriously disrupted."

The role of beginning, middle, and end; that beauty is the result of the harmonious proportion of parts; how the power of "discovery" and "reversal" function as pivot points in the best stories.

Story is magical. When Coleridge's Ancient Mariner intones " 'There was a ship' quoth he . . ." we are at the beginning of story and we, like the Wedding Guest, yield to its enthralling power—"listen[ing] like a three years' child."

Thomas Wyatt's poem "They Flee from Me" establishes the essential conflict of story in the pronouns of its opening line: "They flee from me that sometime did me seek." And his second stanza goes on to reveal the extraordinary focusing power of story: "but once in special, / In thin array, after a pleasant guise. . . ."

Conflict is essential to story—without conflict there is no dramatic tension. As Blake says: "Without Contraries is no Progression." This conflict at the source of story is what the poem resolves, as in the Renaissance motto, "Harmonia est discordia concors" (Harmony is discord reconciled).

Hollywood's oldest formula for story corresponds well to Aristotle's terms if not his spirit: boy meets girl, boy loses girl, boy gets girl. But the conflict that is the essential ingredient of story needn't be something out of melodrama. What is essential to story is that there be at least two centers of energy, two poles of awareness around which the conflict can organize itself. In poetry, the mere presence of two discrete pronouns (such as Wyatt's "They flee from me") is sufficient to create the tension that story will resolve.

When Stanley Kunitz counsels young poets to "polarize their contradictions," he is proposing that one source of dramatic conflict can be ambivalence within the individual. Such a formula is related to Yeats's remark—"out of our quarrels with others we make rhetoric, out of our quarrels with ourselves poetry." It is the self-quarrel of attraction and repulsion vis-à-vis sensuality that galvanizes Eliot's "The Love Song of J. Alfred Prufrock."

But of course, the dramatic conflict is just as likely to concern two figures in the world, as in Robert Hayden's "Those Winter Sundays," where father and son enact their tragic dance of misunderstanding and fear.

Or the self is at odds with the external world; either the social/political world, as in Yeats's "Lapis Lazuli" or "Among School Children," or the natural world, as in his "The Wild Swans at Coole."

Yeats provides further insight into the nature of story when, in a letter written a few weeks before his death, he speaks of trying to put everything he knows into a single sentence and arriving at "Man can embody truth, but he cannot know it." The *embodied* meanings of event, gesture, and deed are how story expresses its truths.

Story is the embodied truth of contraries seeking resolution. Story, in poetry, is seldom concerned with the elaborate and unpredictable contingencies of the world we live in; those belong to fiction. Nor is story in poetry narrative (a larger, looser term). In story, events constellate around a single conflict (Aristotle's "unity of action").

In the twentieth century, the psychological century, Freud has proposed specific archetypal stories such as those underlying the Oedipus complex and the Electra complex. More broadly, he has drawn our attention to the family triad (father, mother, child) as a rich source of urgent stories. Sometimes poets have organized them as a two-person conflict, as in Plath's "Daddy" or Adrienne Rich's "Snapshots of a Daughter-in-Law"; other times they have been dramatized with triadic richness as in Louis Simpson's "My Father in the Night Commanding No," Stanley Kunitz's "The Portrait," and Roethke's "My Papa's Waltz."

Structure

The structural temperament expresses itself in pattern making in a profound sense. This temperament can manifest itself in either open or closed structures. By open structures I mean such things as metrical lines or the infinitely extensible form of rhymed couplets. A poem consisting of metrical stanzas is also an open structure. A closed structure would be something like a sonnet, a villanelle, or a sestina, all of whose defining limits can be seen as approaching an ideal.

In order properly to appreciate the structural temperament, we must realize that for poets of this temperament the beauty of pattern is itself a form of meaning. The transcendent aspirations of such a temperament bring to mind this passage from Plato's *Philebus:*

> The beauty of figures which I am now trying to indicate is not what most people would understand as such, not the beauty of a living creature or a picture; what I mean . . . is something straight, or round, and the surfaces and solids which a lathe or a carpenter's rule and square produces from the straight and the round. Things like that . . . are beautiful, not in a relative sense; they are always beautiful in their very nature, and they carry pleasures peculiar to themselves and which are free of the itch of desire.

A statement from a structural perspective: "The correction of prose, because it has no fixed laws, is endless; a poem comes right with a click like a box" (Yeats in a letter to Dorothy Wellesley).

The structural temperament will always place great emphasis on the conscious pattern-making intention of the poet. The epitome of this, almost a parody, is Edgar Allan Poe's essay, "The Philosophy of Composition," in which he elaborately sets forth his construction of "The Raven."

To poets whose gift is for structure, structure is *primary,* an essence. It isn't something imposed on the poem, not even something chosen in the ordinary sense of the word. It certainly is wrong (how much blood has been spilled on this false issue) to contrast structure with free verse, as if it were simply an aesthetic choice rather than a fundamental form-giving impulse in certain poets. Ezra Pound, usually so perceptive about poetry, is uncharacteristically dismissive of "symmetrical forms." Intent as he is on promulgating a new sense of rhythm and a new idea of the nature and role of the image, he betrays a significant lack of sympathy for the structural temperament when he warns, "don't put in what you want to say and then fill up the vacuums with slush." In fact, Pound also rejects the other limiting impulse, story, having incorporated "the great discovery of the French symbolists," which was "the irrelevance and hence the possibility of abolition of paraphrasable plot." Given these rejections of the limiting temperaments, it's not surprising that Pound's "three kinds of poetry" (melopoeia, phanopoeia, and logopoeia, from the essay "How to Read") in fact only represent the two limitless temperaments, melopoeia corresponding to music, phanopoeia to concrete imagination, and logopoeia to abstract imagination. Such blindness to the role of the limiting impulses had severe consequences for Pound's own later poetry as it struggled to find a convincing and cohering form.

That the great majority of poems written in English since the sixteenth century have aspired to metrical regularity and used a pattern of rhyme and stanzaic repetition does not mean that they are all products of structural temperaments. One need only consider Donne, whose temperament is clearly centered in imagination, the flow of one image or idea into another. If lasting poetry demands metrical regularity, then Ben Jonson was right and Donne did "for not keeping of accent, deserve hanging." But Coleridge comes closer to Donne's genius of imagination when he declares that its power and purpose is to "wreathe iron pokers into true-love knots."

Music

The musical temperament manifests itself in the individual qualities of syllables (pitch, duration, stress, loudness/softness), in syntax, and in assorted sound effects (assonance, consonance, alliteration, and subtler phenomena) as they interact to create the poem's aural and rhythmical structure.

Music in poetry is irrational; it works directly on the emotions, regardless of the purported content of the language. Primitive and powerful. Dionysus's flute rather than Apollo's lyre—more ecstasy and trance than measure and order. Thus Plato bans from his ordered republic certain musical modes (and the poems associated with them) because they have the power to generate undesirable emotions in their hearers.

The cadences of evangelists, orators, and demagogues—the undeniable, even physiological response, but casting a deeply ambiguous moral light.

Primitive in an emotional sense, but also ontologically primitive in the individual—the infant's joy in the babble and coo of sound, the child's pleasure in nursery rhymes. When Coleridge insists that "the sense of musical delight, with the power of producing it in others" is an essential prerequisite for a poet, he places musical pleasure at the very center of poetry.

No matter how carefully you analyze Hart Crane's "Voyages" in terms of imagistic unity, the fact remains that music makes the poem cohere. There is no question that thematic patterns are developed and fulfilled in Keats's "To Autumn"—but its power and unity derive from the same source as its pleasures: a masterful manipulation of sound and rhythm. We hear it in the elaborate musical/emotional parabolas of Roethke's "The Lost Son."

Music shares with imagination the difficulties of closure. In many completed and fulfilled patterns of sound and rhythm, there is still something left over, some vowel, say, that calls out across the poem's final period to its fellow in the silence beyond, asking to go further, to generate new possibilities and combinations. When Keats, in *Endymion,* deliberately and constantly enjambed his couplets, he created a self-defeating structure, especially since he had no story grip on the poem— and so it flowed ("You will be glad to hear that within these last three weeks I have written 1000 Lines" he writes to Haydon), formless, a sweet meander.

And yet, when a poem of musical temperament resolves success-fully, it does so by a powerful marshaling of its inherent qualities, as in the extraordinary last line of Hopkins's "Thou art indeed just, Lord": "Mine, O thou lord of life, send my roots rain." The two heavy internal pauses, the alliteration, the fact that each of the last four monosyllables is heavily stressed, the assonantal thread of the long "i" (mine, life, my), and the extraordinary variety of vowel pitch playing off against this assonance—all these factors impinge on the line with an authority that can only be followed by silence.

Imagination

A poet can, and frequently does, possess both an abstract and a concrete imagination, but sometimes there is a peculiar antipathy among these poets of imagination, for instance, the hostility and condescension Pound and Williams (both finally poets of abstract imagination in my opinion) felt toward Whitman, a poet of decid-edly concrete imagination.

A few poets of imagination: Donne, George Herbert (abstract imagina-tion), Blake in his Prophetic Books, Wordsworth, Whitman (concrete imagination), Dickinson, Rimbaud, Pound, William Carlos Williams, Eliot, George Oppen, Pablo Neruda.

With imagination, as with music, it is easier to recognize its pres-ence as the dominant form-giving temperament in particular poets than it is to characterize the temperament itself. Why is this? Perhaps because an individual poet's imagination moves in ways so peculiar and particular to him or her—so Wordsworth would seem to say in the very poem in which he endeavors to set forth both the principles and processes of his own imagination:

> Not only general habits and desires,
> But each most obvious and particular thought,

Not in a mystical and idle sense,
But in the words of reason deeply weigh'd,
Hath no beginning.

(The Prelude 2, ll. 232–37)

Even when we can trace an individual poet's way of moving by imagination, it doesn't mean that we can pull back and generalize about the process of imagination itself, in part because it *is* a process and has a way of quicksilvering through our hands—we're like Menelaus trying to capture the metamorphosing Proteus in book 4 of *The Odyssey*.

Having said that, it's worth looking at section 6 of Whitman's "Song of Myself" in order to watch an imaginative temperament unfolding explicably and inexplicably in language. In the opening lines, the poem (and the temperament) frees itself by associative "guesses" from an analytical, descriptive stance toward reality:

> A child said *What is the grass?* fetching it to me with full hands,
> How could I answer the child? I do not know what it is any
> more than he.
>
> I guess it must be the flag of my disposition, out of hopeful
> green stuff woven.

(ll. 1–3)

And then launches into the dizzying and audacious metaphors that are the poem's lifeblood:

> Or I guess it is the handkerchief of the Lord,
> A scented gift and remembrancer designedly dropt,
> Bearing the owner's name someway in the corners, that we
> may see and remark, and say *Whose?*
>
> Or I guess the grass is itself a child, the produced babe of the
> vegetation.

(ll. 4–7)

We can analyze Whitman's leaps: that he consolidates the general term "grass" into a rectangular shape with "flag" and this suggests "woven" and the two together result in the image of the handkerchief. But what analysis is adequate to the awesomely condensed implications of the resulting image: God (as a woman?) has flirtatiously dropped the perfumed handkerchief we know as grass so that we, according to the elaborate rituals of assignation or courtship, might thus seek out the divine creator? And this is only three lines—no sooner presented than cast aside for a further image, and another one after that.

How then does a poem governed by the imaginative temperament overcome its own centrifugal impulses and finally cohere? Again, the Whitman poem might give us one important answer—even the wildest, most free-ranging imagination has its themes and obsessions, which it tends to circle around. When, in line 12, Whitman introduces this metaphor for grass—"And now it seems to me the beautiful uncut hair of graves"—he has stumbled upon one of his fundamental thematic obsessions: death. For the remaining twenty-one lines of the poem, the imagination circles in an obsessive spiral around images of graves and death. This fierce spiral shape is not the scattering violence of a tornado, but that of a whirlpool sucking into its centripetal vortex the most disparate objects. And there at the still point of the whirlpool's bottom, one passes through (as if it were really the narrow part of an hourglass) and catches a glimpse of the expanding calm beyond—"All goes onward and outward, nothing collapses, / and to die is different from what anyone supposed, and luckier."

Eros and Thanatos are two deep channels in the wide river of imagination, and quite often the two channels join and roil together their currents. It's easier to generalize about a poet of concrete imagination like Whitman, whose poems are frequently in contact with Eros and Thanatos and their lesser attendant mysteries and emotions, than about someone like Pound or Oppen, whose poems of abstract imagination give the impression of being freer from the cohesive or focusing power of these two major human obsessions. Perhaps one could argue that abstract imaginations are characterized by a "train of thought." Literalizing that dead metaphor for a moment, we might say that each thought, idea, or didactic anecdote is a baggage or passenger car—a discrete unit yet linked to its counterparts and propelled by another discrete unit, the engine, which has energy sufficient to give the whole train movement and purpose.

A Few Thoughts for Poets

It's possible to imagine a poet who proceeds entirely by instinct, one poem succeeding another in a dazzle of ignorant bliss. But all real poets also exist in the long spaces between poems, where a lot of thought takes place. A poet is always trying to decide who he or she is and might become. To me, the notion of the four temperaments holds the promise of an underlying pattern that can orient and guide a poet as well as a critic.

The first issue is always one of self-knowledge or self-recognition. Once a poet has a sense of his or her fundamental temperament, the possibilities for growth are twofold. The first is to go further into the gift, but such a decision carries with it the risk of narrowing as well as the promise of deepening.

The second direction is to expand. Such an expansion can be under-stood as the poet's struggle to nurture and develop the other tempera-ments in such a way that their energies and constraints enrich his or her poems. Again, no one can hope to have all four temperaments in equal strength, but the goal will always be to have all four tempera-ments present, though some will arrive as gifts and others must be learned and labored for.

Contributors

Joan Aleshire graduated from Harvard-Radcliffe in 1960 and received her MFA degree from Goddard College in 1980. She has published two books of poems, *Cloud Train* (AWP Award Series, Texas Tech Press, 1982) and *This Far* (QRL Poetry Series, 1987). She has taught in the MFA Program for Writers at Warren Wilson College since 1983, and has served, periodically, as that program's acting director.

Marianne Boruch's most recent poetry collections are *Moss Burning* (Field Editions, Oberlin College Press, 1993) and *Descendant* (Wesleyan University Press, 1989). Her collection of essays, *Poetry's Old Air*, appeared in University of Michigan's "Poets on Poetry" series in 1995. She teaches in the graduate writing program at Purdue University. The essay reprinted here received the Terence Des Pres Award from *Parnassus* for the best essay published in 1993.

Carl Dennis teaches in the English Department of the State University of New York. He is the author of six books of poems, most recently *Meetings with Time*, published by Penguin in 1992. His other books of poetry are *A House of My Own*, *Climbing Down*, *Signs and Wonders*, *The Near World*, and *The Outskirts of Troy*.

Stephen Dobyns has published eight volumes of poetry and sixteen novels. His most recent book of poems is *Velocities: New and Selected Poems, 1966–1992* (Viking Penguin, 1994). His most recent novels are *The Wrestler's Cruel Study* (Norton, 1994) and *Saratoga Backtalk* (Norton, 1995). His mystery novel, *Saratoga Fleshpot*, was published by Norton in 1995. *Common Carnage*, a book of poems, will be published by Viking Penguin, and his book of essays on poetry, *Best Words, Best Order*, will be published by St. Martin's Press. He is completing a book of short stories: *Dead Men Don't Need Safe Sex*. He teaches at Syracuse University in Syracuse, New York.

Reginald Gibbons has published four books of poems—most recently, *Maybe It Was So* (University of Chicago); his fifth, *Sparrow*, will be published by Chicago. His other books of poetry are *Roofs Voices Roads*, *The Ruined Motel*, and *Saints*. He has also published a novel, *Sweetbitter* (Penguin) and a collection of short fiction, *Five Pears or Peaches* (Broken Moon Press); has edited *The Poet's Work: 29 Poets on the Origins and Practice of Their Art*; and has published a translation of the work of Luis Cernuda. He has been the editor of *TriQuarterly* magazine since 1981, and also teaches at Northwestern University.

Allen Grossman is the author of seven books of poems, *A Harlot's Hire, The Recluse, And the Dew Lay All Night Upon My Branch, The Woman on the Bridge Over the Chicago River, Of the Great House: A Book of Poems, The Bright Nails Scattered on the Ground*, and *The Ether Dome and Other Poems: New and Selected (1979–1991)*. His criticism includes *Poetic Knowledge in the Early Yeats; Summa Lyrica: A Primer of the Commonplaces in Speculative Poetics;* and *Against Our Vanishing: Winter Conversations with Allen Grossman on the Theory and Practice of Poetry* (ed. Mark Halliday). He has been the recipient of a Guggenheim Fellowship, the Witter Bynner Prize of the American Academy and Institute of Arts and Letters, and a MacArthur Fellowship. For years a professor at Brandeis University, he currently teaches at Johns Hopkins University.

Louise Glück teaches at Williams College. Her most recent collection, *The Wild Iris* (Ecco Press, 1992), received the Pulitzer Prize; a new collection is forthcoming from Ecco in 1996. Her other books of poetry are *Firstborn, The House on Marshland, Descending Figure, The Triumph of Achilles*, and *Ararat*. She is the author of *Proofs and Theories: Essays on Poetry*.

Robert Hass is the author of three books of poetry, *Field Guide* (Yale Younger Poets Award, 1973), *Praise*, and *Human Wishes*, and a book of essays, *Twentieth Century Pleasures* (winner of the 1984 National Book Critics Circle Award for Criticism). He has collaborated with Czeslaw Milosz on translations of the Polish poet's poems, and has published translations and editions of Japanese poetry, as well as an edition of the poetry of Robinson Jeffers. The recipient of a MacArthur Fellowship, he teaches at the University of California at Berkeley.

Tony Hoagland's *Sweet Ruin* was the winner of the 1992 Brittingham Prize in poetry from University of Wisconsin Press. He has received two grants from the National Endowment for the Arts, and the John C. Zaharis Award from *Ploughshares* magazine and Emerson College. His criticism and poems have been widely published. He teaches at Colby College.

Heather McHugh is Milliman Writer-in-Residence at the Creative Writing Program of the University of Washington in Seattle, and a core faculty member of the MFA Program for Writers at Warren Wilson College. She was educated at Harvard University and got her MA in English literature at the University of Denver. She is the translator of *D'Aprés Tout: Poems by Jean Follain*, and, with her husband Niko Boris McHugh, collections of poetry by Blaga Dimitrova and Paul Celan. Her most recent books are *Hinge & Sign: Poems 1968–1993* (finalist for the 1994 National Book Award) and a collection of essays, *Broken English: Poetry and Partiality*, both published by Wesleyan University Press. Her other books of poetry are *Dangers, A World of Difference, To the Quick*, and *Shades*.

Gregory Orr is professor of English at the University of Virginia. He is the author of six books of poetry, most recently *City of Salt* (University of Pittsburgh Press, 1995); other collections are *Burning the Empty Nests, Gathering the Bones Together, The Red House, We Must Make a Kingdom of It,* and *New and Selected Poems.* He is also author of two books of criticism, *Richer Entanglements: Essays and Notes on Poetry and Poems* (University of Michigan, 1993) and *Stanley Kunitz: An Introduction to the Poetry* (Columbia University Press, 1985).

Michael Ryan's books of poetry include *Threats Instead of Trees* (Yale Younger Poets Award, 1974), *In Winter* (National Poetry Series winner, 1981), and *God Hunger* (Lenore Marshall/*The Nation* Prize, 1989); a memoir, *Secret Life,* was published in 1995. He has received awards from the Guggenheim Foundation and the National Endowment for the Arts. He teaches at the University of California at Irvine.

Ellen Bryant Voigt has published five volumes of poetry— *Claiming Kin, The Forces of Plenty, The Lotus Flowers, Two Trees,* and *Kyrie.* A graduate of Converse College in Spartanburg, S.C., where she later received an honorary Doctor of Literature, and of the University of Iowa Writers' Workshop, she founded and directed the low-residency MFA Writing Program at Goddard College and teaches in its relocated incarnation at Warren Wilson College in Swannanoa, N.C. She has also taught at Iowa Wesleyan College and M.I.T., as well as many writers' conferences and NEA-sponsored residencies around the country. Voigt's widely anthologized poems have appeared in *The New Yorker, The Atlantic, The New Republic,* and *The Nation* as well as numerous literary journals; received two Pushcart Prizes (Best of the Small Presses), the Emily Clark Balch Award from the *Virginia Quarterly Review,* and the 1993 Hanes Poetry Award from the Fellowship of Southern Writers; and appeared in the *Best American Poetry 1993* from Scribner's. A recipient of grants from the National Endowment for the Arts and the Guggenheim Foundation, she was a 1993 Lila Wallace/Woodrow Wilson Fellow.

Alan Williamson teaches at the University of California at Davis. His most recent books are *Love and the Soul* (poems), 1995, and *Eloquence and Mere Life* (essays), 1994. He is also the author of *Pity the Monsters: The Political Vision of Robert Lowell* and *Introspection and Contemporary Poetry.* His other books of poetry are *Presence* and *The Muse of Distance.*

Eleanor Wilner is the author of four books of poems, *Otherwise* (1993), *Sarah's Choice, Shekhinah* (all from University of Chicago Press), and *maya* (Juniper Prize, University of Massachusetts Press, 1979), as well as a book of visionary imagination, *Gathering the Winds* (Johns Hopkins University Press, 1975). Her work appears in numerous anthologies, including *The Best American Poetry 1990* (Collier/ Macmillan). Currently a MacArthur Fellow, she teaches in the MFA

Program for Writers at Warren Wilson College and is a Contributing Editor for *Calyx: A Journal of Art and Literature by Women.*

Renate Wood was raised and educated in Europe before receiving a PhD from Stanford University and an MFA from the Program for Writers at Warren Wilson College. Her collection of poems, *Raised Underground,* was published in 1991. She lectures occasionally at the University of Colorado in Boulder. Since 1991, she has been on the faculty of the Warren Wilson MFA Program.